RIPOFF

Books by Steve Allen

Bop Fables
Fourteen for Tonight
The Funny Men
Wry on the Rocks
The Girls on the Tenth Floor
The Question Man
Mark It and Strike It
Not All of Your Laughter, Not All of Your Tears
Letter to a Conservative
The Ground Is Our Table
Bigger Than a Breadbox
A Flash of Swallows
The Wake
Princess Snip-Snip and the Puppykittens
Curses
What to Say When It Rains
Schmock, Schmock
Meeting of Minds
Chopped-Up Chinese
Meeting of Minds, Second Series
Ripoff

RIPOFF

A Look at

Corruption in

America

by

STEVE ALLEN

with Roslyn Bernstein, Ph.D.

and Donald H. Dunn

Lyle Stuart Inc.

Secaucus, N.J.

Queries regarding rights and permissions
should be addressed to Lyle Stuart Inc.
120 Enterprise Ave., Secaucus, N. J. 07094

Published by Lyle Stuart Inc.
Published simultaneously in Canada
by George J. McLeod Limited
Don Mills, Ontario

Manufactured in the United States of America

Library of Congress Cataloging in Publication Data
Allen, Steve, 1921–
    Ripoff: a look at corruption in America.
    Bibliography: p. 267
    1. United States—Moral conditions. 2. Business ethics. 3. Corruption (in
politics)—United States. 4. Corporations—United States—Corrupt practices. 5. Judicial corruption—United States. I. Title.
HN90.M6A44   170'.973   79-14663 ISBN 0-8184-0249-0

To

Hank Messick
John Daly
Marty Philpott
Ralph Salerno
and other courageous soldiers
in the war on crime and corruption

Acknowledgments

I wish to thank Don Dunn and Roz Bernstein, who have been of invaluable assistance with writing, editing and research. I'm indebted to Bill Clago for information about the history of corruption in the U.S., and to Dorothy Iavello, Pat Forney and Rose Avallone for their tireless—and sometimes, I'm sure, tiresome—typing services.

It may occur to the critical reader that I have indulged in rather over-much quotation in documenting my thesis. Such inclusion is deliberate, by way of demonstrating that a good many scholars, journalists and other social critics share my concern. Nothing would make me happier than to learn that the present modest effort has encouraged readers to consult more reputable authority on the subject of our growing national scandal.

Lastly I underline my debt to scores of investigative journalists who in concentrating on one specific aspect of corruption have provided much of the raw material from which I have drawn factual information.

S.A.

Contents

Foreword
by Roz Bernstein and Don Dunn   9

I   *The Problem*   19

II   *The Historical Background of Western*
            Corruption   41

III   *Blowing the Whistle on Crooked Cops*   47

IV   *The Push-Button Thieves*   67

V   *Lotsa Luck in the Stock Market*   81

VI   *Politics: The National Scandal*   89

VII   *The Sickness in the World of Medicine*   121

VIII   *Five-Finger Discounting: The Shoplifters*   133

IX   *Cheating in the Schools*   149

X   *The Ethics of Show Biz*   159

XI   *Corruption Is Old in New Jersey*   177

XII   *Corrupting a Labor Union—It Doesn't Take
       Much Work*   189

XIII *Moral Rot in the Military Service*   207

XIV   *Foul Balls and Errors in the Great American
       Games*   217

XV   *Let the Buyer Beware—of Dishonest Ads*   235

XVI   *Who's Got the Solution?*   251

Foreword: The Man Behind the Anger

By Roz Bernstein and Don Dunn

That's right. *Ripoff,* a Look at Corruption in America, by Steve Allen.

Steve Allen? *The* Steve—?

Yes, the comedian. The composer with more than 4,000 songs to his credit. The TV host who created the *Tonight Show,* and who appears all over the dial to the present moment—doing guest shots on *Good Morning, America,* dramatic shows, *Today*—with Merv Griffin, Johnny Carson, his own comedy specials, and serving as moderator par excellence on the unique *Meeting of Minds* on the Public Broadcasting Service network, a show that presents Plato, Luther, Aquinas, Voltaire, Socrates and other historical characters discussing important social questions. Yes, the same man who plays concert halls and theatres everywhere, who's married to actress Jayne Meadows, and—

That Steve Allen? Writing a book about corruption?

We can almost hear the amazement, the questions in your mind as you think about it: *Why in the world is Steve Allen writing about corruption and moral collapse in America?*

A serious enough topic, to be sure, massive in scope, one that could require years of research by philosophers, jurists, criminologists and sociologists in order to arrive at a conclusion.

Just who does Steve Allen think he is—daring to tackle such a weighty issue?

Well, Allen is a citizen of a country he has long believed to be the greatest on earth. Like many of us he is saddened and angered at the depths to which financial crime has permeated our society.

To say that he deplores corruption in America is to put it mildly. As he explains his 30-year interest in the issue one becomes aware of his sense of outrage.

"One of the first instances where I felt compelled to take some sort of action," Allen has told us, "occurred early in the 1950's. I remember opening an issue of *Life* magazine and being brought up short by a dramatic photograph.

"The picture was that of a man swathed in bandages, lying in a hospital bed. He had been savagely beaten, left on the verge of death by a couple or Organized Crime 'enforcers.' Why? Simply because he had spoken out at a Lutheran church meeting against the installation of pinball games in a candy store near a neighborhood school."

The photograph angered Allen so much that he took a public stand that very day. At the time he was appearing on the CBS-TV network with a daily program of comedy and conversation. Millions of viewers were accustomed to tuning in for a regular dose of jokes, music and chatter. Now Allen gave them something different.

"I propped the *Life* picture up and told our camera director to hold a close-up on it while I spoke my feelings on the matter. (The director was Gene Kelly's brother, Fred.) I explained that professional gamblers with mob connections were not merely genial Damon Runyon types but animals willing to resort to terror, murder and atrocity. We received a considerable amount of congratulatory mail afterwards."

Two years later Allen was the original host of the "Tonight Show." Although the program's format today is heavily oriented toward show business, under Allen's direction it had considerably more scope. On certain nights the now standard talk show formula would be followed, but on others the program might consist largely of jazz music, a political debate, a scripted drama, almost anything. One night Allen requested and was granted an extra thirty minutes of time for a special program: a two-hour documentary on the subject of Organized Crime and its influence in one city, New York.

"I called my staff together," said Allen, "and told them we would devote an entire program to a discussion of how deeply corruption—and organized crime—were woven into the fabric of America life." Allen worked for weeks on the script with the enthusiastic cooperation of Walter O'Mara and William Keating, two investigators connected with the New York City Anti-Crime Committee, chaired at the time by Spruille Braden.

When word of the project leaked out, however, Allen began to feel certain pressures. There were no overt threats, he recalls, nothing that could be brought to the attention of the police or district attorney. But there were "hints" and "suggestions" that the planned program might be better forgotten, or that—if it did get on the air—it should not be too specific.

"There was one name in particular in a list of bums I knew had links with Organized Crime," the entertainer remembers. "I eventually got the message that if I mentioned the name on the air, I might regret it. Faced with pressures from several sides, I decided to delete the man's name in order to get the program on the air at all. I agreed to refer to him only as 'Mr. X.' "

The move was, of course, masterful. Confronted with a public condemnation by Allen of a dozen-or-so clearly identified Mafia members and one mysterious "Mr. X," the headline-hungry New York papers naturally became curious about the identity of the one person whose name was held back.

"Jack O'Brian of the *Journal-American* called to ask if the omitted name was Benny Levine," Allen recalls. "I told him he was right. Levine was a former professional hoodlum who—his friends told me—had gone straight and was now a respectable leader in the garment industry."

Several years later *The New York Times*, in its issue of June 5, 1958, ran a story headlined "17 Arrested Here in Narcotic Raid; Top Racketeers Among Those Held on High Bail."

> Racketeers and hoodlums were among 18 persons arrested yesterday as members of a reputed multi-million dollar-a-year narcotics ring ... *also held in 35 thousand dollars bail was Benjamin Levine, 63, who owns a $150,000 home at Atlantic Beach, Long Island. Levine, a one-time confederate of the gar-ment racketeers Louis "Lepke" Buchalter and Jacob "Gurrah" Shapiro, was said to have planned the financing of the narcotics traffic.* (Italics provided)

Allen sent clippings of the story to some of Levine's friends who had phoned him.

Allen had made his point the hard way. And he was prepared to pay the price. Although he is in considerable demand as a nightclub performer there are certain hotels and clubs—either controlled by mob associates or people sympathetic to them—where to this day he is not asked to appear, twenty-five years after his anti-crime documentary.

Favorable public reaction to the telecast encouraged Allen to devote other programs to serious problems in American society. Early in 1955, for example, long before the drug culture was a topic for the Sunday supplements, his Tonight Show staff put together a production that included interviews with addicts, displays of equipment used by junk-ies, films on withdrawal and an interview with the director of health from the New York City Health and Welfare Com-mission.

Again—long before the recent interest in "blacklisting," highlighted by the memoirs of Lillian Hellman and the film *The Front*, starring Woody Allen—Steve Allen did a program on AWARE, an organization which existed "to expose Com-munists and other leftist members of the acting profession."

Recalls the performer: "Actress Faye Emerson and

newspaper columnist John Crosby took part in a lively debate with Godfrey P. Schmidt, president of AWARE, and Vincent W. Hartnett, one of the authors of *Red Channels*, the paper that promoted the blacklist. By taking the story to the air we had done some good."

Allen was again infuriated when labor columnist Victor Riesel, who had appeared on his anti-crime telecast, was blinded by a man Allen describes as "one of the acid-throwing hoodlums of the sort who infest the union movement." When he used his television program to discuss blatant corruption and crime in such labor unions as the Teamsters and the International Longshoreman's Association Allen again heard from anonymous phone callers.

"Lay off, pal, or you're next," said one. Then, after stink bombs were set off in the TV studio one night, another call came: "Those could have been real bombs, y' know."

The tires on Allen's car were slashed a few nights later.

The incidents happened long ago, but are not forgotten by either Allen or his critics in the underworld. A couple of years ago Allen and his wife Jayne were invited to a small Hollywood gathering where the film *The Godfather* was shown. Certain other guests had connections that had long been of interest to federal law-enforcement agencies. The next morning, in a scene straight out of that especially bloody moment in the film, one of the comedian's secretaries found the enormous severed leg of a horse on his doorstep. Allen, not intimidated, sent an equally unmistakable message back to one of the party's guests.

Interviewing the humorist on his longtime repugnance toward crime and corruption we discovered that he is unaware of precisely when and where it began. "Obviously," he told us, "the subject has troubled me for years. Perhaps it goes back to my boyhood in Chicago. Even as a youngster, it was difficult not to be aware of the depths of unlawfulness there; it was the home territory of Al Capone, a moral monster and multiple murderer who nevertheless literally ran the city. Thinking back, there's a school that comes to mind in this connection, St. Joseph's Institute, a boarding school in La Grange, Illinois. There, I received one of my earliest lessons that life is violent, often unfairly so.

"Since the school's student body was recruited partly from broken homes, it had its share of bullies. Sometimes they played cruel initiation stunts on newcomers or smaller boys. I had heard stories of the kinds of things that went on and vividly remember that the prospect of being blindfolded, beaten, and forced to eat what were said to be worms so terrified me that I spent the better part of one weekend lurking about the school building, slipping from hiding place to hiding place like the Hunchback of Notre Dame, desperately trying to avoid the open schoolyard where I knew attacks were taking place.

"From that day," Allen concluded, "my reaction to the less savory elements of society has, I suppose, been more pronounced than that of the average person. Perhaps it was that sort of experience which has led me, on occasion, to speak my mind publicly on certain issues—particularly those where bullying or cruelty are involved."

Over the years Steve Allen—the concerned citizen, not the TV host with the razor-sharp wit—has developed voluminous files on, among other things, Organized Crime and corruption. Today such files fill an entire room in his home. It is not enough, he realizes, to use an occasional television appearance to speak out against the growing tide. The facts—at least some of them—have to be laid before the American public.

"I have long felt that it is possible to speak out against the things that one perceives as harmful, and to improve the world—if only a bit—by doing so," Allen told us in a calm voice that seemed filled with an inner strength. "Words *can* bring about change. The record of history is clear on this."

Theoreticians and fatalists alike might shrug and turn away from the factual reporting that Allen offers to illustrate his thesis that there is almost no corner of American life untinged by wrongdoing. "These problems have been with us since the beginning," they might say. "What's the point of going over them one more time?"

There is a point, Allen believes. His purpose in clarifying it is self-evident in the following pages. And he's right; everywhere one looks now there *is* evidence of moral collapse. At our military academies, for example, long regarded as impenetrable bastions of honesty and morality, massive cheating scandals have shaken the foundations.

In the ensuing chapters Allen sheds light on various kinds of corruption—shoplifting, political and business graft, illegalities in medicine, law, and the market-place.

"At this late date," he says, "we all must examine our consciences, encourage our children in their quest for better, saner lives, call each other to account. Somehow we must become as concerned about moral pollution as we are about the pollution of our air and water."

The reader already, of course, has seen hundreds of separate media stories dealing with instances of corruption. But it is important to collect such disconnected reports and make one case of them. What follows is not intended as a formal moral treatise. It is not an expert document by a professional criminologist, nor a plea for the formation of a Utopian state. It is merely one man's earnest appraisal of a serious national scandal. "The way to begin improving such a damnable state of affairs," Allen argues, "is to first lay out a simple analysis of it. Secondly we must make individual commitments to take a stand on the issue, before we are all inundated by it. It's no longer just a good-guys against bad-guys situation. I repeat: we all must examine our consciences. Only when guilt is realized can it be erased. This is no less valid for societies than for individuals."

RIPOFF

Chapter *I*

The
Problem

I

Since this study deals primarily with corruption, it therefore makes only passing reference to abuses of freedom. There is an obvious interrelationship between the two, however. Criminal excess leads inevitably to the growth of restrictive legislation. But law and order, obviously necessary, can become so encompassing that freedoms are restricted. The heart of the problem is that too many people who consider themselves among the elect now act as if they believed that any method of earning money, short of armed robbery, is condoned. To the extent that this attitude is dominant our nation almost becomes one vast den of thieves in which most men prey upon their neighbors, justifying their own thievery by the argument that they themselves are being robbed by others.

I do not propose, however, to take much of the reader's time in sermonizing. This book deals with a bill of specifics, which will dramatize the moral far more effectively than could abstract argument.

It is fundamental to an understanding of the case I am

about to present to grasp that it is *not* based on a Puritan attitude towards human behavior. I hold that there is profound wisdom in the old Negro song title, "It Ain't What You Do, It's the Way That You Do It." I do not believe that there is anything inherently evil about taking a drink, placing a bet on a football game or horse-race, playing poker or bingo, going to a burlesque show, kissing a pretty girl, or any of the other harmless activities that shock a few religious Fundamentalists. It is obvious that one can enter the domain of evil by carrying any of the above-mentioned practices to excess; it is certainly wrong for an alcoholic to take a drink, for a compulsive gambler to throw away his family's rent money, to rape pretty girls instead of kissing them, etc.

I do not even consider it my business if an adult makes himself dreamily blissful by using marijuana, any more than it is my business if another adult makes an ass of himself by passing out from drinking Scotch whisky. In other words, I am, as the cliché has it, no prude.

All of which strengthens the point, that it does not require the morality of a Sunday-school teacher to be shocked at the ethical climate presently prevailing in the United States.

Pick up your newspaper. Turn on your television set or radio. Glance through any newsmagazine. Daily, there is news of graft and corruption. The stories deal with bribes to politicians, crooked lotteries, police payoffs, fixed athletic contests, payola to radio disc jockeys, nursing-home scandals.

In an effort to escape the dismaying revelations, we may turn to the financial pages to read about the solid, socially-responsible world of business. There, too, we find news of the arrests and convictions of some of the nation's most powerful businessmen who make speeches extolling the moral superiority of free enterprise—apparently making a secret price-fixing deal or authorizing a bribe or political slush-fund as soon as they've stepped off the podium.

It is impossible to specify a single reason for the growing prevalence of immoral and illegal enterprise in America. Crime exists, corruption exists; they always have, always will. But we must not give up looking for answers even though the search must now be conducted in the context of such other disturbing symptoms as growing violence, an ever-enlarging number of rapes, murders, armed robberies, muggings, and cases of savage child abuse.

There are, then, other kinds of corruption than the financial—as Watergate demonstrated—but to deal with all of them would be impossible within the confines of even a very sizable book. In the limited area of sexual morality, for example, it would be impossible for one reader to keep up with the flood of depressing literature pointing to the moral collapse of our society. To refer to but one aspect of the larger problem, psychologist Hank Giarretto, who has organized a child sexual-abuse program for California's Santa Clara County Juvenile Probation Department, has noticed a sharp increase in cases of incest. In 1971 30 cases came to his attention. By 1976 he was dealing with 270 cases annually. As of 1978 the number had jumped to almost 600! The findings are understandably disturbing to Giarretto. "I believe," he says, "that incest is now epidemic in America."

So, while it may be that a general ethical and moral crisis is evident, the present study will nevertheless restrict itself to the area of financial corruption.

Parenthetically it may be asked why, if practically all the information related here is already a matter of public record, even the average informed reader has not perceived the seriousness of the problem. The explanation is simple enough. We see what we are interested in seeing, rather than what is really about us, since the multiplicity of such particulars forces the human brain to a constant process of selection. Ten men may walk into the same room, but they do not all see the same things in it. The attention of one will be drawn to wallpaper and draperies, another may notice a pretty woman, a third the gardens outside the window, a fourth a piano in the corner, a fifth will observe books lined on shelves along a wall, a sixth the relative lack of light, etc. Just so, the average person, in reading a paper or newsmagazine, perceives what his interests dictate. It is time now for all of us to be actively concerned with the problem of financial corruption. We do, after all, pay for it. One would have to be blind not to see the examples at all levels. Consider the following random sampling.

*How many of us have witnessed a neighbor wheel a shopping cart across a supermarket parking lot and casually toss it, along with the groceries, into the trunk of the family car? An isolated instance? Not according to the Kroger Co., which loses 10,000 carts—each worth $40—every year.

*When we go to the public library (which I, like others raised in a less prosperous time, was taught to revere), do we borrow books and "forget" to return them? The average library loses between 300 and 500 books each year—an annual national loss that amounts to $25 million! Imagine it, $25 million worth of books disappearing at a time when few librarians can afford to replace them, when libraries are being forced to curtail their hours or close completely.

*In Detroit, which God knows needs responsible welfare and housing programs, arrests for bribery among Housing and Urban Development agency officials had, by the close of 1977, resulted in over 200 *convictions*. How many crooked operators went unconvicted or undetected is not known. Real estate con-men have made fast and unethical profits in housing programs, in several cities, by acquiring dilapidated buildings at low cost, bribing officials to appraise them at more than their worth, and installing poor families on mortgages that were federally insured. When the arrangements fall apart, as thousands have, everybody loses but the original sharpster. You lose, too, reader. It's your tax money that goes down the drain.

*In 1964 a manager of the internationally powerful Bechtel Corporation, a giant of the construction industry, secured a right-of-way for a project by bribing a New Jersey official. In 1975, according to a *Newsweek* report on the history of Bechtel, five of its employees were indicted for extorting kickbacks from sub-contractors on a power plant project in Calvert Cliffs, Maryland. Refreshingly, however, Bechtel fired the men involved and would appear to be one of the more honest firms in its industry.

*The Anheuser-Busch Company, which produces the popular Budweiser beer, was forced by the Securities and Exchange Commission in 1976 to reveal at least one reason for the beer's impressive sales records. The company confessed that its representatives had made cash rebates and other payments totaling approximately half a million dollars to beer-retailers between 1971 and 1975. This was not merely a case of poor corporate judgment. The officials responsible were perfectly aware that they were violating the marketing regulations of the Federal Alcohol Administration Act, which prohibits payments or gifts to influence liquor stores, bars, grocery and other retail outlets to favor one brand of beer over another. Anheuser-Busch, in 1978 fined $750,000 for such offenses, released the standard corporate cop-out specifying that "the settlement was undertaken to avoid the possibility of further protracted proceedings and does not constitute an admission of non-compliance by the company or its employees."

*Then there's the case of an interesting operator named Meshulam Riklis, whose Rapid-American Corp. (Schenley Whiskey, Botany 500 Suits, Lerner Shops, etc.) has of late attracted increasing attention from the Securities and Exchange Commission. The company, plagued by numerous lawsuits, lost money in 1974 and '75 and earned a very modest profit in '76. Its stock, as a natural consequence, had fallen steadily and its general health had become shaky. But Rapid-American's board of directors, which Riklis had carefully staffed with relatives and other close associates, paid him, in 1975, $915,000, which included a $550,000 bonus! A top Wall Street analyst, according to *Newsweek*, has observed, "Mr. Riklis makes a lot of money for himself, but not necessarily for anyone else."

*In May, 1976, Robert P. Beasley, having just resigned as principal financial officer of the Firestone Tire and Rubber Company, was revealed, by the Securities and Exchange Commission, as having administered an illegal $1.1 million political slush fund authorized by Firestone. That sort of crime, we now know, had become rather common under the Nixon and probably earlier administrations as well. But what made the Firestone-Beasley case of more than usual interest was that Beasley, at least in the opinion of a New York federal grand jury, had paid out the greater part of the money not to eager politicians but to himself. Before retiring Beasley gave $206,101 back to Firestone's treasury. The company sued him for $625,000 unaccounted for as of that time.

*A 600-page report to the Alaska Pipeline Commission, released late in 1977 after an eight-month investigation, revealed that an incredible $1.5 billion spent on the $8 billion project had been wasted. "Poor management" was the phrase employed to explain the huge loss, but when one looked behind that abstraction it became clear that what was involved was, in the practical sense, widespread thievery from pipeline supply warehouses, union featherbedding and goldbricking on an enormous scale, and similar evils that went "largely uncontrolled," according to the report.

*Columnist Hugh Sidey, who seems to know more about American presidents than anyone else, wrote in *Time* that he was told by a former aide to Lyndon Johnson that the Texas politician may have won election to the U.S. Senate in 1948 by several hundred dishonest votes. "Of course they stole that election," said the confidant. "That's the way they did it down there." So much for political morality in the true-blue, 100% *Amurrican*, country club-conservative state of Texas.

*Slum-landlords have long justified their failure to provide tenants with attractive decorations and furnishings by the assertion that any valuable articles not nailed down would in due course be pilfered. The excuse is, God help us, entirely valid. But discussions of the point frequently are based on the assumption that the problem is peculiar to low-income neighborhoods. Perhaps it was once so. According to a story in the December 5, 1968, *Wall Street Journal*, gypsy morals prevail on the right side of the tracks as well. Managers of some of the country's most exclusive apartment buildings report that their tenants steal, rip up building property, and generally remove anything they can lay hands on.

"You won't believe what these people do," complains one manager, whose well-to-do tenants steal tables, couches, potted palms and paintings as regularly as they pay their rent. One of the most attractive new building complexes in a swank Los Angeles neighborhood was losing lobby ashtrays faster than they could be replaced. The solution: the trays had to be glued to the coffee-tables.

A new luxury apartment project in San Francisco was losing picture frames, valued at $25 apiece, every few days until it resorted to gluing the frames and prints together and bolting the units to the wall. In New York, Chicago and other major cities the problem is no less serious. Besides stealing pictures, mirrors, ashtrays, small chairs and other easily transportable items, tenants, when moving out, will frequently remove such other building-owned items as ice-cube trays and sink faucets. A New York psychologist, Harold Greenwald, has a theory to explain why well-heeled renters stoop to petty pilferage.

"The tenants are angry at having to pay such high rents," says Dr. Greenwald. "Stealing is their way of getting back." Greenwald's theory may well throw light on the motivation behind the thefts. It makes no comment about the dissolving ethical standards of an ever-growing segment of our society.

A particularly tragic side-effect of the understandable fear, on the part of landlords, that tenants will steal anything they can get their hands on came to light when a fire in a downtown Los Angeles hotel in December of 1978 killed five people, although several fire extinguishers that might have saved their lives were nearby but under lock and key. "The reason the damned fire extinguishers were not on the wall was because the . . . [tenants] were always stealing them and throwing them under the building," said builder-manager Frank Cline.

*One of the more shocking examples of mindless avarice concerns the John F. Kennedy Center for the Performing Arts, opened in September, 1971, in Washington, D.C. The imposing white marble structure, which stands not far from the Lincoln Memorial, attracted hundreds of thousands of visitors in its first few months of operation. NBC Newsman John Chancellor pointedly observes that "these tourists are not wild-eyed mobs from the inner-city slums, or motorcycle gangs from the suburbs, but nice, middle-class folks, the kind who visit the FBI building when they come to the capital." These middle-class Americans, in Chancellor's words, "have stolen the place blind: the faucets in the washrooms, the chandeliers, the curtains, everything is being stolen."

Within three months after the Center opened, tourists had picked it clean of all ashtrays, all salt and pepper cellars in the restaurant, great amounts of glassware, dishes and silverware. Pieces of valuable curtains were snipped off, chandeliers were stripped of glass, faucets in the washrooms detached and stolen, even brass plates around electrical fixtures pried loose.

"It's incredible," Chancellor says, "people have walked off with plants, taken every single menu in the place, napkins, even pieces of carpets in the halls have been cut up with knives and taken away for God-only-knows what purpose."

Does Chancellor foresee a wave of public shame putting a stop to the thefts by visitors? No. "Their piranha-like rapacity for anything portable," he says, "is a bit frightening, and their numbers will only grow."

A late 1978 conference called by the National Crime Prevention Association heard Merrit Kanner, executive of a Miami-based security agency, explain that U.S. hotels and motels currently are suffering a loss of some billion dollars annually from thefts by guests, employees and professional criminals. At least one out of three guests, Kanner says, takes something believing that "taking is not stealing." But thefts at present involve far more then the traditional towel or ashtray. Some guests cart away furniture, wall-bolted pictures, lamps, heavy bedspreads. Fifty percent of all hotel room thefts, it appears, occur in unattended rooms; very few involve forcible entry. Many hotel guests simply do not turn in their keys when they leave and apparently some of them later use the same keys to commit outright robberies.

    *Americans have been stealing each other's automobiles or parts thereof since the days of Henry Ford. For almost half a century professional specialists have operated in the field. The significance of this for the present study lies in the fact that the number of middle-class, well-paid customers who knowingly do business with criminal car-theft professionals is growing. Several years ago Lee Burdin, staff reporter of *The Wall Street Journal*, related the case of a 40-year-old New Yorker who had his heart set on a particular model, a Buick Electra, but couldn't afford one until a friend told him how.

"It's easy," the man whispered. "First you give me $1,000 and I'll sell you a stolen used Mustang. I'll re-steal it, and you'll collect $2,000 from your insurance company. With the $2,000 you buy a stolen Cadillac Coupe de Ville from me. I'll re-steal it and you'll collect $5,000 on the insurance. Then you can go to a legitimate auto dealer and buy the Buick."

The case came to light as the result of a New York police investigation of organized auto-theft rings. The National Automobile Theft Bureau (NATB), investigating arm of over four hundred insurance companies, reports that auto theft has risen faster than any other crime category in the United States, and estimates that 800 million dollars worth of cars were stolen in this country in 1968, 22% more than in 1967, and double the amount just five years before! According to more recent estimates, there are now over 300 professional car theft *gangs* active around the country.

The working-methods of most of these bear slight resemblance to those of the car thieves of the 30's and 40's, who concentrated on plain-looking, medium-priced models and maintained well-hidden car-body shops to alter the cars' appearance before attempting to put them back on the market. Today's gangs deal openly in Cadillacs, Chevrolet Corvettes, Ford Thunderbirds and other flashy models. Nor do the professionals bother much anymore about altering the appearance of the cars they steal.

Police officials are most concerned that today's auto theft teams could not successfully operate without the *connivance of their customers*, who are willing to take the risk of being arrested themselves, and knowingly do business with professional criminals, to save a few hundred dollars on the price of a car. The majority of buyers of stolen cars, reports Robert Sadowskie, deputy chief of the Queens District Attorney's Rackets Bureau, are *middle-income people with no criminal records*, "but they have larceny in their hearts; they want something for nothing."

According to Irving B. Guller, Associate Professor of Psychology at John Jay College of Criminal Justice in New York, middle-class people are increasingly willing to go along with such schemes because of "the growing publicity about how rich people are making it by skirting the law . . . To a lot of people, owning a Caddie amounts to 'making it' and there's *a growing belief that once you make it, no one will care how.*" (Italics added)

Statistics from the NATB show that in 1975 there were 1,000,500 such thefts in the United States, an increase of 2% over 1974. This means that there is a car stolen in the United States every 30 seconds, or that as of 1975 one out of every 130 registered vehicles in the country was stolen! Most auto thefts, of course, are perpetrated by young people and do not represent an organized business practice, but hundreds of thousands are connected with an ongoing market-activity supported by the American middle-class.

By 1978 the dominant development in the car theft industry had become the "chop shops," out-of-the-way garages where the bodies of stolen cars are torn apart and the parts sold on a nationwide black market.

Sold to professional criminals? No, to allegedly law-abiding body shops and auto dealers, who use the parts to repair vehicles damaged in accidents. According to Federal law enforcement estimates close to 40% of the 975,000 passenger cars stolen in the U.S. during 1977 were dismantled in "chop shop" operations.

*As for garages and auto-repair shops, the picture is no brighter. I recall that some years ago Ed

Sullivan, wanting to have a troublesome carburetor repaired, tried three New York garages, where he was charged $36, $26, and $32. Almost despairing of finding a New Yorker who could properly fix his car, he went to Werner G. Maeder, Jr., on the West Side. Maeder, who comes from Switzerland, told him he had been robbed by the three other garages because little or no work had been done on the carburetor, which still had a gaping hole in it.

The CBS network's superb "60 Minutes" program in the summer of 1978 conducted a survey showing that vacationing motorists have a good chance of being ripped off by roadside gas station operators when they pull in for service. The vicious criminal racket is perpetrated by station operators in collusion with crooks called "50 percenters," who offer their services in return for a 50-50 share of whatever business they handle. The arrangement is, of course, profitable for the station owner because the 50 percenters are so adept at fleecing unsuspecting out-of-state motorists.

The out-of-state factor is important because even if the average victim discovers he's been swindled he's unlikely to return several hundred miles at a later date for a court trial. Preferred victims for these thieves are women and older people, neither of whom generally know enough of matters mechanical to realize they are being robbed. It's important to note that there is no question here of simple judgment or honest error on the part of the mechanics or station attendants. The gasoline industry and law enforcement agencies are perfectly aware that the question is one of criminality.

Some years back, to test the integrity of repair shops, the *Reader's Digest* conducted a now-famous survey of gas stations and garages. The investigators disconnected a single wire in an engine and asked the stations to repair whatever was wrong. *63% of the mechanics approached charged for repairs they did not make.* The *Reader's Digest* team concluded "we were lucky if they didn't take out the new fuel pump and replace it with a used one."

In March 1978 Joan Claybrook, of the National Highway Traffic Safety Administration, told the U.S. Senate Commerce Subcommittee that almost 40% of the money spent on car repairs—a figure in excess of 20 billion dollars a year—was wasted because of faulty and sometimes fraudulent repair-work, poor owner maintenance and new car design.

"We believe," she said, "that slightly more than half of the 20 billion dollar waste results from fraudulent, incompetent or unnecessary repairs performed by the repair industry." One of the more familiar forms of consumer dollar waste, Ms. Claybrook said, involved packaged deals in which the car owner is told he needs a tune-up when in reality only one bad sparkplug needs replacement. "Outright fraud by repair facilities," she said, "is common."

*In a time when the daily edition of any metropolitan newspaper carries more than enough news of greed to turn the stomach, the 1977 discovery in Boston of a wide-spread arson ring nevertheless attracted special attention. After three years of investigation by Boston journalists—for the most part not those connected with that city's major papers—police arrested 33 men—not just street thugs, not full-time professional criminals, but rather landlords, insurance officials, lawyers, officers of the fire department, and others alleged, as we say, to be part of a vast arson-for-profit conspiracy. Mark Zanger and other young journalists conducted a relentless and heroic investigation which in time tied supposedly law-abiding landlords with organized crime figures, including a known arsonist, George Lincoln.

*A Catholic order, the Palatine Fathers of Baltimore, raised 20 million dollars during a two-year period, spent most of the money on a direct mail campaign, and passed less than 3% of it along to the hungry children whom contributers had assumed they were benefiting!

The priest who created the fund-raising Palatine Fathers' brochures—showing starving children with swollen stomachs—the Reverend Guido John Carcich, was charged in January of 1978 in a 61-count indictment with misappropriating nearly 1.4 million dollars donated for the poor and with concealing records of almost 15 million dollars in secret bank accounts.

Carcich and his fellow operators had argued that such large financial holdings were necessary to insure the financial security of the overseas missions conducted by the order.

The investigation, however, revealed that Carcich did not follow the usual procedures in such cases, investing in well-established securities, but rather put money into such unusual enterprises as the Orleans Inn and the Red Coconut Trailer Park in southwest Florida and the Yellow Bird, Bahama Seas and Bon Aire motels, also in Florida. Father Carcich himself made unexplained trips to Las Vegas, accepted new cars from his friends and—incredibly—lent the suspended Maryland governor Marvin Mandel $54,000 to help finance Mandel's divorce!

Earlier a shocked public had learned that the famed Father Flanagan's Boy's Town in Nebraska was increasing its financial position by over 16 million dollars annually while spending comparatively little on child care. These and similar scandals within the churches led to the preparation of a bill in Congress that would require charities to make public precisely how much of their received contributions actually go for charitable work. It is difficult to see what anyone— much less a church official—could find objectionable in this but the fact is that both Protestant and Catholic spokesmen have opposed the bill vigorously! It is significant that the proposed legislation, which was sponsored by Representative Charles H. Wilson (D-Calif.) was enthusiastically supported by the American Heart Association, the American Lung Association, the Save the Children Federation, the National Kidney Foundation and other prominent and ethical charities.

Then there's the case of Rabbi Leib Pinter, who in May of 1978 pleaded guilty of having given $5,000 in bribes to Congressman Daniel Flood of Pennsylvania for Flood's assistance in obtaining federal money for a multi-million dollar poverty agency and aid for a planned school in Israel.

(Flood, of course, was already in trouble since by that time a Federal Grand Jury convened in Philadelphia was investigating charges that the Congressman, a colorful former Shakespearean actor who sports a silent-movie sort of moustache, had collected more than $100,000 in influence payoffs in recent years. Congressman Joshua Eilberg, another Pennsylvania Democrat, was also involved in the inquiry.)

James Lien, Carson City, Nevada's, "Man of the Year" in

1970, mayoral candidate of 1972, and former deputy chief of the Nevada tax agent department, was sentenced to a four year prison term after his conviction on charges of embezzling nearly $19,000 from St. Peter's Episcopal Church, of which Lien was treasurer, over a five-year period.

*Then we have the interesting state-of-affairs in the Texas oil fields, where the recent shortage of drilling equipment has led to a black market for bulky stolen equipment the value of which, according to Houston police, may be running as high as $50,000,000 a year! It is important to grasp that the thieves are not simply full-time scrap metal dealers; 70% of the thefts, according to police lieutenant J. B. Bradley, are *inside* jobs. Needless to say, the stolen equipment is sold back to other "law-abiding" oil field operators.

*That there are presently a good many crooked lawyers can come as a surprise to no one past the age of ten. Even a weeks's casual reading of papers in any American city with a population larger than 100,000 will provide instances of all sorts of minor and major criminal activity engaged in by legal professionals who are perfectly aware of what the law says about their offenses. Instance: In November of 1972 a Los Angeles attorney, Perry J. Walshin, was convicted in New York of planning to smuggle $80,000 worth of cocaine into the United States from Colombia, South America. Walshin earlier had been found innocent, in a Los Angeles trial, on charges of pimping and pandering in connection with the operation of Los Angeles area massage parlors though his co-defendant in the trial, attorney David DeLoach, was convicted and sentenced to a year in jail.

Three-piece-suit Organized Crime, needless to say, could not function without the vast battery of lawyers it employs. Under the American judicial system the worst criminal in the world is entitled to a legal defense; no one takes exception, therefore, to the fact that Mafia and other syndicate hoodlums hire lawyers to protect their interests. But there is a considerable difference between this and the full-time businesses that some lawyers run simply defending top-level criminals or conducting business affairs for them. As Jim Drinkwater, courageous reporter who wrote a bril-

liant series of investigative articles for *Overdrive*, an independent truck drivers' monthly, has put it, "The old time
hoodlums have gone into all kinds of legitimate business,
especially in California. A hefty chunk of their money goes
into real estate development, and who knows what else
they're doing? It's really just a way to wash money. In the
old days, during Prohibition, they beat people in the head.
*Now that they've got millions of dollars they hire lawyers
instead.* They've become a lot more sophisticated."

Miami lawyer Lewis Williams was arrested near that
city's International Airport in January of 1978 on multiple
drug and firearm charges after narcotics investigators reported he had sold them a pair of steel cans containing a
million dollars worth of cocaine.

Then there's the case of Barry Marlin, lawyer-financier
charged with defrauding hundreds of United Airlines pilots
of at least 12 million dollars. In March of 1978, Marlin was
sentenced to three years in prison in Chicago after pleading
guilty to six counts of a Federal Grand Jury indictment
charging him with mail fraud in connection with investments in a Paradise, California shopping-center that existed
only in his own devious mind.

Or consider David D. Trebilcock of Woodland Hills,
California, who, at year's end, 1978, was arraigned in Federal Court in Los Angeles in connection with the armed
robbery of five L.A. area savings and loan association offices.

Unethical legal practices in one state, Florida, have become so notorious that one of the state's better papers, *The
Floridian* of Sarasota, on April 2nd, 1978, ran an admirable
report on the situation, naming a good many names. "Lack
of public trust in lawyers," the *Floridian* explained, "coupled with increasing complaints of lawyers misusing trust
funds . . . persuaded Florida Supreme Court Chief Justice
Ben Overton last year to order a special committee to recommend new procedures for disciplining unscrupulous lawyers."

Sample cases: Harry B. Duffy, Fort Lauderdale lawyer,
disappeared in June of 1976 at approximately the same time
that $750,000 in trust funds he had managed appeared to be
unaccounted for.

Jacksonville lawyer William B. Dawson III was disbarred by the Supreme Court in 1975 for "making monetary advancements to clients for purposes unrelated to the conduct of their litigation, coupled with receipt of property in circumstances that would raise suspicions that the property was in fact stolen." Writer Thomas Oldt says, "Of the nearly 2,000 complaints falling into the ethics category made to the [Florida] bar last year very few filtered through the probable-cause and into the trial stage. In fact, seven lawyers were disbarred while nine were suspended and nine more were issued public reprimands." Over 40 others were privately reprimanded. How many were equally guilty but not detected is, of course, unknown.

*The House Select committee on aging reported, in December of 1978, on a six-month investigation which revealed that elderly Americans had become the victims-of-choice of hard-sell pitches and empty promises by health insurance salesmen.

"We have found," said committee chairman Claude Pepper (D-Fla.), "that many unscrupulous agents have been preying on the fears of the elderly and selling them three, four, five and sometimes as many as thirty different health insurance policies. The sad part is that these policies are duplicative and largely worthless. They generally contain a clause which says that only one policy will pay."

Aged Americans are spending $1 billion a year on such unnecessary insurance, the committee said.

*A separate book could be written on the corruption associated with the American military effort in Vietnam. In fact one has been written. It's *The Greedy War*, by James Hamilton-Paterson (David McKay Company), a true story, packed with more adventure and excitement than most novels. Its hero—if that's the right word for him—is a remarkable man named Cornelius Hawkridge. *The Greedy War* deals primarily with the American and South Vietnamese thieves, black marketeers and hijackers who took money out of your pocket, in your capacity as tax-payer. The U.S. was ripped off for so many billions the actual amount will never be known.

The remarkable thing is that the story of the outrage would never have come out had it not been for one courageous individual, Hawkridge, a one-man truth squad whose charges have been documented by *Life* magazine and by confidential testimony before a U.S. Senate investigating committee. He was an eye-witness to American supply ships being stripped before they even got to dockside in Vietnam ports. Trucks, television sets, weapons, even tanks were hijacked. That this would happen at all is dismaying enough, but in many cases the stolen military equipment was eventually sold to the enemy.

Another reason *The Greedy War* will make you angry is that it tells not only how profiteers made billions in Vietnam but how American fighting men—who were being shot at, maimed for life, killed—were also ripped off by being sold shoddy merchandise in PX's and other shops in Vietnam.

In his testimony before the Senate Permanent Subcommittee on Investigations, Hawkridge said, "I was outraged by what I saw in Vietnam—the corruption, the filth, the thievery, the profiteering on other people's misery. But when I reported what was happening, I was told to shut up, to quit being a trouble maker!"

There are certain people so constituted that if they hear the slightest criticism—even this long after the fact—about the American war effort in Vietnam, they immediately assume the critic must be a Communist.

In fact Cornelius Hawkridge is as dedicated and intense an anti-Communist as one can be without being locked up for erratic behavior. He's a middle-aged native of Hungary who spent 7½ years in Russian and Hungarian Communist prison camps before escaping to the United States, the kind of anti-Communist who, when he went to Vietnam, thought he could do something meaningful and positive to fight Communism. But what he observed in Vietnam turned his stomach.

A figure once portrayed as heroic by the American press, former South Vietnam Premier Nguyen Cao Ky, in July of 1976 revealed that during his brief residence in the United States he had come to an accurate-enough assessment of American financial morality. While addressing an audience of Indianapolis businessmen Ky was asked why the South Vietnamese government had been unable to rally the Vietnamese people to its cause. The government, Ky explained, was "weak, corrupt and made too many errors." He exempted himself from the condemnation. "I was not corrupt. Perhaps that is the only thing I regret, because *I have realized—after 14 months in this country—the value of money, whether it is clean or dirty.*" (Italics supplied.)

II

It has been a common assumption in the United States for more than half a century that the essential superiority of Capitalism to Communism is on the moral plane. But when one considers such disheartening facts as those earlier cited, it is clearly time to examine the national conscience. For example, how do our chambers of commerce feel morally about industrial espionage? Corporate losses through spying and the theft of goods and processes now run to over two billion dollars a year. Espionage is heaviest in the electronic, drug, petroleum and toy industries, but goes on almost everywhere.

Who hires the spies? *Other big companies.*

It is a philosophical commonplace that the morality of large groups is inferior to that of the individuals who comprise them. A nation, for example, will lie, murder, cheat, steal, commit almost any crime if it is imagined that doing so will preserve it, while it imprisons its citizens for doing the same things. Just so, a corporation—particularly a very large one—has no nerve-center of moral sensitivity. Even its leaders come and go. Consequently men who might be reluctant to employ nefarious methods for their personal gain may have no qualms about employing dishonest means to serve the end of corporate profit. It is an accepted part of "the system," the system we call Free Enterprise. So is the corruption of politicians by management. Consider the average state legislature in the United States. Locate "The Illinois Legislature, a Study of Corruption" in the September 1964 issue of *Harper's*. If the body described is even remotely typical (and I believe it is), then God help this country.

Republican Representative Nobel Lee, dean of the John Marshall Law School of Chicago, who had served eleven terms in the Illinois House, estimated that *at least one-third of its members accepted payoffs and bribes.*

These were, of course, politicians, who have always been regarded as a bit suspect by the very constituencies that vote them into office. But what about ordinary citizens who regard themselves as law-abiding?

I shall refer only in passing, incidentally, to crimes committed by the truly poor, such as petty thievery, shop-lifting of basic foodstuffs, even serious street crime. It is all deplorable enough, but at least such offenders can claim the desperation of poverty as an excuse, can argue that when they join an undisciplined gang of looters or put their hand in the till in any other way they are only getting back either their own or that which they have been denied. They deserve, needless to say, to be arrested and appropriately dealt with. Other studies, however, have been written on that subject. I restrict myself here, for the most part, to white-collar crime, to the corruption of people in the middle or upper economic brackets, living in comfortable apartments and homes, driving expensive cars, holding good jobs, and still so greedy that they have to get their paws on *more*.

One thing clearly standing in the way of moral progress now is the absurd belief that there is something somehow *holy* about our economic processes.

It is a monstrous affront to common sense to imagine that Andrew Carnegie, to take just one industrialist at random, was a moral equivalent of St. Francis. The American people are too intelligent to assume that John D. Rockefeller or Henry Ford were as worthy of respect as Abraham Lincoln or Thomas Aquinas.

Again: we must be honest about what Capitalism is. It is a generally free-market structure in which it is perfectly possible for honest people to make a living, to make a profit—possible, for some, to accumulate great wealth. But it is a structure under which considerable advantages also can accrue to the ruthless, unscrupulous and dishonest person.

Some of the individuals who have gone the furthest under Capitalism, of course, are those who combine the best and worst qualities. Carnegie, for instance, attained his position of power at the turn of the century in typical "robber baron" fashion. He was, among other things, a thief and a scoundrel, who rose not only by his penchant for thrift and sound business dealings, but by lying, stealing and ruthlessly crushing all who stood in his way.

A government investigation in 1893, instigated by the Secretary of the Navy, revealed that at Carnegie's Homestead plant the company had deliberately cheated the United States navy by failing to temper steel for armor plate evenly and properly. Former employees of the plant, including men long-accustomed to Carnegie's methods, expressed shock as they revealed that "blow-holes, which would probably have caused the rejection of plates by Government inspectors," had been plugged and concealed. In addition, they said, plates which had been selected for ballistic tests had been specially re-treated so they would seem to be better and tougher than the group of plates they represented.

Carnegie's tactics were not much different in his dealings with rivals. When he was trying to bring the Pennsylvania Railroad to its knees he called in a young employee, a man whose prior reputation was spotless. "I must know the exact rebates that are being paid to our competitors," Carnegie said. "How you are going to get them I don't know, and I don't care. But I must have them."

As a biographer of the industrialist later observed, "From that day to this no one has ever learned how the young man obtained the closest guarded of all railroad secrets." But it can be assumed that the man stole them, bribed for them, or otherwise got them in an underhanded fashion. As a reward, he was given a partnership in the Carnegie Steel Company.

There have been visible improvements in the world of business since the day of the Robber Barons, but as John Kenneth Galbraith points out in his informative and witty *The Age of Uncertainty*, the changes are largely ones of manners, not of morals. One would have to agree that a modern oil man would cringe if an associate said, "The public be damned," as Vanderbilt once did. Today, notes Galbraith, even the most ruthless predator must present himself as a public benefactor.

The change is cosmetic at best. On the moral side, the way such "financiers" as Robert Vesco, Richard Nixon's close friend C. Arnholt Smith, and the operators behind Investors Overseas Services and Real Estate Fund of America work to separate money from widows, orphans and fools does not, says Galbraith, represent "a quantum step up to righteousness from Vanderbilt and the Erie gang [which] bought judges."

Great U.S. corporations have bought politicians at home and abroad, he contends—in much the same way that the infamous Pavel Ivanovich Chichikov travelled over Russia a century ago buying the bodies of dead serfs and, neglecting to mention that they were dead, used their ownership as security for loans from a bank. Is that, asks Galbraith, so much different from the activities of Stanley Goldblum, who inflated the value of the stock of a company known as Equity Funding Corporation by creating phantom purchasers of insurance policies?

(John Birchers and Young Americans for Freedom, take note: I prefer our system to the Communist alternative. It affords a higher standard of living than that prevailing in any Marxist state, and is compatible with essential freedoms—of the press, of assembly, of movement, of philosophical belief—to an extent that totalitarian systems, of the Right or Left, can never tolerate.)

But holy? Sanctified in any sense? Nonsense. The loose structure of economic practices generally connoted by the terms free enterprise or capitalism is useful, practical, productive. That is one side of the ledger. But to refuse to examine the other side is stupid. Capitalism has also been responsible for the worst sort of selfishness, cruelty, suffering, poverty, hunger, sickness, thievery and chicanery of which man is capable.

This book, then, is among other things an exercise in

patriotism. I am infuriated by what the thieves, corporate and individual, are doing to my country. I want to preserve our system, perpetuate it, but purify it. There is dirty linen. The thing to do is launder it, in public and promptly, not deny its existence.

The alternative, in the long run, could be the collapse of what we have long cherished as the American way of life.

To which some ignoramus will rise to inquire "Do you think people are any more honest in Mexico, France, Italy, or elsewhere?" I neither know nor—in this context—care; but the question implies an acceptance of my thesis.

As children we knew that there were evil or dishonest men, but we assumed that they were in the minority and could be easily identified. It is remarkable how persistently we adhere to this early bias through our adult years. Perhaps by the age of 30 we begin to assume that the lawless minority is not as small as we once supposed. As the years pass now it is difficult to escape the conclusion that it is not the lawless but the law-abiding that are in the minority.

Chapter *II*

The
Historical
Background of
Western
Corruption

The American culture did not create the problem of corruption. Its origins are unknown. The Old Testament prophets frequently pointed to its corrosive effects on their societies. To adequately outline the historical scope of the evil would require the preparation of a library. The reader may nevertheless consider helpful a few brief comments concerning the historical background.

In the 16th century, during the reign of Emperor Charles V, the great European powers, as we have come to know them, were beginning to assume their general geographical outlines. France in the west, England in the north and the Hapsburg Empire in Central Europe—larger and more powerful than the individual provinces and city-states of which they were comprised—began to maneuver for power like three mighty mastodons. "Simultaneously," observes Egon Fridell in *A Cultural History of the Modern Age*, "there developed and expanded a large-scale corruption-system of quite new universality and unscrupulousness, possible only in an age of money-economy." It was at this time that gold and politics were united in that inseparable alliance which is characteristic of the modern age. Charles V, King of Spain, became Emperor, not because he was the most beloved or the most qualified—Frederick the Wise, the elector of Saxony, Francis I of France and Henry VIII of England were also contenders—but, as Fridell explains, "simply because the great banking-house of Fugger guaranteed him the sums he had promised the Electors. In other words, even then the greatest power was not Spain or France or England but the financier."

As for the North American continent, there was a degree of corruption from the time of the first European settlements. The native Indian was at once perceived as an easy mark and frequently swindled.

No doubt for the most part those who escaped Europe's tyrannies to establish the good life here possessed the virtues attributed to them by historians. Their diaries, however, reveal that heroism and high moral purpose were not unanimous. Captain John Smith complains that some of his people scuffled around looking for gold and wouldn't work at much else. Partly as a result, corn for the following winter was in short supply. The initial communal experiment was replaced in 1618 when the London Company, the Queen's franchise for Virginia, decreed that private ownership of property was legal. They also included a provision granting fifty acres of land to a settler, fifty acres for each family member and fifty for each worker and tenant on the property. Corruption invaded the Virginia countryside when certain residents started keeping double books. A fast pen established many a Virginia farm or plantation whose occupants today enjoy the inherited fruits of their ancestors' dishonesty.

After sheaves of tobacco became Virginia's monetary unit of exchange, corruptors learned the trick of paying debts with inferior leaves, while holding the good tobacco for future sale. Later in the century our Revolutionary War brought new opportunities for financial chicanery. The story of the flooding of a whole society with printed notes which later inspired the phrase "not worth a Continental" is known to almost every school child. Some historians feel that had the Colonists lost some would have been indicted for willful fraud. A case can be argued that despite the ideals of

Thomas Jefferson and the signatories to the Declaration of Independence, the war itself—as is the case with all wars—greatly increased corruption. This included untrammeled profiteering by some "sunshine patriots" who saw a chance to draw scarce precious metal sovereigns into their own pockets. Some farmers gladly did business with the British military simply because they paid in gold whereas Washington's armies made purchases with paper money. No wonder Washington blistered the Congress for employing financial means which kept him and his ragged troops constantly on the verge of starvation.

Alexander Hamilton, father of the U.S. Treasury, troubled about the Continental notes, decided to restore order by paying off one cent of hard money to the dollar. When word of his intentions got around, certain politicians and their friends in the know profited. Hamilton was not among them.

During the early years of American history, however, partly because of the influence of the high ethical standards—though not always behavior—which accompanied the founding of our nation, and partly, too, because the opportunities for dishonesty were less common than they are presently—fraud was relatively rare.

By 1837, when the American economic network had become more complex, consequently enlarging the opportunities for dishonesty, the *New York Sun* was moved to ask, "Is there no way to reach the knaves who have control of the city with checks made out in the form of bills on banks in which they have not a dollar deposited?"

Frank Gibney, in his perceptive account of country-club level dishonesty in the U.S., *The Operators*, says, "Later 19th-century progress brought the operators into the big-time. By the 1890's, the old-time 'Robber Barons' had become operators in the grand manner. During a meeting of 17 railroad presidents in J.P. Morgan's house in New York City, one of their number, J.B. Stickney, delivered himself of the memorable observation 'I have the utmost respect for you gentlemen individually, but as railroad presidents I wouldn't trust you with my watch out of my sight.'

The years between 1832 and the closing of all the nation's banks by Franklin Roosevelt in 1933 were marked by numerous financial improprieties in banking.

Big-city corruption in time became almost a special American art-form, which leads us to William Marcy "Boss" Tweed. As head of the New York department of public works, Tweed put together an organization known as the Tammany Ring that elected its own candidate for Mayor in 1865, a coup Tweed followed by dictating the election of his own Governor of New York. An 1871 investigation by a group of seventy public-spirited citizens, led by Samuel Tilden, later an unsuccessful candidate for the Presidency, resulted in the indictment and imprisonment of Tweed.

Needless to say, the power structures, both political and financial, which exert unsavory influence over our great cities have not changed much through the years. Their methods now are more sophisticated than Tweed's. But where Tweed played with hundreds of thousands of dollars, city bosses now play with billions.

Journalistic crusaders of the sort that exposed Tweed are not common enough, though there are exceptions such as the *Washington Post*'s Woodward and Bernstein, descendants of the journalists of the Upton Sinclair type whose stories about conditions in the Chicago stockyards shortly after the turn of the century led to urgently needed reforms. The packinghouse giants then wallowed in corruption largely free from "government interference" on behalf of American consumers. It was easy to buy government inspectors who approved hogs riddled with disease. Rank smelling meat shoveled from packinghouse floors found its way into sausage casings. The same financial greed occasioned brutalities inflicted upon slaughterhouse workers who when they objected to ill treatment were beaten by company goon-squads including—God help us—policemen.

Similar conditions obtained in the coal mines of the East, Midwest and West. Most mining families were trapped into lifetime bondage by debt. And everywhere, of course, such corruption asserted itself through legislators owned by business tycoons. In the oil industry John D. Rockefeller demanded and received preferential freight rates, foreclosed on his best friend and explained that if he had not done so someone else would have. He formed a corporation so powerful that finally when the stench of his enterprise could not be tolerated even in compromised government, a Federal Judge, Kenesaw Mountain Landis—later to become Czar of Major League Baseball following the Black Sox players bribery scandal—ordered Rockefeller's Standard Oil Company broken up.

Henry Ford, exalted as the man who put America on wheels, had an "ethics-be-damned" attitude. He employed his own partly-criminal Gestapo to spy on workers and pushed his men until they dropped. Meantime, he corrupted the automobile industry by forcing cars on his dealers at such a rate that they were sometimes forced to discard ethical considerations to keep up with Henry's demands.

By the 1920's the country had entered the period of the prohibition of alcoholic beverages, a well-intentioned but hare-brained scheme that made almost our entire society corrupt and put the Mafia and other organized criminal elements into a position of power that has never since been weakened.

Chapter *III*

Blowing The Whistle on Crooked Cops

It takes only a few seconds to utter one of the most noble phrases that can pass the lips of an American citizen, the sentence in the Policeman's Code of Ethics that goes: "I recognize the badge of my office as a symbol of public faith and I accept it as a public trust to be held so long as I am true to the ethics of the police service."

So long as I am true to the ethics. More and more, it appears, many officers begin to be *un*true as soon as they lower their right hand after subscribing to the oath.

Let me state a relevant prejudice: I like policemen. As a class they are admirable. Since childhood, I have held them in the same regard as selfless firemen, soldiers and sailors, athletes. A policeman's work is dangerous, his pay is low, his courage obvious. When I hear a prowler outside my house at night, I call for a cop. Until my community—or the world— becomes a great deal more civilized, I want policemen out, in force. I do not agree with people who smugly assume that every cop's honor is for sale for a ten-spot or that all police-men are incipient Fascists.

In a word, I am pro-cop. I'm aware that police corruption exists, but I still find it easy to be sympathetic to the men and women who slide into the corruption trap. Lonely foot-soldiers, they find themselves lured with a free cup of coffee to warm their chilled bodies; next comes the free meal, and then perhaps a few dollars to keep an extra eye on the restaurant or to look the other way when the restaurant owner books a few bets on the side. And so it goes, and grows.

Corruption—of all kinds—is generally a matter of a slow process, rather than a single, large dramatic act. That I understand.

But that's as far as I go. I will not give sympathy to the individual who lets his greed totally override his judgment and sense of honor. A cop who cooperates with Organized Crime, moonlights in narcotics, operates his own burglary ring, is a criminal *disguised* as a policeman.

But surely, corrupt policemen are in the minority? I hope so. In some cities it's an open question.

There are enough instances of corruption among the police to fill volumes, rather than a single chapter. The range of criminal acts committed by the men and women sworn to uphold the law extends from shaking down prostitutes to testifying falsely in court in order to let a racketeer or drug dealer go free. Corruption can be internal—such as paying bribes to precinct clerks in exchange for extra days of vacation—or such as planting false evidence on a suspect in the hope of winning a swift conviction and a promotion to a higher grade level.

This last process, known as "flaking," is part of a police jargon that itself suggests the depth of corruption in the profession. There are, for example, the "meat eaters"—cops who actively solicit bribes—in opposition to the "grass eaters," the ones who accept payoffs that just happen to come their way.

Ordinarily when one thinks of police scandal, the mind focuses almost immediately on the long-time bastions of corruption, New York and Chicago.

New York first, then.

An entire library could be accumulated on the history of police corruption in New York City. Rumors, charges, in-house investigations, grand jury investigations, and police department shake-ups have been so common over the years in our largest city that the situation has to assume enormous proportions before it is any longer considered front-page news. It assumed precisely those proportions in 1971 when dishonesty by police officers became so widespread that the public finally became interested.

The question remains: why do cops go wrong? Part of the answer is greed, wanting something extra without working for it. Policemen are in many instances underpaid. Every city, town, and village should regularly study police salary levels and consider pay increases. Still, every officer knows the pay he is going to make when he subscribes to that oath—and there is not a word in it about ignoring the public trust "in the event that I can pick up a few dollars on the side."

Our society will have to wrestle with the problem of finding ways to counteract the long-established philosophy of the dishonest officer, described by Walter Arms in *Pay-Off*. "The crooked cop, somewhere along the line, begins to feel he's a member of a privileged class . . . He believes that he is above censure and penalty and assumes that the graft he is taking is part of his salary." The Knapp Commission report—a massive 283 page study—has stated that "over half of the police force took graft in 1971."

"Over half . . ." That conclusion startled even the investigators who dug into corruption over a 31-month period, after a citizens' committee was commissioned by former Mayor John V. Lindsay and headed by Whitman Knapp, a Wall Street lawyer.

"Over half . . ." And yet, out of a force of thousands, the Knapp Commission's efforts resulted in the indictment of just ten policemen and a series of charges against eleven others. This despite the welter of information provided by Sgt. David Durk and the now famous officer Frank Serpico, whose role was embellished in a popular motion picture and a television series based on his exploits.

"Over half . . . " Thousands of policemen, said the Commission, were involved in graft, classified as both "clean" and "dirty." "Clean graft" meant accepting such ordinary blandishments as free meals, free liquor, an occasional tip in cash. "Dirty graft" could range from routine payoffs made by pimps and narcotics pushers to a share of the spoils from a successful burglary.

Among the tales that startled the New York investigators was that of Waverly Logan, a member of the Preventive Enforcement Patrol, who began his tour of duty as an idealistic policeman. Soon he was tempted by the easy money that could be made by shaking down narcotics dealers and gamblers. At times, Logan told the Commission, he made as much as $3,000 a month—merely by holding out his hand. On the average, he said, he could augment his policeman's pay by $1,500 monthly.

Logan's story was not a case of an honest man's seeing the light. He volunteered to talk only after he was discharged from the force for accepting a bribe of $100. Hoping to negotiate a deal the officer sought reinstatement by offering to provide the Commission with narcotics information gleaned from informants wired with tape-recorders and radio transmitters.

One outcome of the electronic eavesdropping was the revelation that a number of narcotics officers had become pushers themselves. In one film surreptitiously made by the investigating team a policeman received four bottles of whiskey from an informant who was given in return an envelope filled with heroin. Where had the heroin come from? It was not determined but, as the "French Connection" case illustrated, it was not unusual for drugs confiscated in legitimate raids to disappear from police vaults and find their way back into the underworld traffic.

Other testimony unearthed the fact that the members of the force who were "on the take" were benefiting to the tune of some $60,000 worth of free meals and hotel rooms annually. The prestigious New York Hilton Hotel alone gave some 80 cops 144 meals worth $2,500 in six months.

Paul J. Curran, chairman of the State Investigation Commission, revealed that his force had found 17 different ways in which the New York police had become involved in corruption. They had accepted bribes, said Curran; they had extorted money and narcotics for ignoring violations of the law; they had themselves supplied heroin for sale; they had actively sold heroin; they had purchased drugs from Organized Crime sources; they had retained money or drugs found in raids and searches; they had protected narcotics operators from arrest; they had tipped off violators about impending raids; they had framed suspects in order to meet arrest quotas; they had interceded with fellow officers to get charges dropped or reduced in behalf of suspects; they had tried to bribe prosecutors; they had lied in court under oath, and they had intentionally filed weak affidavits to help suspects escape prosecution.

One of the mainstays of the investigation was William Phillips, who, during the public hearings into police department corruption, was asked how many plainclothesmen in the city were receiving payoffs.

"To my knowledge, every one." He explained that the payoffs came not only from professional gamblers, but also from saloon owners, contractors, truck operators and even foreign embassies.

When asked if there would be any difficulty in determining specifically which officers were accepting bribes, Phillips explained, "In this department you could make a phone call, and in five minutes you would know who the individual is, what his hobbies are, and if he takes money."

A veteran of 14 years' service on the force, William Phillips explained to Knapp Commission members the operation of the payoff structure. He told of being assigned to Harlem duty in 1961 and said that almost immediately he was approached by a well-known gambler.

"You get $20 a day," he quoted the gambler as telling him and his partner. "Everyone is taken care of." His six-month tour of duty in Harlem, Phillips explained, netted him a total of $6,000. He said that of the 16 plainclothesmen he worked with in the area, he knew personally that 14 of them were taking payoffs. As for the other two, he added, "their reputations were not established—they were new. When they found out how much money we were making, they wanted to get on the band-wagon too."

In return for the bribes, Phillips explained that the numbers racket was allowed to operate in Harlem but that once in a great while an arrest would be staged, with the racketeers' cooperation, to impress police brass and to delude the public.

One of the most shocking of Phillips' allegations came about when the question was raised as to what would happen to racketeers and gamblers if they did *not* bribe the police. Phillips explained that *they might find incriminating evidence planted on them by plainclothesmen.* "But," he hastily explained, "most of the Harlem racketeers encountered no trouble, because they had been dealing with the police for so many years."

A public that is to a considerable extent itself dishonest tends to be tolerant to a degree concerning bribery on the part of officers when the money comes from gamblers. But when it comes from the heroin market, even many cynical New Yorkers begin to worry. In August of 1971 Police Commissioner Patrick V. Murphy charged that dozens of police officers had accepted $10,000 bribes from heroin pushers in recent years to turn their backs on the drug traffic.

One disturbing aspect of the problem of police corruption that has so far apparently escaped public attention concerns the conduct of officers and agents after they quit their jobs. A long time straight-arrow government investigator has told me that "a surprising number of these guys quit and go to work for people with unsavory connections." According to another report I've picked up, a former top officer of the Los Angeles FBI office has since gone to work for people with out-and-out mob connections. A relevant instance is that of Henry Schwind, former Treasury Department agent, who after leaving government service became managing director of Las Vegas's Frontier Hotel, then under Howard Hughes ownership, and was ultimately, in 1974, fined $10,000 and placed on five-year probation in Las Vegas federal court on charges of income tax evasion.

Returning to the Knapp Commission investigation in New York, another city cop, Edward Droge, Jr., declared that all but 60 out of several hundred policemen working in a Brooklyn ghetto area took bribes. When asked how he had gotten sucked into the whirlpool of corruption, Droge replied that it was easy: "On my first assignment, I was asked to overlook a drunk-driving arrest in return for free meals and a $10 bribe."

Almost before he knew it Droge was receiving generous contributions from gamblers, tow-truck operators, check-cashing firms, supermarkets, even city marshals involved in eviction proceedings.

The evidence accumulated in recent decades indicates that the cop with his hand out is practically as well known as Dick Tracy, Columbo or Kojak. Look back some two decades before the Knapp Commission filed its voluminous report and study the file on one Harry Gross, a bookie.

As the largest operator in the New York City borough of Brooklyn, Gross was paying off policemen with bribes amounting to *more than $1 million a year.*

Each of the runners that worked for him throughout the city passed along some $300 weekly to the cops in his neighborhoods. Gross himself took care of the police brass with special generosity. When investigators finally questioned the bookie about his activities he boasted about the valuable tipoffs furnished by some of the highest police officials.

To indicate the outrageous extent of the Gross affair, one person uncovered by the investigation was James Reardon, a former police detective—who resigned after seven years on the force to become (are you ready?) Gross' business manager. Reardon, who had been earning a few thousand dollars a year as a law enforcement officer, had bought himself a large home in exclusive Westport, Conn., where he employed several servants. He also owned two luxury automobiles.

The story of the Gross payoff scandal was described in a book by Walter Arm, and although *Pay Off* was written more than twenty years ago, much of it reads like an up-to-date indictment of the police in New York or other major cities.

But didn't the Knapp Commission lead to a general cleanup, new anti-bribery regulations? One of the outcomes of the Knapp investigation was the establishment of an elite undercover unit, the Organized Crime Control Bureau, that was supposed to prevent graft problems in cases involving narcotics, gambling, and vice. In 1977 *The New York Times* reported that Irvin Cardona, a detective on the 241-member force, had been demoted to the rank of police officer and transferred to a patrol assignment in Brooklyn because he ostensibly had passed confidential information to bookmakers.

Cardona, assigned to the bureau for six years, had access to department files on gambling investigations. Investigators learned that his brother-in-law was an important bookie in Queens and Nassau County. Evidently the only thing that prevented criminal charges from being lodged against the officer was the fact that the evidence against him, having been obtained by tapping his telephone, might be inadmissible in court.

During the course of the Cardona probe, it was brought out by Chief Charles E. McCarthy, head of the bureau, that all officers assigned to the unit were questioned about their finances and their families before they took their posts. However, McCarthy said, he did not believe that the questionnaires given to the men asked for information about their relatives by marriage. Once an officer was assigned to the bureau no further background checks were made unless a complaint was lodged against him. Obviously there is room for improvement in departmental procedures.

Cardona was only one man. Chief McCarthy emphasized to the *Times'* reporter, Selwyn Raab, that the transfer of 40 other detectives from the bureau was "unrelated" to the Cardona problem. Let's hope so.

But the problem is national. Take Chicago. Please!

During the 1950's comedian Mort Sahl used to draw a big laugh when he told his coffeehouse audiences that the streets of Chicago were "the last outpost of free enterprise." Everyone knew what he meant; traffic officers were openly soliciting bribes from motorists throughout the city. Many college students, knowing that they could be stopped for a marijuana search or for simply wearing their hair too long in

Mayor Daley's conservative kingdom, kept a five- or ten-dollar bill neatly folded atop their driver's licenses.

A former Michigan State University student I spoke to recently told me he was stopped while driving on the near North Side side of Chicago one winter night a few years ago. He presented his license with a ten dollar bill attached to it, since he knew it was a common method of dealing with such problems in Chicago.

"Oh, no," one cop said, "just the license. Put that ten back in your pocket."

He was instructed to go sit in his car, which he did, feeling appropriately guilty. After a few minutes they called him back.

"A judge won't be able to see you until Tuesday," one of the officers said. "How much you got on you?"

The student told them all he had was 20 dollars. The officers accepted it.

During the 1960's the open-handed attitude of the Chicago cops changed somewhat after Orlando W. Wilson took over as the head of the department. After he retired, however, in 1970, the situation worsened. A three-year investigation turned up countless instances of corruption. The probe was carried out by the Chicago Strike Force, federal prosecutors affiliated with the Organized Crime Section of the United States Department of Justice. Its efforts resulted in *more than 60 police officers being sent to prison*. They would have been joined by a good many others if a number of wrongdoers had not managed to exchange their testimony for immunity from prosecution.

An excellent survey and analysis of the increasingly serious problem of police corruption is Herbert and Allan Beigel's *Beneath the Badge* (Harper & Row), an account of the 1970-to-76 investigation into police department scandals in Chicago, an investigation that resulted in more indictments and convictions of police officers than any in American history. The authors touch on an important point when they say, "Dishonest cops don't cause corruption. By imposing its social mores and system of values on the officers, and rewarding them not for strong will and character nor for serving and protecting, but rather for going along, for letting things pass, *it is the public that actually causes the corruption.*" (Italics added.)

Journalist William Brashler writes, in the book's foreword:

> I had real pity for these men—one told me that the first thing he learned on the job was to pay a sergeant $2 a month to forget the mandatory hourly call-in from a beat telephone box . . .
>
> These same men have always tried to convince me that money was thrown at them as they went about their day . . . The public demanded corrupt cops, and it offered 'clean' money, they contended, gratuities, favors, tips, gestures of good faith . . .
>
> But it went much deeper than that, I discovered, and became much more vicious . . . the massive government investigations of organized police scandals . . . have been based on illegal, aggressive police activities in the areas of bribery, extortion, conspiracy, and perjury. Cops become bullies demanding 'dirty' money totalling hundreds of thousands of dollars. They took it from two-bit tavern keepers and silk-suited syndicate hoodlums; they filtered it from the lowest ranks of the department to the highest levels of command.

Added to the original petty street-graft, Brashler explains, is action generated by syndicate figures who need police contacts that will overlook watered drinks, the selling of stolen merchandise, gambling and prostitution. "In no time money is passing from a mob lieutenant to a police lieutenant. No longer is the pay-off phenomenon a natural, mutual big-city reality, but a scandal of damaging proportions which aligns the police with organized crime and altogether undermines law enforcement."

An interesting measure of the degree of corruption in such cities as Chicago is the reaction of many of its city hall and police officials to Jack Muller, the remarkable police officer who had for years performed his duties on the assumption that laws should apply equally to everyone, the highly-placed as well as the lowly, the rich as well as the poor. Muller has put parking tickets on the cars of the Governor of Illinois, of Mayor Daley, of Superior Court judges. In his biography, *I, Pig*, written with Paul Neimark, Muller relates that he once ticketed his own car that had been illegally parked by a friend.

"It's on the level of traffic corruption where you get your first breakdown in law-and-order," he explains. "If someone can fix a parking-ticket with a cop or a judge or a politician, it won't be long before everything else is being fixed, all the way to who runs for President of the country."

Muller's strong dislike for law-breakers was nurtured in his early years when he saw neighborhood toughs extort money from his mother after threatening to vandalize her fish-store. Obviously such a conscientious officer stirs up considerable antagonism in a city like Chicago, by no means all of it from professional criminals. A frequent source of discomfort to his superiors, he has nevertheless persisted in his law-enforcement philosophy even after being transferred to quiet parts of the city where it was thought he could cause little or no trouble. In 1958, when he unsuccessfully competed for the office of Cook County Sheriff, city health inspectors began harassing his father-in-law's bakeries! Disgusted that Daley's officialdom would stoop to such base tactics, Muller stationed himself outside the Board of Health building and ticketed almost every auto that left the parking lot without coming to a full stop at the street.

Since the beam of his honesty circles a full 360 degrees, Muller has as good an eye for police corruption and misbehavior as he has for any other kind. As regards the Chicago police riots during the 1968 Democratic Convention, he says, "Personally, I didn't go for much of the antics of the Conspiracy Eight defendants, but if you've been around the courts as long as I have, you know what the Bobby Seales and the Abby Hoffmans were raving about. You'd have to be deaf, dumb and blind not to see that our judicial system in America is rotten."

Read Neimark and Muller's *I, Pig*. What it reveals about Chicago will turn your stomach.

It would be comforting for the millions who live outside the nation's largest metropolitan areas to believe that police corruption is a problem for large Eastern or mid-Western cities only. It is, of course, most common in such communities. In Baltimore in early 1973 six city police officers and two former officers were arrested and indicted—along with a number of gamblers—in a major police scandal. According to U.S. Attorney George Beal a special federal grand jury handed down three criminal indictments charging that monthly cash payments of $100 had been made to the officers over a period of several months "to obstruct enforcement of the criminal law with intent to facilitate gambling business."

Dr. Albert J. Reiss, a Yale University sociologist, reports: *"There is extensive corruption in almost every major and many medium-sized police departments in the United States."* Everyone has seen accounts of police illegalities in Washington, D.C., Philadelphia, and Detroit, but pick up newspapers from such cities as Reno, Nevada, Albany, New York, Louisville, Kentucky, and Little Rock, Arkansas, and the news is bad there, too. In October, 1964 in Bristol, Connecticut, for example, ten members of the 59-man Bristol police force were suspended in connection with an investigation of a series of burglaries going back at least seven years.

In Los Angeles in 1977 a detective was suspended on charges that he willingly cooperated with burglars he was supposed to be arresting. Then there's the police captain in Little Rock, Arkansas charged with procuring women to work as prostitutes. Or the police lieutenant in Reno accused of taking a $5,000 "loan" from a local businessman who operated a string of bars.

Oklahoma? The state's name suggests blue skies, acres of waving grain, fearless cowpokes. But this bastion of god-fearing and "silent majority" people has its own crooked-cop problem.

Not only is the story of what happened in Oklahoma sickening at face value, it also reveals the fallaciousness of the argument that all professional gamblers are basically decent people who just want to be left alone to engage in a business that appeals to millions of citizens.

During the 1960's the "basically decent" gamblers of Oklahoma caused the state to be gripped in a reign of terror and lawlessness unequalled since the days of the Wild West. And *they did it with the help—overt and otherwise—of a number of Oklahoma policemen.* According to authorities who worked to unravel the scandal, the state's central location helped make it the center for one of the biggest stolen car operations ever uncovered. But the millions of dollars earned by car thieves were peanuts compared to the profits of crooked gambling operations run under the protection of the police.

The public was first made aware of the situation in 1969 when William Bliss was appointed Assistant District Attorney of the community of Tahlequa in the eastern part of the state. After six months in office he was marked for death, according to authorities, by five men who independently ran their own gambling and liquor businesses. Each, according to testimony given a Muskogee County federal grand jury, contributed $8,500 to have Bliss killed!

On June 26, 1969—according to a *Wall Street Journal* report—Bliss stepped into his pickup truck in front of his home. That he was not killed in the explosion that shattered the front of his vehicle was a matter of luck; the would-be murderer had done a clumsy job of placing the bomb. The Assistant District Attorney's two young children narrowly escaped death in the incident. The man suspected of planting the bomb was killed in 1971, presumably to prevent his testifying in the case.

The second attack was made on Tulsa District Attorney S.M. Fallis, Jr. A bomb planted in his car destroyed the vehicle and seriously injured Fallis. He survived but now walks with a cane.

On February 2, 1971 a 28-year-old teacher, Mrs. Don Bolding, was killed by a bomb intended for her husband, who had been scheduled to testify against Tahlequa saloon operator Rex Brinlee, Jr. Brinlee was involved in the stolen truck and car racket. Bolding courageously testified and Brinlee was convicted.

A few weeks later the fourth attack occurred. Mrs. Cleo

Epps, old-time illegal liquor dealer, was shot and stuffed into a septic tank three weeks after she gave *secret testimony* to a grand jury.

Arles Delbert Self, 41-year-old construction worker, was the fifth victim. He testified before a grand jury and later was shot in the head while asleep in his one-room apartment. Vernon English, the man believed to have planted the bomb meant to kill William Bliss, was found burned to death in a locked tavern, apparently the victim of murder, not long thereafter.

The criminal element had assumed so much power by the early 1970's that Gov. Steve Hall, fearing for his own family's safety, installed elaborate alarm systems in his private car and the governor's mansion in Oklahoma City. Everywhere he looked Hall saw danger. In Muskogee, for example, that rather sleepy innocent-appearing town of some 40,000 inhabitants.

The degree of Oklahoma police involvement—*on the side of criminals and against the public interest*—is outlined by Nicholas Gage in *The Mafia Is Not an Equal Opportunity Employer.*

> Muskogee, a town of thirty-seven thousand, was portrayed in the top country music song of 1970 as the model city of the American "silent majority," where drugs, hippies, and draft card burnings are unknown. In that year Muskogee got a new city manager, Leonard Briley, and a new police chief, George Kennedy, thirty-two. *Two previous police chiefs had quit after one had had his automobile bombed and the other had had his home fired upon after they tried to move against rackets that were controlled by "underworld elements" in the town.*
>
> Some of the fifty-two men in the city police department rebelled against the discipline imposed by their new chief. With the backing of the new city manager, Kennedy dismissed or suspended nine policemen. In October, 1970, wives of policemen began picketing City Hall to demand the ouster of Briley and Kennedy. In November, Briley said that "an underworld element" might have been stirring up trouble within the police department.

On December 10 Kennedy announced that he had learned of a plot by underworld elements and city policemen to burn the music store belonging to a city councilman who had come out against corruption in the city. *On December 30 he dismissed three more policemen, and four days later the councilman's music store was burned.* The fire chief said that the $100,000 fire had been caused by arson. *A few minutes before the flames enveloped the store, a police car had been seen speeding away.*" (Italics added)

New Orleans, Louisiana, is another major city in which the honor of the police department has come to be regarded as something of a joke by local residents. In the early 1950's 25 police officers were indicted for bribery and conspiracy to protect organized gambling and vice, though the indictments were eventually thrown out on technical grounds after long delays in prosecuting the cases.

While there is no reason to assume that the situation improved during the following years, it was nevertheless not until 1969 that the scandal erupted into the public consciousness when *22 policemen were charged with actually operating a burglary ring!*

The almost science-fiction, B-movie twist of policemen augmenting their income as burglars will, of course, sound familiar to residents of Chicago, where in the early 1960's at least eight members of the force became accomplices of a professional thief named Richard Morrison. When the officers were finally arrested, four large vans were needed to haul away the stolen goods they had cached at their homes. In the ensuing investigation Morrison explained how officers had cooperatively driven him around Chicago in squad cars, locating the stores to be looted and helping to clean them out.

New Orleans and Chicago are by no means the only cities where uniformed police have moonlighted as burglars. In 1959 Columbus, Ohio, detectives investigating a series of robberies discovered that some of their fellow officers were involved. Eight officers who worked the 11 P.M. to 7 A.M.

shift were arrested and charged with safe-cracking and robbery.

In 1960 six Reno, Nevada, policemen were charged with
first-degree burglary.

Seattle citizens can be grateful to Stanley Pitkin, a
young U.S. Attorney whose courageous efforts led to the
indictment of Assistant Chief of Police N. E. "Buzz" Cook
for perjury. Although the police official denied knowledge of
payoffs going on around him, a veteran officer named David
Jessup testified before a Federal grand jury that Cook paid
him $50 a month—supposedly as his share of the graft pay-
offs coming into the department. Other top officers, according to the witness's testimony, were getting as much as
$1,000 a month.

Pitkin also investigated gambling payoffs to members of
the sheriff's office in King County, which includes Seattle
and its suburbs, and discovered that these law officers were
collecting even more than the men pounding the city pave-
ments.

The investigation revealed, too, that the payoffs were
not merely a matter of small-time operators asking the police to overlook minor infractions of the law. Organized
Crime, Pitkin indicated, played a significant role in the
widespread corruption. William Colacurcio, whose brother
was indicted on charges of conspiring with two Seattle gamblers to transport gambling equipment interstate, was involved. Colacurcio, a major distributor of jukeboxes in Seattle, is a reputed intimate of Carlos Marcello, Louisiana Mafia
boss.

Pitkin had a good word for the area cops, however.
Though some were taking payoffs, the amounts involved
tended to be relatively small. *The big money went to political figures in city and state posts.*

Taking note of the Seattle scandal, Aaron Kohn, managing director of the Metropolitan Crime Commission in New
Orleans, was pessimistic about the future. Perhaps aware of
what happened in his own city after widespread corruption
was exposed, he says: "The thing that would be unique in
Seattle would be for the police scandal to evolve into sweep-
ing corrections. In most cities it's just swept under the rug."

The uninformed might assume that the combination of public outrage, plus the guilt and shame of those policemen whose criminality was exposed, would bring about a situation of reform and improvement. The facts are otherwise. *The record of police reform in most American cities has been dismal.*

A cab driver in Seattle is reported to have said—in words that are echoed daily all over the country: "The cops have been getting paid off since the beginning of time and they always will."

Certainly there is evidence to support the pessimistic view. Crooked cops are exposed, demoted, discharged. Occasionally—very rarely—they are jailed. The cries of public indignation die down, and things return to normal. Too often, "normal" means business as usual—and that means bribery, graft, and corruption.

One relatively bright spot in the picture is the Federal Bureau of Investigation. Since 1924 only one FBI employee has been convicted of a felony. That dubious distinction belongs to one Irene Kuczynski, a young woman who served as a clerk-typist for the bureau in Newark, N.J., for two years at the start of the decade.

Her crime, she admitted, was to steal copies of documents relating to the investigation of John DiGilio, prominent member of the New Jersey crime family of Joseph Zicarelli. She delivered the documents to her husband, who, in turn, sold them to DiGilio. In a seemingly unrelated incident, two potential witnesses against DiGilio—Vincent Capone and Frank Chin—were murdered in what appeared to be a 1970's style .22-cal. mob-ordered hit.

When the illegal activity of Mrs. Kuczynski was exposed, however, some former FBI agents contended that her exposure pointed to corruption within the bureau. She was only a clerical worker, say the ex-lawmen, and therefore was thrown overboard so that the agency could point out how carefully it polices its own people. If the woman had been an important agent, they argue, the case would never have gotten into the news.

Journalist Nicholas Gage, author of *The Mafia Is Not an Equal Opportunity Employer* and *Has the Mafia Invaded the FBI?* notes that whenever questions arise in regard to the integrity of agents the bureau has a general solution. Its policy, Gage says he was told by a former FBI man, is not to probe too hard for answers. "The agents were transferred, retired, or forced to resign, and the reputation of the bureau was preserved."

Something like that appears to have happened not long ago in the bureau's field office in Las Vegas. Some youthful agents there protested to the Justice Department attorneys that their superiors had become cozy with a number of the bosses in the town's gambling casinos. There was no sharp investigation. After a cursory inquiry a spokesman released the statement that "no evidence of criminality or serious misconduct" has been found.

Still, after the denials were part of the public record, a new man was sent to take over direction of the office and several Las Vegas agents were censured.

In another case the New York City office of the bureau came under scrutiny. Four years ago an agent named Tony Villano charged that another agent had taken a payoff of $10,000 from a Mafia source, one John Caputo, who had been arrested on gambling charges. An investigation was carried out—and the whole matter was dismissed as some sort of "Italian vendetta." Villano, it was said, didn't get along with the accused agent and was trying to discredit him.

During the course of the inquiry, stories were modified, reversed, and revealed as complete fabrications. Still Villano was transferred to Philadelphia; the man he accused of taking the payoff was shifted to Boston. Within a few months Villano chose early retirement; the other agent returned to the New York office.

Another agent, Joseph Stabile, the first active FBI man ever charged with a felony, was indicted in September 1978, in connection with the government's claim that in 1973 he took a $10,000 bribe from Caputo, described as a member of the *Frank Tieri crime family*. Agent Stabile again pleaded innocent. He was indicted on charges of perjury when he denied receiving the bribe. The second indictment charged him with representing part of the alleged bribe as a loan from a relative.

According to Dennis Dillon, who studied the case as head of the Brooklyn Federal Strike Force, the investigation was bungled from start to finish. Transferring the men involved was not the answer, he says, noting that "Both the bureau and the agent himself are left under a permanent cloud of suspicion."

The idea that the Mafia could infiltrate the nation's most honored anti-crime organization is repugnant but the information collected by author Gage over recent years cannot be casually dismissed. Gage details the fact that *nearly two dozen murders have wiped out a group of FBI informants and potential witnesses to Mafia-and-bureau links within the last two years.*

The killings—most carried out with .22-cal. automatic pistols—include that of Frank "Bomp" Bompensierie, an influential Mafioso said to be the bureau's most highly-placed underworld informant, and Edward Lazar, murdered after he became an FBI informant in Arizona. Other inside sources such as Frank Chin and Vincent Papa were wiped out in shootings that served to sidetrack investigations of criminal elements within the bureau.

And, notes Gage, since the death of Frank Bomp, nearly half of the paid informants providing valuable information to the law officers have "dried up"—making it more difficult to bring Organized Crime to the bar of justice.

It is not a reassuring picture, not in any aspect. The cop on the beat, senior officers, narcotics investigators, members of the till-now respected Federal Bureau of Investigation, even investigators sworn to ferret out corruption in the ranks of the lawmen around them—all tainted.

Chapter *IV*

The Push-Button Thieves

In November of 1978 the FBI arrested a California computer consultant accused of swindling $10.2 million from the Security Pacific National Bank and converting the bulk of the money into Soviet diamonds, which were then smuggled back into the U.S. Stanley Mark Rifkin, 32, who had worked for Security Pacific, pierced his employer's security systems and on October 25th transferred $10,250,000 to an account of his own in New York. He promptly transferred the enormous sum to a Zurich, Switzerland bank account, flew to Switzerland, bought $8,145,000 worth of diamonds from Russalmaz, a U.S.S.R. state diamond company, and hurried back to California. Rifkin, of course, was not simply a common con-man or professional burglar but a computer-programming specialist who was able to commit grand theft by virtue of his professional expertise. As such he was by no means a rare bird; merely a new and increasingly common type of thief.

Until a decade or so ago a burglar's primary tools were a crowbar and screwdriver, and his attire at work was said to consist of a dark shirt and an old pair of trousers. On occasion he might carry a revolver that more often than not was intended to be used only to frighten a victim.

That, of course, was before the dawning of the computer age.

Today's late-model sneak-thief has no use for weapons or the implements needed for breaking and entering—not when he can use electronic technology to help him commit his crimes. And, far from wearing old clothes designed to make him invisible, he is often dressed in a custom-tailored suit that draws envious glances from the corporate executives who toast him at lunch and dinner. Inwardly the computer criminal might have the same greed and fears that a second-story man has when he sets out on a night's work, but outwardly the electronic thief can display a cool demeanor, knowing that his trail is nearly impossible to detect.

What makes the computer criminal especially dangerous is that he can steal even if his victim is hundreds or thousands of miles away. Merely by pressing the keys of an electronic terminal linked to a distant computer he can reach into your bank account and withdraw your savings, order merchandise from the fanciest stores and charge it to your credit card account, steal confidential information about you—what your credit rating is, for example, or which days you're likely to be on vacation from your job—and use it as an aid in other crimes.

In business, the computer criminal can steal important trade secrets and client lists from competitors. If he wanted to operate on the highest level of all he could theoretically "steal" the entire U.S. missile system, which is controlled by computer.

Computerization in America has led to the training of some two million citizens as programmers, operators, and advisors—a sizable force of people intricately familiar with the workings of these electronic marvels, some of whom seem to be learning the computers' capacity for crime. In the past twenty years computer crime itself has grown into a major industry. Although it has been called "the crime of the future," it's already here. The U.S. Chamber of Commerce estimates that some $100 million annually is being stolen with the aid of computers; other estimates place the figure as high as $300 million!

The total might be even greater since only one out of every 100 computer ripoffs is detected. And the size of the theft can vary immensely. Federal crime statistics show that the average amount missing from banks and other financial institutions in typical fraud or embezzlement cases is $19,000, but the average amount stolen, in a mid-70's survey of computer crimes, was $450,000! A young accountant in a California hospital used a minicomputer to transfer small sums—always less than $4—from the federal withholding accounts of his fellow-workers to his own account. By tampering with each month's payroll he built up a large tax overpayment that entitled him to a sizable refund. Where the accountant stole only a few dollars at a time (from dozens of co-workers), the masterminds behind the now-classic Equity Funding fraud used a computer to make off with some $2 billion!

Psychologists are probing the makeup of the computer criminal to see what makes him tick. Researchers contend that some people delight in using the electronic machines to steal, in a kind of personal protest against the regimentation and impersonal efficiency that confronts them in contemporary life. People angered by finding their electricity cut off by an unheeding computer, or told "computer error" after their 10th phone call to complain about a department store overcharge, can become criminals if the opportunity presents itself, believes one student of the problem.

In some instances computers themselves become victims. Three years ago a computer operator at the Charlotte Liberty Mutual Life Insurance Co. in North Carolina blasted away at the office computer with a gun; instances of similar attacks have been reported throughout the country. Computers have been short-circuited by a car key or screwdriver, they've been doused with gasoline and set afire, and at least one has been bombed. Damages in these last-cited instances ran from $585,000 to $2 million.

Turning a computer against society—the society that created it—has another appeal, too, in that crime by computer is non-violent. It produces no bloodshed, no gaping wounds. So it may have fascination for the crook who abhors physical confrontation. It also has a lure for the well-educated person who can respond to the challenge of using his or her brainpower to outsmart a machine.

Most important, computer crime boasts the advantage of being almost impossible to detect. And even when a computer crime is uncovered, the guilty individual frequently receives minimal punishment. Computer thieves get lighter sentences than the perpetrators of crimes of the same financial magnitude that are executed by conventional means partly because the courts, in many cases, have difficulty determining the value of exactly what has been stolen.

Take the recent case of two trusted employees of a Sperry Univac office near Philadelphia. Matthew Palmer, Jr., and David E. Kelly, knowledgeable about computers, had succeeded in teaching one to store and print complex musical arrangements. The printout manuscripts were sold to record shops and rock bands. During a three-year period, the two men allegedly cheated Sperry Univac out of computer-time worth $150,000. They might still be operating if a conscientious fellow worker had not turned them in.

The "merchandise" in another case of computer crime was somewhat more tangible. Taking advantage of the fact that the traffic flow on much of the nation's railroads is governed by computers, a small band of crooks programmed a Penn Central unit to detour 277 freight cars to an out-of-the-way siding in Illinois. There the cars were stripped.

Computer schemes can be highly intricate. One of the most complex computer frauds to date was pulled off by a man called "James Harlow" described in a fascinating account by author Thomas Whiteside that appeared in *The New Yorker*. As chief accountant at a large firm, Harlow succeeded in manipulating the company's computer to deposit substantial sums in phony bank accounts.

To carry out his scheme Harlow first had to convince his firm that it should adopt a completely computerized accounting system. For several years before he made the proposal he had been studying computer technology—going so far as to rent an IBM 402 and other equipment for home use.

When he felt that he was thoroughly familiar with the subject, Harlow set up his own computer service bureau under another name.

When his management decided to go along with their accountant's suggestion that an outside computer service could speed things along, Harlow's service naturally was chosen. Ostensibly Harlow performed routine accounting functions until the day he became enraged over a reduction in his annual bonus. To get back at his bosses, he began diverting funds to himself under the guise of increased costs.

Since costs at the firm fluctuated significantly from season to season, and since Harlow was so skillful in spreading his "personal increments" over a wide variety of products, his plan worked efficiently. Soon he was taking roughly three-fourths of 1% of the corporation's gross revenues for himself—and no one noticed! With a straight face, he delivered convincing reports to the financial board—neglecting to mention, of course, that he was funneling company funds into 14 dummy accounts that provided him with some $200,000 a year.

What went wrong? Actually, nothing. Harlow grew rich and fat, a little tired, and decided to put an end to his system. But he had a problem. To straighten things out, he would have to show that the company's many suppliers had *reduced* their prices and—especially in a time of soaring inflation—that would attract undue attention.

While he pondered the situation the accountant heard rumors that the Internal Revenue Service was about to investigate the company. Acting fast, he wrote checks on the company's account and deposited them to the accounts of various officers and executives, hoping to make it look as if others were behind any irregularities. When the checks came back from various banks Harlow destroyed them, effectively getting rid of the evidence. When no one noticed the sudden infusion of funds into numerous accounts Harlow decided to call attention himself to the fact that "something funny" was going on at his company. He deliberately overdrew one of his own dummy accounts to start the investigative ball rolling.

As smart as he was, Harlow saw his complicated plan

unravel in a mass of contradictions. He eventually was sentenced to ten years in San Quentin. The sentence, by the way, is the most severe ever handed out for a computer crime. Upon release in 1974, the accountant settled with the IRS for a token sum of a few thousand dollars. He then settled down as a data-processing consultant for several California companies! All of his computer work these days, he says, is strictly legal.

Another computer criminal who appears to have profited remarkably from his illegal efforts is a young man named Jerry Neal Schneider. If you don't recall his name—and it was in the headlines not long ago—the Pacific Telephone and Telegraph Company will never forget it. Jerry Neal Schneider is estimated to have used a computer to steal $1 million worth of electronic equipment from the company.

At 21 Schneider was a computer buff like many other youngsters in the nation. To get supplies for his homemade devices he collected junk discarded from a phone company supply storeroom near his school. Over the years he picked up seemingly useless pieces of equipment, various instruction manuals, and guidebooks that explained how Pacific Telephone bought equipment from Western Electric Co., a major supplier.

Since he knew that equipment was ordered by telephone through computers and delivered to various storage locations at night, Schneider worked out a system that enabled him to tap into the Western Electric computers and order his own equipment. To learn the proper codes, the young man visited Pacific Telephone's headquarters in the guise of a free-lance writer working on a story. Once he had the necessary information, he tested the system by ordering such simple things as wastebaskets and desk phones, arranging with the distant computer for delivery to a drop-off point he selected.

It worked, so well that within a year Schneider needed ten employees and a six-thousand-square-foot warehouse for his stolen equipment. And he had a flourishing business going, selling the equipment at discount prices to a long list of customers.

His plan, too, was practically foolproof. Computers ordinarily do not make mistakes and have no conscience that nags them if they are turned to illegal use. But Schneider made an all-too-human error: he turned down an employee's request for a raise. The angry worker, seeking revenge, tipped the police. The result: Schneider's den of thieves was suddenly filled with stunned investigators trying to inventory the stockpiles of equipment.

Our electronic wizard was lucky, however. The prosecution could prove only that $5,000 worth of the equipment was actually stolen, although the estimates of how much had passed through Schneider's hands ranged up to $1 million worth! The young thief was sentenced to a modest sixty days in jail, and actually had to serve only forty. He settled a civil suit brought by Pacific Telephone for $8,500, and then—brazenly—set himself up in business as a computer security consultant.

In addition, Schneider sold his story of the phone company ripoff to a motion picture producer for a sizable sum. Look for his tale at your neighborhood theater. Perhaps your children can learn that frequently in this corrupt society, crime not only pays; it pays handsomely.

When he is operating within a giant corporation, the computer criminal knows that he has the advantage of time on his side. He might be able to get away with his misdeeds for years before anyone discovers anything amiss. Most managerial types, he knows, are not familiar with computers and their special terminology. Furthermore, even if a top executive discovers something wrong, he will not rush forward with charges until a long and careful investigation takes place. One reason: rumors of internal fraud or mismanagement of corporate finances can cause the stock of a company to plummet.

Which brings us to the biggest and most intricate of all computer crimes, one that required an 18-month investigation to uncover: the Equity Funding scandal that surfaced in

1973, and which involved hundreds of millions of dollars in funds that were "illegally transferred."

Books have been written on this incredible case, as well as countless magazine and newspaper reports, but it is likely that no one—not even the people behind the fraud—will ever have a clear idea of how much money was lost by numerous investors. To provide an insight into how complex a computer crime can become, it might be worthwhile to study at least the outlines of the Equity Funding operation.

Based in Los Angeles, Equity Funding Corp. of America was a unique organization that sold mutual fund shares and insurance policies to the public. Under its plan a customer's payments were recorded as investments in a mutual fund program. At the same time Equity Funding itself paid life-insurance premiums on the customer's policy, and recorded its payments as *loans* to the customer—loans on which the customer's mutual fund shares served as collateral. The economic theory behind the intricate arrangement was that the customer could utilize his liquid assets—the mutual fund shares—for investment purposes as needed, rather than having his money locked up entirely in insurance premiums.

It sounds like a "something-for-everyone" scheme but it was legal.

Things seemed to go smoothly for the company and its customers for a few years, with the mutual fund shares increasing in value as the stock market went up. But in 1969 the operation began to expand—and any expansion program calls for heavy spending. To get money, Equity Funding (largely under the direction of its chairman, Stanley Goldblum) began to sell some of its insurance policies to other insurance firms. The idea was that the other companies, paying a flat sum at time of purchase, would continue to receive future years of premium payments from the policy holders.

But Equity Funding did not have enough policy holders of its own to get the huge amounts needed for its expansion program. It solved the problem in a way as simple as it was dishonest. The company's computer was ordered to print out *fictional policies* on people whose names were chosen at random from various sources, including the Chicago telephone directory.

Each of the bogus policy records consisted of a computerized listing that gave the holder's name, age, sex, amount of coverage, monthly premium, and an identifying number. All of the records were kept in a fictitious grouping known as Department 99—a number borrowed, perhaps, from "Agent 99" of the television series, *Get Smart*—whose scripts sometimes dealt with criminal masterminds who turned computers to nefarious uses.

At a touch of a button the Equity Funding computer could print out any number of fake policies to be sold—along with a few real ones thrown in for a cover-up—to reinsuring companies. When the number of bogus policy records in the computer began to dwindle, it was a simple matter to feed in additional phony names and start over again. When the whole business exploded, *some 22 insurance company employees would be convicted of "inventing" 56,000 fake policies with a value of more than $2 billion and reselling them to outside firms!*

It might seem that with the firm's records crammed full of fictitious policy holders, who supposedly were pouring millions of dollars worth of premium payments into company coffers each month, any half-awake auditor could have uncovered the fraud. But it is not easy to follow the labyrinthine trails within a massive computer.

The computer criminals made the trail more complex by occasionally "killing off" one of their fictional policy holders. This produced additional paperwork, which in turn became a morass of bits of information inside the computer's memory bank, as "death benefits" were supposedly paid to the heirs of the deceased. Since there were no deaths and therefore no heirs, there was no money going out. To account for the fact that its computers *said* that $1.2 billion had been paid in the form of death benefits over the years, the Equity Funding operators had to prepare additional fake policies that were supposedly bought by *new* investors—who mysteriously put exactly $1.2 billion *into* the company's coffers.

By 1971 the operation had grown to mammoth size. Any company that could pay out such massive amounts and still not show any decrease in its assets seemed a good buy for investors. More and more money was coming in but the payrolls had to keep growing, too, in order to keep up with the size of the ever-expanding fraud.

A lot of cover-up work had to be done. Each phony policy holder had to be provided with references and records, including medical examination reports and credit rating information. With the number of fake files climbing to 50,000, an entire office had to be rented on Maple Drive in Beverly Hills just to accommodate them.

Still the auditors did not catch on.

How could they? All policies that were coded with the nonexistent *Department 99* were automatically excluded by the computer from any printouts that the auditors needed to investigate the company. Without the files, the auditors had a complete story, they thought. Even if someone had noticed that there seemed to be more money coming in and going out than there appeared to be findable, there was no way to account for it. Meanwhile the stock of Equity Funding kept going up.

It might still be climbing if a former employee of the company—an honesty-freak perhaps—had not decided to tell his story to Raymond Dirks, a Wall Street insurance analyst. Dirks, who had advised some of his customers to buy Equity Funding stock over the years, immediately reversed his bullish opinion of the company and told officials of the New York Stock Exchange that something suspicious was going on at the California concern.

Until Dirks's charges were made, several Wall Street firms had been touting Equity Funding shares. It was a "glamour issue," one of the high-fliers in the stock market, apparently as solid a buy as IBM, Xerox or Polaroid.

Overnight the picture changed. Wary investors began pulling out of Equity Funding amid rumors that the conspirators were hastily erasing phony tapes and frantically altering records to conceal their crime. Examiners from the California Insurance Department rushed in to impound records and try to untangle the mess. What they discovered stunned even the most hardened investigator.

They found that of life insurance policies issued with a face value of more than $3 billion, over $2 billion worth were false.

Of some 97,000 policies registered with Equity Funding, approximately 64,000 were for persons who were nonexistent.

And, although the company's latest financial statement showed that it had $737 million in assets, only $185 million worth of the assets were real.

It took several years for the investigators and the courts to follow the tangled trails and to determine what had been done with the millions of dollars that had flowed into Equity Funding's accounts—and mysteriously vanished. Some of the money, it was learned, went to pay for lavish "fraud parties" tossed in posh company suites at which knowing officials laughed uproariously over the phony background documents dreamed up for the mythical policy holders. In the end Goldblum and several other officers were tried, convicted of fraud and sentenced to prison terms. The case had an interesting aftermath.

Ray Dirks, the man who blew the whistle on the whole affair, was himself charged by the New York Stock Exchange with participating in a fraud. Tipped off to the ballooning scandal at the insurance company, Dirks had moved to protect his own customers first—it was claimed—and thus enabled many of them to sell off their Equity Funding stock before the balloon was punctured. In so doing, said the NYSE, he had spread "inside" information to a few favored clients, rather than revealing the truth to the general public.

Perhaps the mildest of the many names levelled at Dirks was "rumor monger." When his actions came under investigation by the Securities and Exchange Commission Dirks saw his business fall off. He was eventually forced to leave his firm, although he had been comfortably established there for more than a year. In an interview with Edwin Newman on television, Dirks was asked if he would act the same way if he were to become aware of a similar fraud at another company in the future.

"Yes," he answered, without hesitation. But he warned that the citizen who points out fraud and corruption in today's society has to be ready to accept brickbats as well as bouquets.

As complex as it sounds, the Equity Funding operation

was not terribly sophisticated in its use of computers. The electronic machines were helpful in concealing information, and enabled the perpetrators to prepare a great mass of fraudulent material in a relatively short time—but the crime did not call for any great knowledge of the actual workings of a computer. Neither did it involve using a computer to conceal from company management what was going on. A large number of people—from Goldblum at the top to dozens of others in the lower echelons—knew precisely what was going on.

Unlike poor men who hold up a grocery store for 50 bucks and get a stiff sentence, Goldblum was sentenced to only eight years at the Federal Correctional Institution at Terminal Island off the California coast. He is looking toward a mandatory release date of April 15, 1981. If the experience of Schneider, "Harlow," and others of their ilk is any indication, he can look forward to a prosperous career as a consultant on insurance fraud. Meanwhile, of course, the thousands of investors who suffered serious losses when his company went bankrupt, or whose savings went down the drain in the collapse of the Equity Funding stock, will have to scrape along in their efforts to rebuild their accounts.

Former computer criminals are not the only ones profiteering from the increasing incidence of electronic crimes. Major accounting firms, such as Coopers & Lybrand, are attracting many new customers for their security services. Special methods have been introduced which it is claimed can detect current instances of computer fraud and prevent future ripoffs. Says William P. Callahan, president of a new company formed in New York City for such a purpose:

"The existing vulnerability of almost every type of business or financial institution to unscrupulous or fraudulent acts places a complicated burden on the shoulders of management. It is the intention of United Intelligence, Inc., or UNITEL, to share that burden in the hope of preventing criminal acts which may prove to be not only costly but embarrassing as well."

Precisely what can be done about the growing computer fraud problem? Donn B. Parker, researcher at SRI International in Menlo Park, Calif., and a lecturer on the subject, suggests that a code of ethics is needed for anyone working with computers. He is greatly concerned that young people are taught to play "games" with computers, and thinks that such activity blurs the distinction between right and wrong. If a computer is ordered to misplace a million dollars, is this a crime—or only a prank?

A Lutheran Sunday-school teacher, Parker is concerned with "the great ethical vacuum in the computer field," and thinks that technologists may have to be licensed or otherwise certified for the protection of the public. Even then, he worries, data processors themselves can be conned into illegal activities by others. "Many computer technologists," he says, "still think they are functioning in a world of good guys. We must make people in positions of trust aware of their responsibilities and sensitive to the possibilities for crime."

It is not going to be easy. While everyone waits for a new kind of ethic to evolve in the computer field, prudent management is considering more complete checks of personnel references, employee bonding, frequent changing of assignments, mandatory vacation periods (during which safety checks can be run in secret), and a variety of other safeguards.

In the near future the situation may worsen. Already more than 200,000 minicomputers are in use, and more are coming on the market daily. Many new low-cost units are in the hands of lower-level personnel who have only just begun to understand what they can make their machines do—at the touch of a button.

In addition to the thousands of individuals who can now be transformed into criminals overnight, the public faces another threat on the computer front: from Organized Crime, which is just starting to study the nation's increasing dependence on sophisticated electronic fund-transfer systems. These systems, which join together retail businesses and huge financial institutions, are the forerunners of a "cashless society" and might lead someday to incredible variations on the old-style bank heist plot.

Rather than confront a nearby teller with a subma-chinegun in hand, the bank bandit of the future might simply plug in a typewriter-like console, set a telephone receiver atop it, dial a number, press some keys—and add a few million dollars from a distant bank's vaults to his own account.

No fingerprints. No speeding getaway car with a telltale license plate.

Perhaps—as Donn Parker argues—the only defense against such crime is a formal code of ethics for computer experts, a code such as those subscribed to by lawyers, physicians, policemen and—

Elsewhere in this volume I'll consider the ethics of lawyers, physicians and policemen, among others.

If that's the standard we're in real trouble.

Chapter **V**

Lotsa Luck
in the
Stock Market

Since this is not in any direct sense a book on Organized Crime—although the reader ought to be familiar with books of that sort—I do not go into extended detail about Mafia and other syndicate criminals. It is common knowledge, however, that, as a *Newsweek* editor has put it, "Any small bookie can bribe the cop on his beat; but *only the Mafia can buy enough judges, politicians and law enforcement officials* to make sure that the nationwide gambling business can operate with relatively little fear of crippling raids, jail terms or the disruptive glare of public scrutiny. As for security, the mob has the ability to infiltrate law-enforcement agencies and provide valuable warning when raids are imminent. It keeps careful vigilance over the conduct of sports—an important function, since no one is more concerned with keeping sports honest than the bookies, the men who could be burned by a fix. In return for such services to lower-echelon gamblers, the top mobsters get the funds to invest in other lucrative activities, from loan-sharking and narcotics-peddling to a number of 'legitimate' businesses such as trucking and handling vending machines and juke boxes. They also get very rich. Bosses who concentrate on gambling are reputed to be among the richest of all Mafiosi." (Italics added.)

Organized Crime, in any event, is the single largest, most profitable American industry.

Comments Leslie Waller in *The Swiss Bank Connection*, recommended reading for any student of American corruption:

> [Organized Crime] is an active, healthy, rapidly growing element in the national economy that is estimated at the moment to employ about 7 per cent of the adult work force in its legal, quasi-legal, and illegal enterprises.
>
> Moreover, it is an element in the economy that provides goods and services for about 15 per cent of the nation. To put it another way, 15 per cent of citizens of voting age in the United States are customers, either regularly or occasionally, for the goods and services of companies controlled by the mob.
>
> As always, these numbers represent conservative estimates and obviously include vast groups of ordinary, law-abiding citizens who have no idea who really owns the concern for which they work or the one from which they buy. Nevertheless, 22 per cent—7 plus 15—of all American adults is a figure of commanding substance, amounting to more than 20 million people.
>
> What many Americans are not aware of is the extent to which the mob now participates in the long-established corruption of the Stock Market.

So widespread is the stock-market swindle as an artform that the book-publishing trade is recognizing the phenomenon. In 1977 Doubleday published *Wall Street Swindler* by Michael Hellerman, with Thomas C. Renner, which this author recommends to those interested enough in the larger problem to learn more of it. Hellerman, a bright young Wall Streeter, was an early success but despite his brilliance was willing to cut ethical corners so sharply that he was eventually barred by the SEC from working as a stock broker. He thereupon moved into the restaurant field which, in New York, almost inevitably means that one will have to mesh gears—willingly or not—with the Mafia. When the organized criminals with whom he became intimate learned of his financial gifts he was encouraged to become a behind-the-scenes stock manipulator. *Wall Street Swindler* gives details concerning the market manipulations of such leading Mafiosi as Carmine Tramunti, Vincent Aloi and Johnny Dioguardi.

The reader might assume however, that such criminal behavior is rare and that while frauds in, say, the door-to-door sales or home-repair category may be common, the situation would be much better in the stock market because men of presumably higher ethical standards earn their living by the exercise of nothing more than shrewd intelligence. The supposition will amuse those familiar with the market. Officials of the Securities and Exchange Commission concede inability to measure the losses through the highway robbery resulting from the sale of relatively worthless stocks, although they know the annual amount runs into the hundreds of millions.

Most stock market swindlers—like thieves generally—are not apprehended. When occasionally a big fish is landed—such as the professional thief Alexander Guterma—what is perhaps most remarkable is not that he was able to defraud several companies and an army of stock-holders, but that he was able to function so dishonestly in the market for *9 full years* before being convicted by the U.S. Government in 1960.

The startling story of widespread dishonesty on Wall Street is well told by Christopher Elias in *Fleecing the Lambs* (Regnery). Elias, who was for six years a staff-member at *Business Week*, editorial director of the *Magazine of Wall Street* and Editor of the *Exchange*, has written a shocking indictment of many of the most reputable firms and executives in the stock market—naming names, as the saying goes.

"Wall Street," Elias observes, "is a world unlike any other—and not a very honest one . . . The rules that govern the Street are written by Wall Streeters, for the reforms of the 1930's merely made Wall Street more cautious, not any less larcenous. Wall Streeters still act as if they are immune to common law, even though their dishonesty is well documented . . . "

Nor does the activity of market thieves stand merely as a moral scandal of which the victims are few. The questionable practices of many in the market, Elias says, "have cost people everywhere billions of dollars."

While the present degree of dishonesty on Wall Street may be unprecedented, the author establishes that larceny was always common there. On May 17, 1792, 24 brokers met under a buttonwood tree and signed an agreement organizing the market, out of which grew the New York Stock Exchange.

The purpose, from the beginning, seems to have been to fleece the average man, the small investor, or at the very least to regard him as only a source of the large revenue needed for the speculation and dealing of the big operators.

Well before and long after the meeting under the buttonwood tree, Wall Street's approach to finance and investing was a matter of powerful, moneyed, and politically connected interests *speculating on the basis of inside information* and thus creating financial speculations that the average man seldom could take advantage of. The men involved in the speculations, appropriately preceded on the Street by resident Captain Kidd, were so ruthless that over the years they sheared the public, and they sheared each other. They clearly regarded the individual's pocketbook as something to be picked and the U.S. Treasury as something to be exploited. They used bribery, payoffs, deceit, and treachery routinely, yet they were pious in the extreme and gave generously to charitable organizations. Taken together, such activity became a template of conduct for the manipulators and lawbreakers who have streamed through Wall Street over the past two centuries: including Jacob Little, Daniel Drew, Jim Fisk, Jay Gould, Cornelius Vanderbilt, J. P. Morgan, John D. Rockefeller and Richard Whitney. (Italics supplied.)

It is easy to become depressed over the fact that such large-scale thieves—for thieves they indeed were, although they were also able to claim other accomplishments—were *among the most socially envied Americans of their time*, which tends to support the hypothesis that we are quite prepared, as a society, to condone thievery; what we will not tolerate is failing at the art.

"From its inception in 1792," Elias says, "the Exchange had been writing its rules solely for its members. . . . The unfortunate truth is that, despite the reforms of the 1930's Wall Street is as avaricious as ever, and the Exchange is its most useful tool. Instead of being brutally overpowering in their treatment of customers, as they were in the 20's, the firms have become more sly, using the Exchange as an instrument through which they evade and ignore the public interest. The Exchange's record of proposing new rules and laws strictly in the public interest is slight . . . One must go back to the Presidency of William McChesney Martin (1938–1941) to find someone who was above the crowd on the floor, someone who took the public interest seriously. Most members and many leaders are men with a peddlar's bent. Their language and bearing suggest quickly to observers that their only interest is to extract as much profit from their membership as possible . . . The brawling, coarse, and irresponsible behavior of many specialists . . . led the New York Times to describe the specialist in this way: 'Unquestionably he is the pig of the marketplace. His nose is dug in, and he cares for no one. His manner is crude and his speech ridiculously full of curses.' "

Fleecing the Lambs is full of specific instances of chicanery. Chapter 8, "Wall Street's Salesmen," refers to the case of Michael DuBroff, an employee of A. L. Stamm and Company, who in 1968 was disciplined for questionable conduct. DuBroff had been censured and suspended from employment for three months by the Conduct Division of the Department of Member Firms for the rather common practice of permitting a favored customer to buy stocks and then pay for them only *after* they had been sold.

James R. Foster, Jr., a margin clerk, had known of

DuBroff's activities but had failed to report them. As punishment he was suspended for one month. DuBroff's supervisor, the branch-office manager Charles Lowlicht, also was suspended, for three months, and was denied a supervisory job with any exchange firm until August 1st, 1970.

The DuBroff case, Elias reports, "was *a single incident among tens of thousands, possibly hundreds of thousands, that occurred in the bull market of the 1960's*. DuBroff's crime, which in the eyes of most of his fellows was that he had been caught, demonstrates the loose ethics and downright dishonesty that are to be found among firms regulated by the New York Stock Exchange. It also demonstrates the type of slap-on-the-wrist penalties that the Securities Industries self-regulators mete out." (Italics added)

One particularly prevalent unethical market practice is known as "churning the accounts" of customers. Thousands upon thousands of cases are documented. A far greater number never come to light. One that did is that of Beverly Hills, California salesman Harry Glicksman, suspended for six months in 1969 by the New York Stock Exchange. He mishandled a customer's portfolio to the extent that turnover had reached 43.7% in the customer's margin account and 12% in his cash account.

As is often the case when business affairs are poorly managed, what is involved is a combination of dishonesty and ineptitude. Elias's chapter 7 reports the chaotic conditions leading to the collapse in Wall Street's back offices in 1968. Papers were regularly lost, stolen, misplaced and mailed to the wrong parties. "As might be expected," Elias says, "the working conditions in the back offices attracted a particular segment of the New York population. Few back office workers were well-educated; many were not very intelligent or ambitious. They were recruited from the outlying boroughs of the city, and many were hired *from Mafia-controlled employment agencies* [Italics added] as was revealed by I. Mitchell Graybard, director of personnel and training for Smith, Barney and Company at a Security Control Conference held in New York in November, 1969. Time and again in 1970 Wall Street brokers reported large thefts traced to the back offices. In December, 1970, for example, a back office supervisor for Scheimman, Hockstein and Trotta was indicted and charged with involvement and theft of 2.3 million dollars worth of securities."

The New York State Legislative Committee on Crime has learned how one million dollars in stock certificates was stolen from just one brokerage firm. It emerged that figures long operative in Organized Crime had gone into Wall Street in a big way, according to one informant, "because there was big money and we are getting more educated people [into criminal ranks] who know how to steal with an IBM machine."

In one instance a young man who was the nephew of a leading Mafioso was held up and relieved of thousands of dollars worth of negotiable securities. The messenger, who came under suspicion, appeared several times before the grand jury investigating the possibility that the robbery had been staged. When the criminals began to fear that the messenger might be revealing too much, he was killed, his body covered with stab wounds.

In May of 1971 seven employees of the Central Certificate office, the world's largest single depository for stocks, a sort of stock bank where 32 billion dollars in securities are stored by members of the New York Stock Exchange, were arrested and charged with the theft of *2.6 million dollars* in stock certificates.

The 14,789 shares of stock—among them 9,789 in Walt Disney Productions, 3,000 shares of International Business Machines, and 2,000 shares of Duke Power Company—were recovered in a raid of a mid-Manhattan hotel-room. Those arrested were Rosemary Ruggero, John Cosenza, Ralph De Cola, Arthur Andino, Ramon Martin, Richard Dieniewicz and Allan Perlin—all in their 20's.

The inside tip that led to the arrest reached District Attorney Frank Hogan from the Senate Permanent Investigation Committee headed by Senator John L. McClellan. McClellan, in commenting publicly about the case, said that *over one hundred million dollars worth of securities are stolen each year from brokerage houses, banks and the U.S.*

mails and that "most of this activity is directed by Organized Crime and is international in scope." The relevance of such information to the thesis of this book is that it would be impossible for known Mafia criminals alone to perpetrate the thefts, handle the paperwork, and subsequent disposal of the stocks. *They are aided at all stages of the operation by white-collar business people.*

Moneysworth, May 3, 1971, tells an interesting story involving Merrill Lynch, Pierce, Fenner & Smith, which sells and buys securities worth $125 billion a year. It is the world's largest investment house and prides itself on catering to the needs of small investors.

Two ladies wrote Merrill Lynch asking for advice. The first said she was a widow, about 60 years of age, and had $40,000 to invest. She had Social Security and wanted a nice nest egg she could retire on, in the form of interest from her stocks. Merrill Lynch replied and suggested shares for her to *buy* which totaled $40,900.

The second lady wrote a week later and told a similar personal story. She had stocks and wondered if Merrill Lynch would suggest she *hold* them. Actually the second lady was in collusion with the first. The stocks she told the brokerage firm that she had were identical to the ones that only a week earlier Merrill Lynch had told the first lady to *buy* as the soundest investment. The reply came promptly. The second lady was told to *sell* her shares at once and go into a Mutual Fund. If she had indeed sold those shares and done the trading through Merrill Lynch, the brokerage firm would have stood to gain $2,425 in commission!

Chapter *VI*

Politics:
The National
Scandal

One of the reasons for the dramatically negative attitude toward politicians which reached a peak in late 1978 was the seemingly endless series of scandals involving officials at the local, state, and federal levels. The race between Mervin Dymally and Mike Curb for the Lt. Governorship of my home state, California, dramatized the predicament. There had long been rumors about investigations of Dymally and his financial affairs. As for conservative leader Curb, who unlike Dymally has presented himself as an almost classic Mr. Clean, the reality of the man would appear to be decidedly otherwise.

New West magazine (November 6, 1978) reported that "when Curb was staff producer for Mercury Records in the 1960's, he was caught billing his employer for studio time that was actually spent working on records for Curb's own independent production company," an offense that Curb's boss told him to his face was "grand larceny."

In the late 1960's, *New West* reports, "Curb negotiated ... with Paramount Pictures to buy prime studio property. When required to come up with a token payment to show his good faith in the negotiations, Curb gave Paramount a bad check for several thousand dollars.... From 1969 to 1971 Curb was twice placed on AFTRA's unfair list ... after AFTRA performers complained of not receiving minimum payment for their services. In 1977 another complaint was filed with AFTRA, this time by members of Curb's own Mike Curb Congregation singing group, who charged Curb had underpaid them $2,400 for a recording session.... In California, Curb has been named, or figures prominently, in 16 lawsuits with a range of charges from breach-of-contract to fraud and conspiracy."

In 1969 Ronald Reagan, then California's governor, appointed Kerry W. Mulligan chairman of the California Water Resources Control Board. Three years later the Governor's office requested Mulligan's resignation after learning that he had served, while in office, as consultant for a private engineering firm. Mulligan, it developed, was charged with considerably more than that—specifically, bribery. Larry Chung, prosecuting attorney of Honolulu, Hawaii, accused him of participating in a $20,000 bribery attempt related to engineering studies for a Hawaiian sewage disposal facility. Charged with Mulligan were Harvey Ludwig, Chairman of Engineering Sciences Corporation of Arcadia, California and Joseph Feeny, executive vice-president of the company.

According to Chung, an undercover policeman was present at two of three meetings between Mulligan and Honolulu's Urban Renewal Coordinator, John Teehan. Mulligan's first meeting with Teehan was in October of 1971. Ludwig accompanied him to the second meeting and Teehan was present at the third, delivering the money according to a pre-arranged plan. "From the second meeting on," Chung explained, "police placed a man in Teehan's office."

Mulligan had been Mayor of St. Helena, California from 1964 to 1967 and before that owned an automobile agency in the same northern California city.

Howard Jarvis, who leaped from obscurity to popularity among conservatives in 1978, was revealed, in a July 25th column by Jack Anderson, as having had his name linked to "at least three shady operations."

"We traced one operation," Anderson wrote, "back to 1964 when Jarvis and two associates, William Morrison and Morton H. Nathan, set up shop in Los Angeles as Business-men-for-Goldwater. With a 'boiler-room' type campaign, they solicited thousands of dollars from businessmen throughout the country with the pretense of raising funds for the Republican presidential candidate . . . the Jarvis front neither had the approval nor the sanction of Goldwater's campaign organization or the Republican national commit-tee. Upon learning of the California scam, G.O.P. officials filed suit to stop Jarvis and his colleagues from collecting money in Goldwater's name. . . . *Not a penny was ever turned over to the Goldwater cause*. Not long afterward, Jarvis and company surfaced again in Arizona as promoters of . . . the National Freedom-to-Work committee. . . . On this occasion they were poaching directly on the territory of a long-established group, the Right-to-Work committee. In in-corporating their committee, Jarvis and his friends adopted the charter of the other group word-for-word. The only change they made was to use 'freedom' instead of 'right.' Reed Larson, director of the Right-to-Work committee . . . in a private May 7, 1978 memo denounced their operation as a fraud. . . . As late as 1976, Jarvis turned up as chairman of the Friends of Hayakawa committee, which raised $57,454 os-tensibly for the senate campaign of California's S. I. Haya-kawa. Yet *the campaign records show that the candidate got none of the money*." (Italics added.)

Reporting further on the case in his column of August 29, 1978 Anderson revealed that following his first exposé Jarvis had come to Anderson's office and "cordially pro-fessed his absolute innocence." Added Anderson, "We have now obtained additional facts that bolster our story. In the investigative files of the Postal Service we have found more evidence of Jarvis' connection with two fly-by-night schemes. One led to mail fraud investigations by FBI agents and postal inspectors."

I can recall certain specific moments in which the enor-mity of the situation I am describing suddenly leaped into focus for me. One such occasion came in 1950 when I moved from Los Angeles to New York to work in network television for CBS. Although criminality was certainly not unknown in Los Angeles I was still not prepared for the situation I found in New York City, which was, to state the matter briefly, that *criminal syndicates and their allies—in politics, in unions, in the police department, in business—were running the city*. Nor were they ruling an unwilling people. Notorious murderers, thieves, sadistic torturers, arsonists, criminal psychopaths, were not looked down upon or nervously tolerated, as would be the case in an ethically reasonable society; they were honored, respected and envied!

When racketeer Frank Costello was released from jail in the early 1950's, he was cheered, by a group of neighborhood children who happened to be in the area, as heartily as if he had been a famous athlete or other national hero. The young people were well aware that they were applauding a notorious criminal, at least as well aware of Costello's criminality as were the countless judges, mayors, congressmen and police officers of the New York area who courted his favor during the years of his dominance in that city.

District Attorney Frank Hogan of New York County, one of the few truly honest public servants of which that community could boast, has said, "We appear to have developed a public morality which condemns—rather than praises—any private citizen who seeks to enforce the laws ... we make a sort of game of it, between law enforcement officials and criminals, and sit complacently by, quite ready to applaud a brilliant stroke on either side."

One explanation of the American tendency to honor the powerful criminal rather than be repelled by him is our irrational infatuation with *Success*, however achieved. Thus we are fiercely critical of the petty criminal, of the narcotics addict driven to hold up a delicatessen or gas station because of his desperate need. We are stern towards the confused juvenile delinquent, the petty burglar, the purse-snatcher. But we seem to admire the *successful* criminal.

Consider what this means. Many of our nation's leading Mafia gangsters are not only known to be murderers, some have killed many times over. But they are still treated with deference in swank restaurants, political clubhouses, business offices, country clubs and resorts, and by no means out of fear. Society will sometimes at last turn away from them in disinterest but this has nothing whatever to do with the heinous nature of their crimes; it is the result of their falling out of favor, in precisely the same way that an athlete or entertainer may fall out of public favor.

While the corruption of which I speak is a national disease, it is not equally serious at every geographical point. It is worse in major cities than in rural areas, although the latter ought not to feel secure at knowing that they are, say, only one-tenth as corrupt as Chicago or New York since the degree of fraud and graft in these two cities is such that many scholars of the question consider their cases literally hopeless.

Chicago's predicament, even as regards degree, is unique in that, while most American cities were founded by largely decent people and only gradually succumbed to more corrupt and ruthless elements, Chicago has been, judged ethically, a hell-hole from the day of its birth.

Ovid Demaris, whose *Captive City* (Lyle Stuart) should be made required reading for all students of city government, says:

> From the moment of its incorporation as a city in 1837, Chicago has been systematically seduced, looted and pilloried by an aeonian horde of venal politicians, mercenary businessmen and sadistic gangsters. Nothing has changed in more than 130 years. . . .
>
> In the beginning the dominant member was the business tycoon, the ruthless entrepreneur out to make a quick financial killing, whether it be in land speculation, railroads, hotels, meat-packing, or public utilities. Pirates like Potter Palmer, Philip Armour, George Pullman, Charles T. Yerkes, and Samuel Insull fed the city with one hand and bled it dry with the other. Then, around the turn of the century, when the population explosion got out of control, the politician gained the upper hand over

his partners in the coalition. It remained for the
gangster to complete the circle in 1933, following
the murder of Mayor Cermak. Today it is nearly
impossible to differentiate among the partners—the
businessman is a politician, the politician is a gangster, and the gangster is a businessman.

Note, parenthetically, that the names of Chicago's notorious Robber Barons are to this day treated with as much
respect in the midwest as were the names of their New York
counterparts.

Corruption, long rife in Chicago at *all* levels of officialdom, would be even more widespread but for the Better
Government Association. On duty for over 50 years, the
association acts as a sort of ombudsman hopefully protecting
the citizens of Chicago against blatant official corruption.
Because financial subscriptions to it are substantial the BGA
is not beholden to any particular donor, and can attack
where others—such as the police—might fear to move.

Even the BGA, however, has sometimes hesitated to
tackle senior officials in the machine of the late Mayor
Daley. But other cases brought by the group have saved the
city millions over the years. Daley tended to regard the BGA
as an arm of the Republican Party, established chiefly to
discredit Democrats.

What about Daley's personal honesty? Well, consider his
high praise for a friend named Paul Powell, spoken at Powell's funeral. "A natural leader who never lost the common
touch, and who was proud to be called a politician." Powell,
a lifelong Democrat, had risen to be State Secretary of
Illinois shortly before he died in 1970. Few people warranted such an endorsement by the Mayor of Chicago. Powell's salary as State Secretary in Illinois was a mere $30,000.
The surprise was therefore great when it was discovered
that $800,000 was tucked away in cupboards and old shoe-
boxes in his home. Other secret treasures were shortly discovered in banks. The total: more than $3 million!

Even many aware that political power in the U.S. often
accompanies financial gain were surprised at the extent of
the funds Powell had been able to hoard. The money drew

claimants, including Powell's red-haired mistress, a buxom divorcee. Equal interest was shown by the state of Illinois, and the Johnson Historical Society, which Powell had asked to preserve his home as a monument—to God-knows-what, unless it be civic disgrace.

Powell's unsavory financial affairs were investigated by two grand juries, the Internal Revenue Service, a legislative commission, and the State Attorney General. As State Secretary, *the deceased had controlled 5,000 party job-holders; in Illinois kickbacks from grateful office-holders are common.* Enormous fees came from horse-racing syndicates, banking and insurance companies, haulage firms, and others for whom the greedy Powell fought so assiduously in the Capitol. As late as December, 1978 *Los Angeles Times* journalist Larry Green reported that Chicago still held the national corruption championship. Selecting just one month—November—Green reported that:

*State appellate Court Judge Henry Dieringer resigned following an investigation of his conduct on the bench.

*Alderman Edward "Fast Eddie" Vrodolyak was reported to have made a $44,000 profit in ten months on real estate he purchased at low cost and which then was rezoned by the City Council Building and Zoning Committee, of which Vrdolyak just happened to be chairman.

*Republican Governor James Thompson fired the county public guardian after the woman had refused to resign in the wake of charges that she grossly mishandled the estates of elderly people declared incompetent by the courts.

*The personal and political finances of Illinois Attorney General William J. Scott were being investigated by a federal grand jury. Earlier it was discovered that Scott, described by Green as "the former golden boy of Illinois Republican politics," had been using a $50,000 cash hoard kept in a safe-deposit box, for personal living expenses.

*A former Chicago public official pleaded guilty to charges that he defrauded a federally funded education program designed to assist children of low-income families.

*A federal grand jury indicted seven electrical inspectors on charges that they accepted bribes in return for overlooking building code violations.

*Four city building department supervisors were convicted on charges that they extorted more than $50,000 from five Chicago construction firms.

*At least 100 *more* city workers were expected to be indicted in a wide-ranging federal probe of corruption in the city's building department.

*James Y. Carter, former Chicago taxi commissioner—and a personal appointee of the late Richard Daley—was found guilty in Federal court of having shaken down independent taxi owners in the city for nearly $150,000.

*Former Judge Hyman Feldman, hired by Mayor Michael Bilandic to rout out corruption, told a city council budget hearing that it might take twenty years to do the job.

*A federal grand jury continued looking into the question as to how the city's two largest taxicab companies managed to win a substantial fare increase last year. A number of city officials had been publicly implicated.

To dramatize for its readers the depth of local political corruption, the *Chicago Sun-Times* purchased a neighborhood tavern. The paper staffed the bar with two reporters, Pamela Zekman and Zay Smith, investigator Jeff Allen, and another investigator, William Recktenwald, who worked for the Better Government Association. The four pretended to be the owners of the bar and set out to acquire the various licenses they would need to operate it. Everywhere they turned—whether they needed a liquor license or a health permit—an inspector's hand was reaching out for a bribe.

The *Sun-Times'* team learned quickly that, for the right price, building violations could be ignored. Shoddy construction, exposed wiring, leaking pipes—no cause for worry if the proper payoffs of anywhere from $10 to $100 were slipped to the various city officials who came to call. When the bar began serving its patrons, another kind of fraud was uncovered: bookkeepers and accountants advised the "owners" to under-report their actual income, so as to avoid paying the full city and state taxes. In a series of articles, complete with photographs of investigators accepting payoffs, the *Sun-Times* estimated that the tax skimming was costing the city of Chicago some $16 million annually!

The figures might suggest that Chicago is different as regards political corruption. No. Things are bad all over. In Miami, Philadelphia, New Orleans, Baltimore, Tucson, New York City, Albany, Washington, D.C.—in city after city—there is an increasing stench.

The state of Pennsylvania, never exactly a model of political virtue, has recently sunk to such a level that the *Philadelphia Bulletin* has run a series of stories under the title "The Shame of the State." *Bulletin* investigators report that from the period 1970 to May of 1978 *239 state officials have been successfully prosecuted.* At least 50 of those indicted or convicted were connected with the administration of Democratic Governor Milton J. Shapp.

An example from Hawaii, one of our youngest states: When Honolulu Mayor Frank F. Fasi was indicted twice on charges of accepting a $5,000 bribe from a developer of a multimillion-dollar condominium built on city urban renewal land, it was reported in the press as just another instance of alleged political corruption. The Fasi indictments also charged that he had conspired to obtain political contributions by passing out non-bid contracts; as the case went to trial the charges became more weighty. It developed that Mayor Fasi and a colleague were accused of soliciting a total of $500,000 in bribes on the $50-million downtown improvement project.

After months of testimony the case ended as so many of this nature do. All charges were dismissed by a Circuit Court judge after the prosecution's key witness—the man who had

been awarded the building contract—refused to testify
against the mayor and his adviser. The witness' lawyers said
that he could not give testimony in the state trial against the
mayor because his statments might be used in a Federal trial
involving mail and income-tax fraud charges.

The general drift of the preceding two paragraphs has
become familiar enough. The terminology of political corruption—*indictment, bribery, contribution, grand jury, tax
fraud*, and *withdrawal of charges*—is commonplace. It was
all there in the case of the Honolulu mayor, even down to
the politician charging that a "political vendetta" was being
waged against him and that his constitutional rights had
been violated.

Ernest Van den Haag, professor of social philosophy at
New York University, believes that many Americans today
have changed their expectations and "no longer accept corruption as part of the political process."

Either that, or a more pragmatic motivating factor has
come to the fore: the pinch of inflation and rising taxes has
made citizens less tolerant of the enrichment of politicians
at public expense. There was near-jubilation, for example,
at the 1978 sentencing of Gordon F. Lawson, postmaster
of Atlantic City, found guilty of helping to mastermind a
$1 million robbery of the Post Office.

Was it only greed that led to Lawson's crime? Not
according to David Egan, one of the burglars who offered his
testimony in a plea-bargaining arrangement. Lawson, said
Egan, planned to use his share of the proceeds from the
robbery to bribe State Senator Henry J. Cianfrani of Philadelphia. The bribe, it was hoped, would lead to the naming
of Lawson as postmaster of Philadelphia. For providing the
burglars with keys and floor plans of the Atlantic City Post
Office, Lawson was sentenced to 25 years in Federal prison.

If Egan's testimony is accurate, it illustrates how pervasive is corruption within the system—and how readily it is
accepted as a way of advancement in politics. Lawson, who
began working for the Post Office department at the age of
17, served as a local postmaster in two Pennsylvania towns
before he was promoted to the Atlantic City post. He had

evidently decided, as he moved ahead in the system, that bribery was the proper procedure for anyone who wanted a better job. Probably he saw enough examples as he climbed the ladder.

As for Cianfrani, once one of the most powerful men in the state Senate, he found himself accused of serious violations of law at about the same time the prosecutors were catching up with Lawson and Egan. The senator, it was said, had given $10,000 worth of gifts, including an expensive fur coat, to Laura Foreman, a reporter for the *Philadelphia Inquirer*. He was also said to have put a woman friend on the state payroll in a "no-work job." A federal prosecutor accused Cianfrani of cheating Pennsylvania tax-payers out of thousands of dollars through his actions.

Cianfrani resigned from the Senate, entered a "no contest" plea to Federal income tax-evasion charges, and provided the government with an "unconditional" plea of guilty to charges of racketeering, obstruction of justice, and mail fraud.

It would appear that in our democratic society, the opportunity for profiteering from corruption increases in geometric proportion with each step a politician climbs in his career. The higher the office, the more hands reaching out and the larger the payoffs. And the indications are that the politician discovered to be corrupt at the very highest levels of government did not suddenly decide to get his "while the getting is good." He probably has been on the take almost from the beginning of his career. Consider Spiro Agnew. Although the depths of his greed were exposed after he became Vice-President of the United States, investigation revealed there had been numerous infractions when he served as governor of Maryland.

Harry Bensen, a Time-Life photographer intimately familiar with American politics from his long White House and other Washington assignments, has told a friend, who does not wish to be personally quoted, that he happened to be present in a typical "smoke-filled room" during the Republican Convention of 1968, at a moment when the question as to whom Richard Nixon would or should select as a Vice-

Presidential running-mate was being discussed. After several minutes a telephone report reached the room. "It's going to be Spiro Agnew," someone announced.

At that an aged man with white hair, who had for several minutes sat silently reading a newspaper while others did the talking, lowered his paper and said, "Agnew? Why, they can't do that. He's a crook."

That this was long before Agnew's venality became public knowledge is obvious enough. The important point is that Agnew was known to be on-the-take by highly-placed Republicans, even before he became Nixon's Vice-Presidential choice. It is, of course, possible that Nixon himself did not know of conservative hero Agnew's unsavory reputation when he chose him but, in the light of what the nation has now had opportunity to learn about Richard Nixon, it would appear that if he did know his only cause for concern would have been whether Agnew was likely to be exposed. Harry Truman, who knew a great deal about Nixon, once said of him, "I don't think he knew the difference between the truth and a lie; I can't understand how he got on as far as he did . . . "

From the more recent trial and conviction of Agnew's successor, Maryland Governor Marvin Mandel, it might be conjectured that corruption is to that state what sunshine is to California. Mandel and five codefendants were accused of engaging in "a scheme of fraud or artifice," which involved the Governor using his official power to enhance the value of a racetrack secretly purchased by the codefendants. How could a governor make a racetrack worth more? By raising the legal limit on the number of racing days allowed in Maryland.

And what could a governor gain by letting the eager bettors in the state step up to the win-place-show windows a few more days each year?

According to his testimony, Mandel's cooperation enabled him to supplement his $25,000 annual salary with some $350,000 worth of gifts! During a six-year period he received clothing, paid vacations, expensive jewelry, investments, loans, payments of insurance premiums and cash. Portions of the payoffs were used by Mandel to help pay the settlement costs of his divorce in 1974 from his wife, Barbara. After 30 years of marriage the governor had left his first wife to marry divorcee Jeanne Dorsey.

The cronies involved with Mandel were W. Dale Hess, state legislator and lobbyist, Harry R. Rogers and William A. Rogers, real estate and insurance promoters, Irvin Kovins, former race track owner, and lawyer Ernest N. Cory, Jr., accused of falsifying documents.

Assistant U.S. Attorney Barnet D. Skolnick, chief prosecutor in the cases of both Mandel and Agnew, convinced a jury that Mandel and others "have been lying . . . in denying their guilt." After one of the longest federal jury deliberations in history, the governor and his colleagues were convicted of some 18 counts each. Among the charges: mail fraud and racketeering.

As for my old home-state of Arizona, the situation is so bad that it differs largely in kind rather than degree as compared to eastern states. The editors of *New West*, in publishing highlights of the 23-part, 100,000 word series prepared by the team of 36 reporters responding to the murder of *Arizona Republic* newsman Don Bolles, comment:

> Laws, even when enforced, are inadequate. The staffing of police and regulatory agencies is miserly. And there is widespread public indifference to corruption.
>
> The activities of Organized Crime figures go largely unwatched; white-collar swindlers waltz through a prosecutorial system marked—until recently—by incompetence, fuzzy or non-existent law and brazen bribe-taking. Public figures, on the rare occasions they are caught, are allowed to resign in lieu of prosecution and the *leaders of the most powerful political machine in the state have set the general standard through a history of profitable and open association with Organized Crime figures.* (Italics supplied.)

Anyone who imagines that such bastions of political conservatism are somehow far removed from organized crime and corruption will be greatly enlightened by Michael F. Wendland's *The Arizona Project* (Sheed, Andrews and McMeel) which, in relating the story of the killing of Bolles says, "whatever it was about the state of Arizona that had so corrupted Bolles' killers, that had *made land fraud the state's biggest business,* that allowed 200 recognized leaders and underlings of organized crime to find exile there, that prompted politicians and businessmen to look the other way—that was the real story." (Italics supplied.)

How does the classic Arizona land fraud work? It is simplicity itself, as described by Wendland: "A hastily formed land company purchases a huge chunk of wilderness, maybe 10,000 acres, for $100 an acre. Next step is the bulldozing of crude dirt roads and the plotting of the land into lots. The 10,000 acres become 40,000 quarter-acre lots. Then—through fancy advertising and lots of slick blue-prints—these 40,000 lots are sold nationwide for $1,000 a lot. That's a $40 million return on a one million dollar invest-ment. By the time sales commissions have been paid, engi-neering and planning costs met, and the heavy advertising budget absorbed, the actual profit is closer to $20 million."

Does the present situation represent a new low in real estate depravity? Not at all. Traditionally, Wendland reports, *Arizona has led the states in the list of land fraud com-plaints received by the interstate land sales division of the U. S. Department of Housing and Urban Development.*

Bolles' death resulted in the formation of a task force to carry on his work. Included were Tom Renner and Bob Greene, both from *Newsday,* a paper on Long Island, New York; Wendland from the *Detroit News*; John Winters from the *Arizona Republic*; and Alex Dreschler and John Rawlin-son from the *Arizona Star.*

The reporters alleged that professional criminals in Ari-zona had powerful friends—including such important fig-ures as Senator Barry Goldwater, the senator's brother Rob-ert, and former Republican State Chairman Harry Rosen-zweig. The triumvirate, it was said, controlled Phoenix and had condoned the presence of various mob figures through personal friendships and business arrangements. The influence of the politicians and of their unsavory friends, claimed the reporters, extended into such neighboring states as Nevada and California.

Denials were prompt. But the Phoenix project presented strong evidence to support its claims, including masses of data linking politicians to crime figures.

There was, for example, a contribution of $5,000 from notorious racketeer Willie Bioff, made to help promote Barry Goldwater's early aspirations. And Goldwater's familiarity with such as Moe Dalitz, Clarence Newman and Gus Greenbaum (a lieutenant of mob financier Meyer Lansky) raised serious questions.

Newman, a gambler, was supposed to have made contributions to the Goldwater campaign. Goldwater was accused of having personally intervened to have a lighter sentence imposed on Newman, as well as having tried to have the convict moved from a Texas jail to one closer to his home.

Then there was Goldwater's relationship with Joseph P. Ceferatti, a former insurance broker alleged to have underworld connections. Ceferatti's rise from gas-station operator to an important insurance broker was said to have been speeded by his connections with Joseph Zerilli, Detroit Mafia boss. In 1973 when the Arizona Insurance Commissioner took away Ceferatti's authority to underwrite low-rate insurance policies for restaurants both Goldwater and Rosenzweig, the Republican State Chairman, spoke up on the broker's behalf.

Another relationship that came under scrutiny by the investigators was the Goldwater friendship with the Funk family, whose members shared ownership of seven dog racing tracks in the state with Emprise Corporation. Emprise has been alleged to be a front for Mafia figures, including Zerilli. According to ex-Congressman Sam Steiger, Goldwater and Rosenzweig had both asked him to "go easy" on the Funks. While the Justice Department was proving the activities of Emprise, Goldwater corresponded with Art Funk and promised to inform him of any relevant findings to come out of the investigation. This took place in 1970, when Richard Nixon's good friend Richard G. Kleindienst, a former Phoenix lawyer—and, according to the Phoenix report, a product of the Goldwater-Rosenzweig GOP organization—was serving as a Deputy Attorney General!

Barry Goldwater personally is likable, charming. He might have been our president. Perhaps he has been guilty only of an incredible carelessness. But the situation in his home state has been shameful.

In their documented report, Phoenix investigative journalists contended that Harry Rosenzweig's sphere of influence extended far beyond the prosperous jewelry store he owned. He was involved in numerous land transactions and stock deals, some of a questionable nature. In one transaction, for example, Rosenzweig and his wife purchased the stock of a company called Educational Computer Systems, Inc., which was then bought—1.7 million shares worth—by Great Southwest Land and Cattle Co. Great Southwest closed its doors April 7, 1972. Shortly afterwards, Educational Computer Systems filed for bankruptcy. One day before it did, however, Rosenzweig's wife attempted to transfer 6,000 shares of the computer company's stock. Rosenzweig denied any knowledge of his wife's business deals.

In another odd arrangement, a company called Capital Management Systems—thought to have been endorsed by Senator Goldwater at Rosenzweig's request—turned out to be a fraud. Property offered for sale included uninhabitable acreage that had only one distinguishing geographic feature—cliffs.

Rosenzweig, the journalists pointed out, was on more than a casual-acquaintance basis with Herbert Lieb, a friend of Allen Dorfman—both of whom had documented ties to organized crime figures. Organized crime ties were also said to exist between numerous people and Senator Goldwater's brother, Robert, who ran the family department store business and was influential in the local GOP. It is no coincidence, says the Phoenix report, that a Goldwater Department Store unit opened in the Desert Inn Hotel in Las Vegas in which Moe Dalitz is influential.

Ned Warren, one of those rare swindlers who would appear to be without a shred of mitigating morality, was—at very long last—in January of 1978 sentenced to a term of 54 to 60 years in Arizona State Prison for grand theft, bribery and conspiracy. Warren had admitted that he misrepresented what were actually cliffside lands in Yavapai County for sale as residential lots, not to wealthy out-of-staters who might be able to absorb such losses but to overseas American servicemen! It is significant that the two states of the Union where for years real-estate confidence men made enormous profits were the conservative bastions, Florida and Arizona. Evil sometimes lurks behind the common cry, "No government interference with business!"

It would appear that the Sunbelt region, now the nation's fastest-growing area, is expanding as rapidly in corruption as in population.

But it is pointless to single out specific cities and states as spawning grounds of corruption when the pattern of villainy is also discernible in the nation's capital. As these words are written, South Korean millionaire Tongsun Park is filling newspaper columns with the names of dozens of Congressmen who accepted his bribes—"envelopes stuffed with $100 bills."

As special counsel for the House Ethics Committee investigating the allegations of influence-buying by South Korea in Washington, Leon Jaworski has already gone a long way in showing that a true sequel to Watergate exists. In the Capitol corridors, where some cynics believe the public never really learns from past scandals, Koreagate's revelations came as no surprise. Members of Congress took favors from Park, the Korean businessman and lobbyist, and from Kim Dong Jo, a former South Korean Ambassador to Washington.

Sources close to Park allege that he gave $190,000 to Otto Passman, one of the most powerful members of the House of Representatives until his defeat in 1977. The money was given, it appeared, to encourage Mr. Passman's support for the South Korean government and Park's own business endeavors. Need it be added that Passman, who served in Congress for 30 years, denied the allegations?

In subsequent disclosures Park indicated that 15 to 18 current members of Congress may be guilty of having violated ethical standards. Benjamin R. Civiletti, Acting Deputy Attorney General, predicted the indictment of a number of former Congressmen—although the expiration of the statute of limitations would prevent indictments from being lodged against many others.

In addition to gifts of cash, American politicians are believed to have been lavishly entertained with dinners, travel abroad, and other favors—and, just as with Watergate, there appears to have been a concerted effort by those involved in Koreagate to cover the whole thing up. There is dispute over how quickly the Justice Department reacted to a Presidential order to look into the South Korean situation. Officials who served under the Ford administration deny that there was procrastination. Carter administration officials claim that the investigation did not get off the ground until they came on the scene.

The ongoing testimony by Park in Washington followed 17 interrogations in Seoul, during which he was questioned as long as six hours a day and took twelve lie-detector tests. Those sessions produced more than 2,000 pages of transcripts for the investigating committees of the House and Senate. And out of it all may come headlines nearly as explosive as the ones from Watergate.

Since this book is intended as a *guide* to corruption in the United States rather than a complete survey of it (a task which would require a boxcar-load of volumes) there are frequent references to other studies in which dishonesty is detailed in specific, limited areas. Another good example would be *The Case Against Congress* by Drew Pearson and Jack Anderson, a compelling indictment of corruption on Capitol Hill. It is important to be familiar with the information it provides because many Americans apparently believe that the recent "housecleaning" adoption of codes of ethics by the House of Representatives and the U.S. Senate grew out of a soil no deeper than that of Watergate and the concomitant sex scandals that attracted so much public attention during the early 1970's. That is not the case at all; political corruption in the United

States starts at the local, neighborhood level. Not every office holder is contaminated by it, but the majority are, to one degree or another. Those politicians who go along with the general wishes of the party machines, which originally put them into power, who demonstrate that while they may have an occasional ethical impulse or two they are nevertheless not rock-the-boat types, will discover that their ascent up the political ladder is thereby greatly facilitated. It is no surprise, therefore, that such a depressing percentage of less-than-saintly servants of the public eventually find their way to Washington.

If we start with the assumption that the American political structure must—granting the traditional exceptions—send a better class of citizens to Washington than it leaves behind in the 50 states, then the degree of corruption in the Senate and the House of Representatives assumes more interesting significance. Pearson and Anderson, whose long experience in the Capitol has placed them in an advantageous position from which to evaluate the ethical conduct of our elected representatives, document the misconduct of those who, having been sent to Washington to create America's laws, have all too often abused their power by placing two interests above those of the American people. The first was their own, the other that of powerful economic forces for whom the representatives were perfectly willing to do favors in return for payment. To quote the book's publisher, "Here are the Congressmen who do the bidding of their campaign contributors, pad their payrolls with friends and relatives, who use Federal Public Works projects to reward their allies and punish their enemies, who promote their own financial interests—through their votes at closed-door committee sessions, and on the floor of the Congress itself. This is a world where conflict-of-interest is a way of life, where private pleasures and conveniences come before the national welfare, where the best find themselves compromised by the venal system—and the worst defy, with impunity, laws of the land."

Are there *any* honest men and women in Congress? Of course. No doubt even those petty and major thieves who work in the Senate or the House spend most of their working hours engaged in ethical pursuits. Even Jack the Ripper spent very little time actually committing murder. "Yet," the authors say, "the honorable men in Congress demean themselves by ignoring the corruption that flourishes in their midst. Many members who might be tempted to speak out against the abuses around them find they cannot. They have been compromised by the small favors they have done, or intimidated by the wielders of power, or bought off by the necessity of seeking funds for re-election, or hushed by a code of comradeship that ignores morality. Their silence is complicity in the deeds of the corrupt."

Read an infuriating book titled *The Real Voice*, by Richard Harris (Macmillan and Company). It tells of the heroic campaign waged by one honest politician, the late Senator Estes Kefauver, on behalf of the American people, a campaign for a new law extending Federal responsibility for the safety and effectiveness of drugs. Here was an instance where a decent, courageous man was trying to perform a politically virtuous act. Perhaps inevitably he paid a terrible price for his virtue.

That the present sordid state of affairs did not prevail in the early days of our nation's history we may assume from a letter written by Thomas Jefferson who, in returning a gift to a Baltimore merchant, wrote: "It is a law, sacred to me while in public character, to receive nothing which bears a pecuniary value. This is necessary to the confidence of my country, it is necessary as an example for its benefit, and necessary to the tranquility of my own mind."

"Over the years," Pearson and Anderson observe, "the words of Jefferson have been ignored and in their place the ideas of John Bricker have been practiced. Bricker, a Republican Senator from Ohio who ran unsuccessfully as Thomas Dewey's Vice Presidential nominee in 1948, was chairman of the Senate Commerce Committee while he drew $35,000 a year from his law firm, which represented the Pennsylvania Railroad. When his conduct was questioned, Bricker responded, 'Everyone knows I'm honest.' "

In considering the problem of corruption in Washington

it is pointless to choose up political sides. Neither the Republicans nor the Democrats have a record to boast of. When Dwight D. Eisenhower became President, his administration proclaimed corruption and graft were to be things of the past; the scandals of the Truman era would not be repeated. The President used the phrase, "clean as a hound's tooth," to express the ethical intent of his team, but in 1955 the unappealing facts of the Dixon-Yates scandal were revealed. What was involved was an effort on the part of powerful members of Eisenhower's administration to aid the private-enterprise power industry by substituting private electric power for a percentage of power from Tennessee Valley Authority sources. One of the tip-offs to the questionable methods used in bringing this end about was that no competitive bidding was permitted.

Three years later a House of Representatives committee looking into activities of the Federal Communications Commission uncovered improprieties in allocating television-station frequencies.

Richard Mack, a resigned member of the FCC, was indicted in July, 1958, on charges that illegal pressure had brought about the award of television channel 10 in Miami, Florida.

About the same time the nation learned the interesting story of Bernard Goldfine, a Boston businessman who was a close friend of Sherman Adams, President Eisenhower's executive assistant. Adams was never able to claim that he was shocked to learn what Goldfine's moral standards were, since the latter's career had consisted of a long history of stockholder's law-suits, charges of conspiracy, and charges of defrauding individuals, city administrations and corporations. One of his holding companies, the East Boston Company, avoided issuing the yearly financial reports required by Securities and Exchange Commission law. In December, 1958, Goldfine agreed to a settlement of $662,000 in a minority stockholder suit against East Boston and an allied corporation for what the stockholders asserted was "continuous looting" of the company's holdings. Goldfine was by no means a rare bird. Crooked business operators of his type have long flourished in the American corporate environment. What made him notorious in 1958 was his close personal relationships with a number of influential Washington officials.

Sherman Adams, for example, had accepted numerous favors from Goldfine, allowing him to pay his hotel bills, accepting expensive coats, rugs, etc. But Goldfine was more than just a crook; he also could boast *chutzpah* in that he charged such gifts on his income tax returns as legitimate business expenses! Such deductions included $3,000 worth of hotel bills paid for Sherman Adams and three fellow Republicans, Senator Paine of Maine, Senator Bridges of New Hampshire, and Senator Cotten of New Hampshire.

Like all efficient businessmen Goldfine made sure that he got what he was paying for. Evidence was revealed that Adams had made telephone calls from the White House on at least two occasions to inquire about the progress of cases coming up against Goldfine in the Securities and Exchange Commission and the Federal Trade Commission.

Walter Lippman, in his column of July 8, 1958, aptly observed, "The argument that money may be accepted provided nothing is given in return is an attempt to befuddle the real issue. It conceals the main point that what is customary and perhaps tolerable elsewhere may be intolerable in the close official family of the President. For those who are at the top, the country has the right to demand a self-imposed standard of conduct which is much higher than the laws against bribery and graft. That was in essence the principle on which General Eisenhower ran for President in 1952. The ultimate power of the state cannot be entrusted to men whose conception of public virtue is that their integrity is adequate if they cannot be convicted of a crime."

Another source that names names and reveals the sordid facts of wheeling-and-dealing, influence peddling, kickbacks, payoffs and bribes is Robert N. Winter-Berger's *The Washington Payoff* (Lyle Stuart). Winter-Berger, a veteran Washington lobbyist, worked intimately with some of the most influential men in Washington, and consequently was privy to the kind of deal-making that his book discloses.

His first chapter outlines a story so shocking that one

literally has difficulty accepting it, even in the absence of naive confidence in the integrity of our elected and appointed representatives.

"During the summer of 1945," the author explains, "I went to work for A. Davis and Sons, Inc., the country's biggest manufacturers of women's suits and coats.... During World War II, the Coat Corporation of America, a division of A. Davis and Sons, had a government contract to make uniforms for the military, obtaining the material on government approval from manufacturers. *Quite a bit of the material was siphoned off to the black market.* [Italics added.] The company did not report these earnings, nor did it pay taxes on them. The Internal Revenue Service discovered the fraud by checking tax reports of other companies, then hit A. Davis and Sons with an action for two hundred thousand dollars in penalties. The owners, Milton and Charles Davis, also faced a prison sentence."

When Franklin D. Roosevelt was still alive, Winter-Berger relates, he had made a personal crusade of prosecuting industrialists who profited from the war illegally. Francis Biddle, the U.S. Attorney General at that time, was known to be of unimpeachable rectitude. Then the Davises hired the New York legal firm of Simpson, Brady, Noonan and Kaufman. Irving Kaufman was a personal friend of Tom Clark, then an Assistant U.S. Attorney and head of the Criminal Division of the Department of Justice.

"After Roosevelt died on April 12, 1945, and Harry Truman succeeded him," Winter-Berger recalls, "rumors spread through Washington that Truman would appoint Tom Clark as U.S. Attorney General. As these rumors reached New York, Charlie Davis told me that Clark himself had telephoned Irving Kaufman and said, 'You can stop worrying now.' Tom Clark was in fact appointed U.S. Attorney General on May 24, 1945. Meanwhile, Lamar Caudle, a Clark protégé, was appointed to Clark's old job, heading the Criminal Division of the Department of Justice. On July 31, 1945 Milton Davis and Charles Davis, the latter of whom was powerful in Democratic circles, pleaded guilty ... to filing a false statement with the Army Quartermaster Corps

. . . the Davises were fined 30 thousand dollars. Nothing was said about the rest of the money. Nothing was said about the prosecution, and there was none.

"About two weeks later . . . I saw Tom Clark himself enter a large showroom at A. Davis and Sons, on the 17th floor of 225 West 37th Street in New York . . . I watched him cross the room and accept a suitcase that was given to him by Charlie Davis, and he walked out with it. After he left, Charlie told me, in bragging fashion, that the suitcase contained 250 thousand dollars in cash. I was stunned. Years later, as a lobbyist, I learned on my own that, in Washington, big favors cost big money. Not long ago, in talking to me, Al Davis kidded that his uncle might have been exaggerating, but he confirmed that the sum had been substantial."

Winter-Berger gives an extended account of the Bobby Baker scandal. Since the facts have been outlined in such detail elsewhere, I will not refer to them here. Perhaps one of the most important lessons to be learned from the Baker mess, however, is that Baker does not appear to have been an utterly unusual character. He blended easily into the ethical climate of our nation's capital and seems to have been able to pick and choose among willing collaborators. He was no small-time crook working in the shadows of obscurity but a Washington big wheel. At various points his gears meshed comfortably with those of more-than-shady Las Vegas characters. Winter-Berger reminds us that in 1963 Baker and a man named Edward Levinson had met to discuss bidding on the gambling concessions at two West Indies hotels owned by Intercontinental Hotels, Inc., a subsidiary of Pan American World Airways.

Levinson held large interests in two Las Vegas casinos and was also a major stockholder in Baker's Serv-U-Corporation. Two other casino owners involved in the transaction were Jacob Kozlof and *Nevada Lieutenant-Governor Clifford Jones, an associate of George Sadlo, business partner of Meyer Lansky, one of the leading figures in the American underworld.*

Winter-Berger reports at length on the unsavory situation in the office of House Speaker John McCormack, whose pipeline to the underworld was Nathan Voloshen, his close

personal aide. Voloshen's key connection with the underworld, in turn, was Congressman John Rooney of Brooklyn.

*Among the various underworld characters welcomed to
Speaker McCormack's offices by Voloshen was Mafia leader
Frank Costello.*

"Nathan Voloshen," Winter-Berger relates, "moved into
the big-time in the 1948 period. At the time, he was a
trouble-shooter for the law firm of Hartman, Sheridan,
Tekulsky and Donaghue. A close friend of his was a prohibi-
tion-era racketeer named Anthony Carfano, more popularly
known as Augie Pisano. 'Little Augie' had made it up the
ladder through his contacts with Al Capone. Voloshen and
Pisano met through their girlfriends. Voloshen was very
close to Shirley Lewis, the then-wife of Irving Segal, a stock-
broker friend of Pisano. Little Augie was also the confidante
of such powerful figures as George Scalise, Frank Costello,
Vito Genovese, Albert Anastasia and Al Capone. Pisano was
having an affair with Janice Drake, wife of comedian Allan
Drake . . . It was in 1948 that Little Augie introduced
Voloshen to George Scalise, whose specialty was labor racketeering."

Scalise had been sent to prison in 1940 on a 10-to-20-
year sentence for stealing funds from the Building Service
Employees Union, of which he was president. The purpose
of the meeting was to bring together two men who could use
each other's connections. Voloshen was ever eager for clients; Scalise needed someone in government who could
make life less troublesome for him and his criminal associates.

"Later Scalise introduced Nathan Voloshen to Bill
Bufalino of the Teamsters Union, and eventually to Team-
sters president Jimmy Hoffa. Voloshen became close friends
with both these men. It was Voloshen, too, who got Bill
Bufalino's ex-convict brother, Eugene, the job of head of the
Rectifying Union on the West Coast."

In the mid-1950's Pisano, Scalise and Sol Cilento, secretary-treasurer of the Rectifying Union, were indicted by
District Attorney Frank Hogan after an insurance broker,
Louis E. Saperstein, had informed a Grand Jury that the
three had taken $299,000 in kick-backs from him, on deals

which they referred to as "investments for the Union's Welfare Fund." Before the trial opened, Saperstein was shot in the head. Much to the surprise of those who had ordered him to be hit, he survived.

Years later—in November, 1968—Saperstein died by arsenic poisoning. Although the autopsy showed that his body contained enough arsenic to "kill a mule" his death was ruled a suicide! Saperstein was killed—by himself or others—at a time when he had been scheduled as the principal witness against Mafia bosses Angelo De Carlo and Daniel Cecere, who had allegedly extorted money from him.

On September 25, 1959 Little Augie—after having had dinner with a group of friends that included Mafia hoodlums Tony Strollo and Anthony Mirra—and Nathan Voloshen—was shot to death in a car, with his girlfriend, Janice Drake.

Tristram Coffin, editor of the *Washington Spectator*, in an important "Open Letter to Congress," August 1, 1977, quoted an editorial from the *Rocky Mountain News* that he rightly observed should be pinned up in the Senate Ethics Committee room as a monument to that committee's shame:

> To the surprise of no one who follows its antics, the Senate Ethics Committee has voted to kill the probe of Sen. Hugh Scott and more than a dozen other Senators who took illegal contributions from Gulf Oil Corp. . . . Under Senate rules, the contributions should have been accounted for and publicly disclosed. Scott and most of the other recipients made no reports. Also, it is a felony for politicians to accept corporate funds. . . . In any case, the committee voted 5-1 . . . not to pursue the Scott affair any further. By a remarkable coincidence, *four of the five Senators voting to quash the inquiry themselves are alleged to have received money or services from oil or aircraft companies.* . . . They ought to cut the hypocrisy and rename their ethics committee . . . Old Boys Protective Association.
>
> There is already a rank-and-file movement to punish those with conflicts of interest. House Demo-

crats broke with the leadership and voted 189 to 83 to remove Rep. Robert Sikes (D-Fla.) as chairman of the Military Construction Appropriations Subcommittee. He was accused by 45 Representatives and Common Cause of "failing to disclose stock holding in Fairchild Industries, a defense contractor; promoting the establishment of the First Navy Bank at the Pensacola Naval Air Station, then becoming the third largest stockholder in the bank; and sponsoring legislation to allow development of Florida property in which he had substantial financial interest. (Italics supplied.)

An interesting case of Congressional corruption was that of one Congressman Dowdy, accused of having accepted a $25,000 bribe in 1965.

During his trial the defense introduced a surprise witness, Leonard R. Wilson, executive secretary of the Citizens Council of Alabama, a white-supremacy group. Wilson, a right-wing segregationist of the sort that often proclaims allegiance to basic American ideals, testified that he had taken time off from his work to drive to Atlanta, Georgia and deliver a $500 campaign contribution from banker Wallace Malone of Dothan, Alabama, who has since died. Wilson swore that, because he had been with Dowdy the whole time at the airport where the congressman was alleged to have received the $25,000 bribe, no one could possibly have delivered such a payment to Dowdy.

It emerged that banker Malone was an associate of Willis Carto, head of the right-wing Liberty Lobby, which contributed over $21,000 for Dowdy's defense. Shortly thereafter the prosecution was able to establish, by records subpoenaed from the Citizen's Council, that Wilson had told his employers that he stayed in Montgomery, Alabama the entire day in question.

Congressman Dowdy was found guilty on all counts.

Another relevant instance came to light in late March of 1978 when a Federal Grand Jury handed down a 35-count indictment charging Congressman Charles Diggs with hav-

ing padded his federal payroll over a 5-year period. Specifically Diggs was accused of raising the wages of three of his
House employees, then demanding kick-backs by suggesting
to the benefited workers that they pay a number of Diggs'
personal bills. He also placed three employees of his family's
undertaking business on the federal payroll, at excellent
salaries. In December Rep. Diggs was convicted.

Not that Washington needed another scandal but in
May of 1978 the General Services Administration, a sort of
combination landlord and supplies-agency, announced its
very belated intention to put a stop to fraud in the GSA's
$2.4 billion-a-year federal building and supply operation.
The announcement came after the FBI had begun investigating payments paid to contractors who submitted bills to
the government for work other than that actually performed, the giving of clothing, color TV sets and stereo
equipment to GSA supply-center managers with the apparent intent to influence their purchases from office supply
companies, the authorization of inferior workmanship, theft
of merchandise, etc.

For revealing important information on the case credit
an obscure painting contractor named Robert Lowry, who
lives in Hyattsville, Md., near Washington, D.C. Unknown to
the news media until mid-1978 Lowry became a key figure
in the investigation of the General Services Administration
scandal—estimated to be costing taxpayers $100 million a
year.

For two years—and while he himself was involved in
the kickbacks and phantom deals that are part of the mess—
Lowry tried to tell his story. He wrote long letters to the
President, congressmen, the FBI, and the newspapers, but—
incredibly—got no results, no action. In March, 1978, when
the *Washington Post* began revealing the scope of corruption within the G.S.A., Lowry came forward with tale after
tale of what he saw, what he was offered—and what he had
taken.

In a *Post* interview he said, "One building manager I
met at a party in 1970 said to me, 'If you're a thief, I want
you. I intend to steal $200,000 this year and if you want part
of it, come see me Monday morning.' I turned him over to

another contractor. I was already doing enough myself that I wasn't all that proud of, and scratchin' my head trying to see how I could do any of it without going to jail anyway."

Lowry wove a labyrinthine tale, wrote *Post* reporter Myra MacPherson, of corruption and subterfuge as contractors wooed G.S.A. building managers in order to get jobs. In exchange for kickbacks the government employees used the taxpayers' money to pay for phantom painting jobs, paying for two coats when only one was applied, or for plastering and repairing of walls that needed nothing more than a coat of paint to look good as new.

To get around the federal rule that any job requires three different bids, a painting or contracting company merely had letterheads printed up with three different names! The G.S.A. employee who was on the take approved the letterhead with the lowest bid, without question. The number of employees involved grew over the years. Lowry first noticed how widespread corruption was when he found that he was not getting any G.S.A. business, no matter how low he bid for a particular job. Finally, he began asking, "How much does it *cost* to be the low bidder?"

One of the things it cost was paying off the building managers. Lowry made the rounds of the men who assigned the contracts and wined and dined them, often running up bills for $200 for two. A typical part of the routine consisted of starting in a topless bar, where the "customer" would get liquored up and ask Lowry to provide the name and number of a girl for dinner and afterwards. Occasionally he was expected to supply enough party girls for a group. One party—for which he furnished liquor and women—for about 16 G.S.A. workers, cost him and six other contractors $6,000.

Feeling uneasy, Lowry decided to stop dealing with the G.S.A. He thought of blowing the whistle but held off, saying, "You wonder who you could tell anyway. You got to ask how high does it go."

It was in 1974, after he lost out on a bidding job to another painter, that he became enraged.

Lowry began writing a series of letters, but could get little satisfaction. "I cannot fathom the government's reluctance to act on these matters," he wrote in desperation. He furnished data in one case to the *Post*, which was checking into the Levcon Construction Co. The G.S.A. had paid Levcon to paint 2.4 million square feet of walls and ceilings in its headquarters building—but the building, according to measurements taken, only had 1.9 million square feet of surface.

His willingness to talk brought Lowry not credit but trouble. Only three or four contractors would hire him for paint jobs, because others feared that if they used him they would be cut off from lucrative G.S.A. assignments. His Great Dane died mysteriously from an intake of chemicals. But he is more at peace with himself now than he has been for a long time, as the scandal widens, despite the G.S.A.'s initial attempts to dismiss it as a localized instance involving only a few wrongdoers. In just three months after the charges of corruption surfaced, 19 major changes intended to correct the agency's problems were ordered by Jay Solomon, G.S.A. adminstrator. One was the establishment of a central procurement office, which means that one small staff of employees will handle all purchases—rather than having buying split up among the central office in Washington and 10 regional offices. While no one can guarantee that the workers in the central office will not continue the pattern of kickbacks and favors, at least it is easier to keep an eye on one office than on a dozen.

Corruption sometimes goes hand-in-hand with bureaucratic stupidity. As part of the G.S.A. investigation it was noted that when the Defense Department wanted to buy Worcestershire sauce for its cafeterias and restaurants, it provided makers with a 20-page document setting standards for the product it wanted. After asking 36 companies to supply bids, it got answers from only two and bought 217,152 bottles of sauce for 20.5 cents per bottle. More recently the department decided not to worry about the specifications and testing procedures and offered to buy a sauce sold commercially on the market. This time four bidders responded, and the agency bought 224,640 bottles for less than 17 cents each. The same thing happened when the Pentagon tossed out a 23-page specification for bath towels and got them 10 cents cheaper than those bought previously. A few cents here, a few cents there—add up to big savings for the taxpayer. And it is not always a cent or two that is being talked about. The Defense Science Board discovered that the Pentagon could save $80 million a year, and get better equipment, if it dispensed with outmoded specifications for electronic test equipment built especially for it and, instead, bought commercially available equipment.

Chapter *VII*

The Sickness in the World of Medicine

In March of 1978 the California Medical Board of the State Department of Consumer Affairs announced the creation of a strike force to put "every dope-pushing doctor in California out of business." Earlier an investigative report published in the *Los Angeles Times* had revealed that hundreds of doctors had become the main illegal suppliers of dangerous drugs, to thousands of mostly young patients across the state. State officials put their finger on the doctors' personal motivation—"vicious greed."

On the national level in late September of 1978 Health, Education and Welfare secretary Joseph Califano spoke harshly of "croakers"—doctors who knowingly accept phony Medicaid cards to prescribe drugs not only to users but to pushers. "The pushers get pharmacists to fill the prescription," Califano said. "Then they sell the pills out in the street. Uncle Sam pays the bills." In addition to the campaign against unethical doctors the secretary also identified a separate effort to target federal employees illegally receiving welfare benefits. 23,000 names had, as of September 27, 1978, been identified as warranting individual investigation.

By the time of Califano's statement some 50 California doctors had been arrested; 332 others were under investigation as a result of the several-month state-wide campaign against drug-dealing M.D.'s.

In late December of 1978 the House Subcommittee on Oversight and Investigations released a report that unnecessary surgery remained "a major national problem," cost almost $4 billion annually and in the one year 1977 led to an estimated 10,000 deaths! The report harmonized with a study released earlier in the year by Blue Cross and Blue Shield of New York, which found that in one out of every four elective surgery cases in which a second opinion was sought the second doctor rejected the first doctor's recommendation for surgery.

Obviously a certain percentage of unnecessary operations are performed not because of financial greed on the part of the surgeons and other attendant physicians but because of ignorance or ineptitude. But no one supposes that the factor of financial dishonesty is totally absent from the picture.

There are, of course, various kinds of crooked doctors. A Baldwin Hills, California psychiatrist and her husband were in March, 1978, arraigned in Los Angeles Municipal Court on 25 felony counts each of medical fraud. The two—Dr. Sara Carter and her husband Kenneth—were accused of one count each of grand theft and 24 counts each of filing false claims in allegedly submitting claims for services totalling approximately $45,000 over a period of a year and a half, according to Deputy District Attorney Barry M. Sax.

From a rising number of such instances we are only recently beginning to realize—with a special sort of shock— that the medical field is just as vulnerable to corruption as business, politics, sports or any other area of human enterprise.

As necessary as they are for millions of people, the federally-funded health programs for the poor and the elderly—especially Medicare and Medicaid—have multiplied the traditional possibilities for medical cheating. As evidence, papers from coast to coast have been filled with stories about "Medicaid mills," nursing home outrages and growing numbers of justified malpractice suits. Headlines about scandals in the medical world are now common. "HEW to Reorganize to Stem Health Fraud" . . . "Doctor Fined $100,000 in Cocaine Case" . . . "U.S. Tracking Medicaid Cheaters" . . . "M.D.'s Ripped Off Hospital for $650,000, Audit Shows" . . . "Medicaid Worst Rip-Off in History, Senators Told" . . . "Doctors to Pay $185,000 to End Kickback Suits?" . . . "26 Indicted in N.Y. Nursing Home Industry," and on and on.

One of the most recent tales of a Medicare-Medicaid ripoff involved our old favorite bastion of corruption, the state of Illinois. An investigation of the program by the Senate Subcommittee on Long-Term Medical Care revealed that *$1 out of every $6 spent by the Illinois Public Aid Department was illegally channeled to unauthorized people!* To prove the corruption, investigators from Chicago's Better Government Association set up a clinic on the North Side of the city, adjacent to ghetto areas. When word was sent to a number of important medical laboratories that the new clinic was open for business, some 13 representatives of as many labs rushed to offer their services. Among the lucrative propositions suggested to the "clinic" were kickbacks of patients' payments, free tests for private "special" patients, free medical equipment, generous salaries for secretaries, even free plumbing and wiring. All the clinic had to do was give the labs its business, and everyone could grow rich. You and I, of course, foot the bill.

Among the abuses unearthed by the establishment of the mock clinic was the labs' offering of two sets of prices for any needed test—*one price charged for private patients and a higher one billed to Medicaid recipients.* An audit of more than 20,000 bills submitted by labs in such instances showed a median overcharge of 116% on the Medicaid tests!

In addition to inflated billing, the investigation revealed that bills were submitted for tests that were either unnecessary or not administered. There were cases of male patients being billed for pregnancy tests, and of white patients being screened to determine if they had sickle-cell anemia (a disease that occurs almost exclusively among blacks).

Frequently outright kickbacks were disguised as "rent"

payments, with the lab ostensibly renting space, for whatever purpose, from the doctor. *Time* reporter Richard Woodbury met with a doctor whose office rent cost him $300 a month, but who received $2,000 a month for supposedly allowing it to be used by a laboratory and a pharmacy. The doctor seemed perfectly at ease when questioned by the journalist on the propriety of the set-up. "I talked to my lawyer," he said. "He sees nothing wrong."

A case that dramatizes the potential for abuse within the Medicare-Medicaid system is that of Flora Souza, owner and director of a $7.5 million health care operation in San Jose, California. Her company was the second-largest provider of health services in the state, and Mrs. Souza was not at all ashamed of her power. A highly visible figure who dressed in white suits and boots and carried a white umbrella on cloudy days, she included among her friends a number of influential politicians: San Jose City Councilman Joe Colla, who supposedly recommended Mrs. Souza to various county officials in return for $36,500 worth of medical supplies purchased from the Colla Rexall pharmacy; and State Senator Alfred Alquist, who advocated legislation that would benefit Mrs. Souza, and whose wife at one point was on the Souza payroll.

There were important friends in the world of medicine, too, such as Dr. Jerome Lackner, director of the state health department, whose father and brother both were members of Mrs. Souza's medical advisory board. There was Albert Fox, a senior Medicare officer in the Bureau of Health Insurance at Social Security headquarters, who aided Mrs. Souza with various matters in Washington, D.C. It is not surprising that Mrs. Souza refused to comment or testify before a Congressional subcommittee.

An investigation into her affairs, however, turned up some surprises. One was that when Travelers Insurance Company, a private company, had been directed to audit Mrs. Souza's books, the company's auditor, Jack Stewart, reported that he had found irregularities. *Within a two-month period, Stewart had left Travelers and joined Mrs. Souza's company as her controller—with a generous stipend of $43,000 and a $15,000 Mercedes, all paid for by Medicare*, which means the taxpayer. Stewart dutifully proceeded to find fault with his original audit for Travelers. It was subsequently rejected by The Bureau of Health Insurance.

The case might have died if it had not been for career auditor John Markin who works in the government's General Accounting Office. He singled out the Souza operation for a routine audit after a cursory glance at figures made him suspicious. "Just from the breakout of the costs," he told Patrick J. Sloyan of *Newsday*, "I could tell that this agency might be abusing the system."

Markin was so relentless in his investigation that he rented a trailer and parked it next to the operation's office. Among other questionable expenses he found on the ledgers were two Mercedes automobiles, three other luxury cars, a $35,000 motor home, $6,000 worth of beauty parlor expenses, a $1,600 brass bed, a $3,500 trip to Hawaii, and annual salaries for three sisters, a daughter, and assorted other relatives of Mrs. Souza. These salaries were, naturally, in addition to the greedy lady's own annual wages—a mere $140,000.

Digging into a pile of business lunch receipts, Markin found one that showed Medicare had paid for a meal that cost $47.47. Searching through the records, he came up with the original tab for the meal; it totalled $7.47, for two cheeseburgers, one beef sandwich, one hot dog, and three Cokes. Someone had used the check to steal $40 of taxpayers' money.

Although there have been suggestions that HEW Secretary Joseph Califano sought to curb the investigation of the scope of the Souza fraud case, the allegations have been denied. As of 1977 the Criminal Division of the Justice Department was on Mrs. Souza's trail, and Califano himself predicted that ". . . there will almost certainly be prosecutions forthcoming."

If Mrs. Souza's case ends in punishment she will be one of the few to get caught. The record seems to show that far more wrongdoers are getting away with fraud than are being discovered. Some of the cases discovered make headlines because they are almost beyond belief. A moral low, of sorts, emerged when charges were levelled, early in 1978, against a nursing home in Middletown, N.Y., that was run by—believe it or not—an order of Roman Catholic nuns.

The State Office of Health Systems Management accused the sisters of having abused the public trust, complaining that Medicaid funds had been used for such things as grooming pet dogs and the purchase of a gift for the late Bishop of Buffalo. An audit of St. Theresa's nursing home in Orange County also indicated that the nuns spent Medicaid money to buy meals that were eaten in a nearby convent and for a course in handwriting that had nothing to do with patient care. Checking into expenditures over a three-year period that ended in 1975, auditors found that $100 had been spent for medicine and "a pedicure" for two dogs kept by the Carmelite nuns, and another $100 had gone for the Bishop's gift. The meals totaled $3,360, and were eaten by nuns who lived in the nearby convent but did not work at the nursing home. All told, *the state rejected about $158,000 worth of bills out of a total submitted for $3.8 million in reimbursement funds!*

State efforts to correct the apparent misuse of Medicaid funds "were met with a reaction by the nuns that varied from indifference to an outright refusal to hear them," the audit said. The auditors also criticized the home for hiring members of its board of directors as lawyers and auditors, contending that this constituted a conflict of interest. Sister Mary Grace, the home's administrator, refused to comment on the charges. But the head of the state investigative office said, "It is our intention to go hard on these types of irresponsible acts and make them public whenever we uncover them."

"Go hard on them." In most such cases that means that a fine will be assessed, a fine which, because there is plenty of cash, can be easily paid.

Consider the case of the Los Angeles physicians whose dishonesty made headlines when they agreed to pay more than $185,000 to settle various civil suits charging them with receiving illegal kickbacks on laboratory tests. The doctors paid the fine, though none of them admitted wrongdoing.

The group had been accused of pocketing illegal rebates from the Damon Medical Laboratory, Inc. According to City Attorney Max Factor they received "a great deal of money, in excess of $4,000 or $5,000 a year each" through their participation in the fraudulent practice. The question is whether the punishment meted out to any of the individuals will affect their conduct in the future. Perhaps they will just be more careful next time.

The range of Medicaid cheaters is wide, to say the least. A HEW investigation, named "Project Integrity," screened Medicaid bills submitted by 231,000 doctors and 44,000 pharmacies. The investigators identified 172 cases classified as the worst offenders: 92 physicians and 80 pharmacists located throughout the U.S. Here are just a few examples of what they found:

*A druggist who dispensed more than 100 pills a day, to the same Medicaid patient, for 204 days.

*A doctor who unabashedly billed one patient for six consecutive tonsillectomies.

*A gynecologist who charged a patient for an abortion, after having previously charged the same patient for a complete hysterectomy.

*In one of the more audacious instances a single internist submitted more than 26,000 bills for a year's worth of medical procedures on his Medicaid patients. Even if the young man worked a staggering 80 hours per week he would have had to complete work on a patient every ten minutes.

More disturbing cases showed up in an analysis of the some 250 million bills submitted to Medicaid by physicians and pharmacists in 1976. The study was conducted by the newly established Office of Inspector General at the Health Care Financing Administration, over a five-month period. Inspector General Thomas Morris and his staff turned up 47,000 abnormalities among the bills! 2,000 suspicious cases were earmarked for further investigation and possible prosecution. One of the most flagrant abuses: a doctor who passed along bills for three hysterectomies on the same patient in the same year.

Throughout the nation individual states are working to hold down the ballooning cost of social services—ballooning, they believe, partly because of increasing corruption. The program worked out by the state of North Carolina with the Los Angeles-based Bergen Brunswig Corp. is one of many remedies being tried almost in desperation. Bergen Brunswig contracted to run the state's Medicaid program on a "fixed cost" risk basis. The company agreed to pay excess costs above the $400 million Medicaid budget, but collects 25% of any savings it achieves through computerization of the program.

Among the goals announced by the company was the reduction of the length of the average hospital stay by North Carolina patients—two days, as compared with 1.6 days by patients in California. Doctors handling Medicaid patients in the state were told that they would be asked to tell in advance how long they expected patients to remain in the hospital, and would have to receive permission to extend the period.

Audits at individual hospitals have unearthed numerous other medical ripoffs. One such inquiry involved the Queens Hospital Center in New York, which lost some $650,000 in a year's time. The sum was for thousands of laboratory tests and prescriptions for patients—lab tests that were conducted and prescriptions that were filled but for which no revenue was recorded. Either the patients were never billed, said an investigator, or the money that came in was "misappropriated." Staff physicians at two other hospitals in the area were believed to be responsible for the losses. Parents used to brag about "My son, the doctor." Some might now accurately switch to "My son, the thief."

One of the most common frauds involves the treatment of private patients at public expense. "Shocked" was the word used by Layhmond Robinson, spokesman for New York City's Health and Hospitals Corporation, when he found that an audit of laboratory and pharmacy records showed many more tests and prescriptions were issued than could possibly have been used by the limited number of patients in one hospital.

The entire area of medical fees is subject to constant

abuse, investigators have discovered. Since the advent of Medicare and Medicaid, doctor's fees have escalated rapidly. The physicians protest that the increases merely reflect inflation: higher costs of rent, nurses, secretaries, insurance and the like. But the truth seems to be that many doctors have raised their rates in the belief that Medicare and Medicaid reimbursements come from an unlimited supply of funds, and they might as well get as much as they can.

Sometimes, particularly for people living on fixed retirement income, doctor's bills are just too steep. A professional ombudswoman, in charge of aiding patients at a highly respected private teaching hospital in the East, recently told about some of her problems.

"These old people come to me in tears," she said, "with their hands trembling and looks of anguish on their faces. Their medical bills for surgery are way beyond what the Medicare and Medicaid coverage will pay, and they don't know what to do. What can I tell them, except, 'Don't pay it!' Sometimes it works. You see, the doctor does not lose out on the deal. He collects what he can from the Government, continues to bill the patient—and eventually writes off the episode as a bad debt."

Many doctors have learned the art of double-billing. A physician taking care of a Medicare patient refers him or her to a specialist. Or a group of specialists. Then the physician bills Medicare for the work done by the specialist, and the specialists submit their own bills. In the welter of bills and forms flooding into agency offices, it is more than likely that everyone will get paid.

Doctors have, of course, learned how to charge the government agencies for work that once was done free. A friend paid a visit to a college chum, now an internist, to get a regular checkup. When he received his bill, he discovered that there was a charge of $10 for removing wax from his ears.

"Don't worry about that," his doctor reassured him. "It's all covered by Medicare."

And it isn't only MD's who must be watched. Medical-dental abuses are legion in clinics and in private practice. "Based on available evidence, it can be conservatively estimated that at *least 15% [of U.S. dentists] are incompetent, dishonest, or both,"* reads a booklet issued by the Insurance Department of the state of Pennsylvania.

        Consider the nation's pharmacies. Remember the friendly neighborhood druggist, who dispensed cherry Cokes and prescriptions with equal ease? Today the man behind the prescription counter is every bit as skilled in the science of cheating as the unethical doctor or dentist. He knows how to charge highly inflated prices for medicines, how to issue fraudulent bills, how to sell free samples of prescription drugs given by pharmaceutical manufacturers for promotional purposes.

Investigative reporters for the *New York Daily News*, chiefly Richard Oliver, discovered in January of 1972 an interesting racket perpetrated by a number of New York pharmacists, who were charging customers for sample prescription drugs distributed by pharmaceutical houses free of cost.

A New York State Board of Pharmacy spokesman, Secretary Albert J. Sica, revealed that the practice had become a serious problem because of the large volume of such drugs in circulation.

"The drug sample," he said, "has become, in effect, an item of commerce." His agency was nevertheless powerless to deal with the situation, he explained, because no legislation had been enacted to deal with the offense.

The problem had come to light as a result of the experience of fire captain George Schofield of Bay Ridge, Brooklyn, who contacted the *Daily News* after reading published articles about drug-pricing abuses in the Manhattan area. Schofield said that he had taken his son, a teen-ager, to a doctor after the youth complained of severe headaches. The physician, in describing a nasal spray, said, "It's very difficult to obtain. Who's your pharmacist?"

Schofield told the doctor he dealt with H. M. Sanders and Son, 8002 Fifth Avenue, Brooklyn. Later in the day he visited the drug-store, had the prescription filled, and was charged $8.89 for the drug, called Redadron Turbinaire.

When he got home Schofield noticed that the word "sample" was stamped on the underside of the spray. Understandably puzzled, he returned to the store and confronted the druggist with the information. An argument ensued, during which the pharmacist said, "Look, what do you care? Your union is paying for it."

As is often the case with unethical practice, there is more to the situation than initially meets the eye. Drug firms do not distribute the samples to pharmacists. They are given *only to physicians*. Consequently druggists can acquire them to sell only from doctors or from the drug companies' own distributors.

A fascinating side-light to the case is that on the same day the *News* published its story the Nixon Administration's Price Commission turned down a bid by the nation's pharmacists to be excluded from the requirement that they post their retail prices.

Chapter **VIII**

Five-Finger Discounting: The Shoplifters

It has become a familiar story in some of the nation's largest department stores, but it still surprised a California woman who recently went shopping in New York City. She had checked into her favorite room at the Plaza and hurried off, wallet filled with credit cards, toward the posh B. Altman & Co. at 34th Street and Fifth Avenue.

"I was on the first of the two granite steps to the store," she reported later, "when the glass doors swung open. Out charged a husky guard in uniform, nearly knocking me down. He raced through the flow of traffic on Fifth Avenue, a tangle of cabs and buses, and disappeared down 33rd Street."

By the time the woman realized what had hit her, the guard was on his way back. In one hand he held four or five expensive Gucci bags and an elegant matching umbrella dropped by a fleeing shoplifter. In his other hand was a walkie-talkie he used to report to someone inside the store that the merchandise had been recovered, but that the culprit had escaped. The guard stopped momentarily to apologize to the visitor for knocking her aside.

How serious a problem is shoplifting? General crime statistics provide a clue. The Federal Bureau of Investigation, in its Uniform Crime Report, disclosed that in 1974 *reported* crimes took one of the largest leaps since the Bureau began recording such statistics. In that one year larceny theft—which includes shoplifting—was up 21%. The jump for burglary: 18.5%. For robbery, 15.1%. As measured from 1969 the three areas averaged almost a 50% increase.

The word "reported" is emphasized in the preceding paragraph because according to experts, perhaps as many as 80% of crimes are not reported and therefore are not reflected in the FBI figures. When the targets are large business enterprises the majority of crimes are never even discovered!

As one narrows in on specific industries the problem comes into even more alarming focus. According to Charles I. Miller, President of Loss Prevention Systems of Cincinnati, a consultant to food stores about what the industry calls "shrink" problems, the estimated cost of crimes to all retailers in 1974 was 5.8 billion dollars! Harold Cohen, assigned to prevent theft-loss for the Wakefern Food Corporation, has an even darker view of the situation. In a book on supermarket security called *The Crime That No One Talks About*, Cohen estimates that the present annual shrink-loss for all retail food outlets is "a shade under $10 billion." That, says Cohen, is "as if the Great Atlantic and Pacific Tea Company had no sales whatsoever for [nearly] two years."

The important relevance of such figures to my study is that *professional burglars and robbers account for only 2% of the total loss*. Bad-check artists, by no means all of whom are pros, count for 12%, and shoplifters for 16%. The majority of the loss comes from employees and vendors.

If you'd like more details about the national supermarket "shrink," write to *Progressive Grocer* magazine and ask for a copy of their February-March 1976 Special Security Report. It includes stories about specific cases, such as that of a steady customer, a mother confined to a wheel-chair, who always shopped with her 14-year old son and—as it turned out—her husband. A manager happened to see an 8-pound turkey disappear under the woman's lap blanket as she rolled down the aisle. When the police arrived they also searched the husband and discovered a police badge that had been missing for 17 years. Part of the con was that on the rare occasions when the woman would be apprehended the husband—unidentified as such—would quickly show up with his badge, "investigate the case," and take the woman and child off in his car.

Parenthetically it's interesting that one of the most reliable sources of information concerning the ethical and moral corrosion of our society is the *Wall Street Journal*, which might have been expected to put the best possible face on the capitalist economy, but which in fact almost daily reveals its depravity.

James MacGregor, staff reporter of the *Journal*, in December of 1968 worked for ten days as a Christmas-time toy salesman at the E. J. Korvette store on Fifth Avenue. The store prides itself that its customers are of higher station than the average American discount or department store caters to. What MacGregor learned during those ten days he will never forget, nor should any concerned citizen.

"I repeatedly saw some salesmen ignore their customers," he says, "feed them misinformation, sell them broken goods and items they didn't ask for, or chase them away with a curt 'I don't have time to talk to you now.' " Rudeness and a certain degree of dishonesty were apparently the worst crimes of the salesman. It remained for the customers to win the contest for criminality hands down.

"The one shoplifter I actually spotted," reports MacGregor, "was a nice-looking woman wrapped in furs. She stole one of the five empty parcels I scattered around one day to test the honesty of my customers. *The five disappeared in 19 minutes!* None of the thieves was caught—the woman was in an elevator seconds after she stole the package—even though a Korvette official says the chain takes 'every known preventive measure' to halt shoplifting. Uniformed guards, plain-clothesmen and TV cameras watch the shopping areas. Every purchase has to be put into a bag which is stapled shut, the sales slip attached to the outside."

Customers aren't the only ones who steal, of course. One Korvette sales girl complained to MacGregor that for 3 days in a row her lunch was stolen from the locker she shared with three other clerks.

Stealing from stores is a crime costing merchants an estimated $5 billion a year.

It costs the rest of us, too, even if we're not the *one out of every ten* that a recent survey suggests has committed a shoplifting crime at one time or another. This particular form of corruption accounts for losses of 1% to 2% of the annual volume in most American stores. The losses get passed on in the form of higher prices on what merchandise remains to be sold.

The problem is everywhere now, from the swank stores and shops in Manhattan and Beverly Hills, to "Ma and Pa" groceries throughout the country.

In Encino, California, one of the more attractive suburbs of Los Angeles, Burt Peck is the proprietor of the Encino Book Shop. He reports on the growing problem:

"I've discovered that kids between the ages of ten and fourteen steal a lot of books. They do it for kicks, at least out here in Encino, which is an affluent area. It's not because they don't have the money. Kids steal paperbacks mostly— but adults steal $25 art and antique books."

The situation at Peck's is not unique. On the campus of the University of California at Los Angeles in the fashionable Westwood district, the man who runs the official university bookstore reported to an investigator from the *Los Angeles Times*, "It's a crazy situation. The shop, in a sense, belongs to the kids. It's not the same as a private neighborhood operation. And yet the stealing has become such a serious problem that we've had to start a public campaign to counteract it. We've got guards, supermarket-style turnstiles, everything. And they're still getting away with it."

The UCLA bookstore is not alone in looking for ways to stem the rising tide of shoplifting by young people in the 18-to-25-year-old age group, which predominates in this particular form of corruption. Similar efforts are being made in every city across the nation.

We shall return later to the subject of the honesty of the younger generation. In the late 60's the argument was common that young people were turning off their fathers' generation because of the older group's materialistic concentration on money and property. It now appears that the young are quite as gifted at thievery as were their parents.

"Ripping off" is merely another term for stealing.

Retailers are also confronted by the problem of "switchers," shoppers who substitute a low price-tag from one item for the higher price-tag on another item, pay the lower cost and carry the more valued item out of the store. Outright thieves, of course, they cost stores millions of dollars each year, but they probably feel as guiltless as the dishonest employees.

In the bargain basement of Woodward and Lothrop, one of the biggest department stores in Washington, D.C., two women browse through racks of clothing and counters filled with merchandise. One is dressed in jeans, the other in a leotard top and slacks. They could be customers hunting for marked down values. Nearby a man with a green canvas bag slung over his shoulder studies a table piled high with sports shirts on sale. Any one of the three could be a potential thief—in truth, all three are watching for shoplifters among the thousands of customers that pass through the store each day.

Woodward and Lothrop, like many other establishments, now provides on-the-job training for an increasing number of private detectives. Once the men and women have completed the course they have the same authority in the store that a policeman has on the street. They carry no weapons, however—only a two-way radio that keeps them in close touch with other detectives if help is needed. According to Lewis Shealy, director of security, they can also carry a nightstick and a canister of the chemical Mace, which can temporarily immobilize a culprit.

If it sounds like something out of a Marx Brothers movie—a plainclothes policeman chasing a fleeing shoplifter and trying to spray him with an aerosol canister—there's

nothing funny about it. The war against store theft is occupy-
ing an increasing amount of time and effort by people whose
talents could be better utilized. Entire industries have
sprung up to provide merchants with anti-theft devices—
such as electronic tags which signal an alarm if stolen property is carried out of the store—all of which increases the cost
of doing business and results in higher prices to consumers.

In Bloomingdale's and Alexander's, New York department stores, an effort to prevent shoplifting involved
putting two-way mirrors into the fitting rooms so that customers could be observed if they stuffed a stolen skirt or
blouse beneath their street clothes. Complaints by civil liber-
tarians and irate feminists resulted in the technique being
rejected after it was discovered.

Other anti-shoplifting devices include a new plastic bag
that is sealed shut once the customer's purchases are placed
inside. The bag can be opened only by tearing it apart, thus
insuring that as the customer leaves the store, he or she does
not casually drop a few additional articles from the shelves
into it.

In special theft-prevention clinics being conducted
across the nation, storeowners are warned never to put two
articles of a pair—shoes, gloves, earrings, etc.—on display,
since a shoplifter is less likely to make off with one. In fur
departments they are also told to dress store mannikins in
coats rather than to simply drape the furs over an arm from
which they can easily be lifted. Sales slips which are discarded by some customers should be retrieved from the
floor or wastebaskets and immediately destroyed, the storekeepers were advised—to prevent shoplifters from getting
their hands on the slips and using them as evidence of
purchase of purloined goods.

Shoplifting methods are so varied that it is almost impossible to categorize them. Small articles may be palmed and
carried out of the store in one hand. Merchandise can be
casually dropped into purses, briefcases, shopping bags, um-
brellas. Special clothing fitted with hooks and pockets on the
inside can conceal stolen items. Loose garments known as
"shoplifter bloomers" can cover up the theft of something as
bulky as a small television set. And there are special de-

vices—such as a "booster box" with a false bottom that fits over large objects—that are brought into play by sophisticated thieves.

One of the most elaborate shoplifting operations was exposed recently in *The New York Times*, which detailed the exploits of a group of South Americans who had joined together to steal merchandise said to be worth $150 million a year! A man identified as "Miguel Contreras," cooperating with the investigators, defended the operation in simple terms: "We Chileans are not the violent type and shoplifting doesn't hurt anyone. The insurance company pays for a store's loss."

As the *Times* reported, teams of shoplifters from Chile, Colombia, and Peru each day staked out the territory they would cover. On a typical day, Contreras was part of a four-man team that set out to hit "all the good stores" on a short stretch of New Jersey highway.

"We'd go into a store like a group of friends and start browsing," the *Times* quoted its informant as saying. "We'd decide the area we wanted to work and I would attract the salesman to another part of the store. I take a regular 36 suit, but I'd ask for a 38. Of course, the suit would not fit, and I'd make some excuse like I must have lost weight to gain time and keep the salesman tied up with me."

While the salesman busied himself with his customer, the friends of Contreras pretended to browse, and "would artfully roll up expensive suits without taking them off their hangers and would tuck them inside the backs of their suit jackets, which were fitted loosely at the top and tighter at the bottom so the suits wouldn't fall out when the jacket was buttoned." The hangers, explained Contreras, were never left behind because they could serve to indicate that something was missing from the racks. Without the telltale empty hanger, it might be days or weeks before the thefts were discovered.

In the half-hour it took Contreras to find a suit that fit him, his partners had wandered in and out of the store several times—as if shopping elsewhere in the neighborhood while they waited for him—and had carried out some 20 suits, sold to a fence later in the day for $50 to $60 each. The stolen suits were deposited in the team's car parked on a nearby lot, stuffed into plastic garbage bags to seem less conspicuous.

After all the trouble on the part of the salesman he did not even get to sell a suit to Contreras. Instead the Chilean would buy something else—an expensive $35 shirt perhaps—so the salesman would remember him as a good customer when he and his friends returned, a week or so later, to make additional "purchases."

The South American teams are fanning out to other cities, and are starting to become organized in a highly efficient way, contends Michael Minto, vice president of Intelligence Services Inc., a private company that tries to deter theft. Minto sees a resemblance between the rival shoplifting rings and the various groups that grew into the Mafia at the turn of the century.

As one indication of the size of the South Americans' operation, an investigator for the United States Immigration and Naturalization Service said that perhaps as many as 1,000 Chileans were involved in it, along with comparable numbers of immigrants from Colombia and Peru. The three groups, it was reported, maintain close ties with one another so that bail can be posted for team members if they are arrested.

Although organized rings of shoplifters and petty thieves existed before Charles Dickens detailed the exploits of Fagin's gang of young criminals in *Oliver Twist*, nearly 95% of all shoplifting incidents are carried out by amateurs, people who—sometimes on the spur of the moment, or having grown weary of waiting for service in a crowded store—simply slip merchandise into pocket or purse and head for an exit. According to one detective most shoplifters have money or a credit card on them when they are arrested and could easily pay for the stolen merchandise.

The question, of course, is why—if most amateur shoplifters have the wherewithal to pay for the goods they steal—why do they resort at times to violence to conceal their crime, and why do they commit the crime in the first place?

The stories of two shoplifters might suggest some answers. One is a 19-year-old woman, the other a 23-year-old man who once worked as a parole officer.

The young woman, a resident of Madison, Wis., was apprehended in a grocery store when she slipped a can of tuna fish—worth about $1—into her purse. Like most youthful shoplifters confronted by an accusatory store manager, she panicked and tried to make up "an insane story about having brought the tuna the previous day and forgetting to take it out of her pocketbook," according to the report of the case in *Seventeen* magazine. Understandably her story was not believed, and the store manager decided to call the police.

What is interesting is the girl's initial belief that the authorities would not punish her. She felt sure that they would accept her apology and, after she had paid the dollar for the tuna, promptly release her.

She was wrong. Angered by a series of shoplifting incidents the manager decided to prosecute. Stunned, the young woman was booked at the local police station after hearing a policeman solemnly read her rights to her. She was fingerprinted and photographed. Then the District Attorney enumerated her choices: she could go to court, plead guilty, and pay a fine for her crime. She could plead not guilty and take a chance on being convicted, and perhaps get a more severe sentence. Or she could attend a special school at night, going four hours a week for a month, to hear lectures on crime-prevention and study the psychology of thieves like herself. If she attended the classes and committed no other offenses during six months of probation, the charges against her would be dropped.

The options represent a recent technique in dealing with shoplifters. Classes are open to adults who have no prior police records. Small groups of about 20 people meet to discuss their individual problems and to hear talks on the shoplifting problem by store owners, policemen, lawyers, even ex-cons. In a small city like Madison, the young lady discovered, there was plenty of reason to take the problem seriously: losses there from shoplifting are estimated at $13 million annually!

But the most revealing statement by the teenage offender was her admission as to why she had shoplifted many
times over the years. It was not because of dire poverty, she
explained, nor for a thrill. It was merely part of her way of
life—because *she had not been caught the first time she did
it.*

In telling her story the young woman kept her identity
secret, but the situation was different with Paul J. Mc-
Garigal, who candidly confessed to his shoplifting record in
the pages of the Lakeland, Fla., newspaper, *The Ledger*.
McGarigal, 23, was arrested after making off with some
tennis equipment from the public courts in Lakeland and
spent a "nightmarish" evening in the Polk County Jail—
something he swears will never happen to him again.

The youthful thief describes the genesis of his shoplifting career in the neighborhood candy store, but believes
that a major factor that contributed to his problem was the
family's financial predicament. He was one of ten children of
a schoolteacher father whose paycheck simply did not
stretch far enough to cover toys and other "extras" for kids.
A baseball enthusiast with no equipment and no allowance,
McGarigal ended up stealing the things he coveted. Today,
aware that he fell prey to a vicious habit, he is sincere in his
repentance and is motivated to help confused parents deal
with their own 8-to-18-year-old offspring.

It is not enough, he believes, to give youngsters life's
material necessities in the hope of staving off their inclina-
tion to take what they want. How many parents of young
shoplifters have cried: "I don't understand it. He has everything! An electric guitar, a 10-speed bike, a stereo, his own
phone, a sportscar, clothes . . ." Obviously giving is not the
answer. Instead, suggests McGarigal, a child should be
taught the value of money at an early age—by providing
him with an allowance, no matter how small. The child
should be urged to "earn" the allowance by performing
simple tasks around the home—emptying wastebaskets,
feeding the dog. The idea that the youngster should work for
what he gets is important, since he or she may thereby come
to understand that very little in life comes free to the honest
adult.

McGarigal suggests, too, that parents should be on the lookout for new things that come into the house unexplained. If 12-year-old Junior shows up with a TV set, which he says he's borrowing from a friend, be suspicious. If your daughter has new earrings, don't be reluctant to ask where they came from. If the answer is slow in coming, counsels McGarigal, do *not* fly off the handle and give her a slap or a spanking. Getting to the source of the item, and—if shoplifting is involved—to the source of the problem calls for tact and the proper application of psychology.

One thing to keep in mind: your child is not the only one involved in these reprehensible actions. Some four million shoplifters are caught every year, but that is believed to be only one out of every 35, which means an astounding total of 140,000,000 separate incidents of theft classified as shoplifting annually.

The average shoplifter is female, age 14–18, from a family with an annual income of more than $10,000. Psychological studies show that people shoplift for various reasons: compulsion, desire for attention, actual need, "kicks," revenge against "the establishment," peer acceptance, a narcotics habit, or other personal problems.

Items shoplifted most frequently: food, jewelry, wallets, cosmetics. Worst times: between the hours of 2 P.M. and 6 P.M. on Thursday, Friday, or Saturday—suggesting that the shoplifter suffers some kind of pre-weekend stress syndrome, perhaps an equivalent of the housewife's "Monday morning blues."

Researchers accumulating information on another giant ripoff, "inside" theft, have discovered the shocking fact that *most employees questioned said they would feel little, if any, guilt about stealing from their employers.* In one survey of 49 people who had made off with company supplies, only two admitted to "stealing" and suffering guilt, while 12 others admitted that although they might consider their action as stealing, they felt absolutely no guilt about it. The majority—33—contended that they felt as innocent as new-born babes. Oswald Spengler thought Western society was doomed. That one statistic suggests he may have been right.

Small wonder, considering the prevalent attitude, that retail employees steal more than *$3 billion a year* from their employers. Although estimates vary, employee theft is said to account for 60% to 75% of all inventory loss by retailers throughout the country.

In June, 1978 the National Council on Crime and Delinquency released statistics that emphasized the seriousness of the problem. Stealing by employees has become so important a drain on the national economy—running to many millions of dollars per year—that approximately half of all American employees are now believed to take part in workplace crime. In an instance cited by the NCCD 62% of the workers at one company—numbering 1,400—admitted stealing at least one hundred dollars in a one-year period (after being promised they would not be fired for telling the truth in response to a direct question).

Employees of a foundry in Buffalo, New York, stole 129,000 pounds of lead by melting it down and casting it to fit the shape of their bodies, after which they walked off their work-premises with metal hidden under their clothing. A prominent drugstore chain, finally driven to apply lie detector tests, was shocked to learn that 76% of its employees had stolen either money, merchandise or both! One of the most startling discoveries of all, according to NCCD, was that banks across the U.S. are currently losing more money to employee fraud than to bank robbers of the more traditional sort.

One answer to the worsening problem of shoplifting is suggested by Arthur Marshall, a Maryland attorney. "All shoplifters," he declares, "should go to jail. Even if it is only for one hour, they should all go to jail."

We have too long treated shoplifting as if it were some sort of easily forgivable, innocuous prank, like a fraternity initiation stunt. Theft, of virtually every sort, is a crime. In Maryland, where Marshall practices, the fact is impressed on convicted first offenders by making them work at cleaning up county parks, roads and hospitals. The pattern might be experimented with nationally. Trying to reform shoplifters by employing them in public works projects could answer two basic needs at one time—providing chastisement for the culprits and enlightening them concerning the individual's obligation to the rest of society.

If little or nothing is done the situation will continue to worsen.

Again, I draw a distinction between shoplifting generally and stealing food truly needed for the sustenance of life. When I was 16 I ran away from home in Chicago and hitchhiked, alone, about the country. The nation was in the grip of the Depression. After a few days on the road I had only pennies left and was desperately hungry. So I went into a grocery store, bought a loaf of bread and stole a can of sardines. Then I walked around the nearest corner, sat down on the curb and made myself about a dozen sardine sandwiches, which I wolfed down, since I hadn't had a meal in two days. That sort of theft is of no moral importance whatever and, statistically speaking, of no interest to the grocery industry. What does concern the industry, since it cuts seriously into profits, is the vast ripoff conducted, for the most part, by middle-class thieves, people who don't have to steal at all to keep body and soul together.

The 1977 black-out in New York City and the extensive looting that came in its wake show how rapidly traditional admonitions against "coveting thy neighbor's goods" can vanish. In the darkness that flooded the city's streets store after store was ransacked. Even heavy merchandise such as hundreds of expensive couches were carried out the front doors of furniture stores. Canned goods by the carton disappeared from supermarkets. Racks of clothing were rolled out of menswear shops, and a trail of discarded hangers was left behind on the sidewalk to show the routes the looters had followed.

The trails were not followed by the police, of course. There was no point in trying to track down all of the thieves, because the booty had been widely dispersed among hundreds of people—among once-decent citizens who saw nothing wrong in taking merchandise at the first opportunity to steal without fear of being caught. There were thousands of looters and relatively few cops.

A small shopowner showed up on the television screen, standing in the center of what once had been an office at the rear of his store. The room was stripped completely bare except for a heavy sofa.

"It was just too heavy for them to carry, I guess," he said, his face caught between a forced smile for the camera and real tears. "I mean, why else would they have left it? They took my lighting fixtures, the faucets on the bathroom sink, the venetian blinds on the showroom window, my file cabinets, all my lamps, chairs, desk, pillows, pencils, pens, paper supplies, even the old clothes that I kept in back for clean-up work. They were a flock of vultures, licking the bones clean after the kill."

He pointed angrily at the sofa. "That's what they left me," he mumbled. "Do you want it? It's yours, if you can cart it away!"

To the shopowner—who, like most of the others hit by the looters, could never recover his losses from an insurance company—looting is no joke. Carting goods out of a store in the darkness is more brazen than sneaking merchandise into a pocket or purse, but it all comes down to the same thing. Simple theft. And, increasingly, children seem to find it a rewarding pastime.

Recently I was told the story of a group of seven-year-olds at a playground in lower Manhattan. They were city kids with street savvy, the kind who know even at kindergarten-level what words like "pot" and "mugging" and "graffiti" mean. Overheard, the youngsters were comparing notes on their personal experiences at a nearby Woolworth's.

"Everytime I go there, I luck out," said the group leader, a cherubic-looking boy with neatly combed blonde hair, well-scrubbed fingernails, and clear blue eyes. "Especially in the toy department, where that lady with the red hair is so dumb and blind."

"Yeh," piped up one of the other boys. "Last time I went in, I got a bag of marbles, a Matchbox racer, a box of

Day-Glo chalk, and a cap gun. You got to make sure you wear the right jacket, though—with plenty of pockets."

A girl with pigtails and missing front teeth interrupted: "That's nothing. I did better 'n that yesterday." Her haul, she carefully enumerated, consisted of two charm bracelets, three ballpoint pens and a red wallet.

"Doesn't your mother notice when you bring the stuff home?" said another girl.

"Nope," replied her friend, flashing a grin. "I say I saved up to buy it, and she never checks."

Then, with total disregard for the adults around them, they began to lay out their purloined valuables on the sidewalk for a miniature flea-market exchange. In broad daylight. Penny-ante stuff to laugh off while we concern ourselves with bigger scandals? Not by a damn sight.

If the small crimes of children are ignored, they will not necessarily disappear with age and maturity. In many youngsters, long after the scrapes and scars of skinned knees and banged-up elbows have faded, there can be permanent moral scars.

Good parents and good citizens must act early to prevent those scars. In the unending spiral of corruption, where minor crimes lead to larger ones, we can no longer afford to cover up the problem. No one can afford to try to protect himself by denying the existence of the problem, as some store owners have tried to do—out of fear that if the public becomes aware of how easily merchandise can be taken by thieves, more thieves will appear on the scene.

"Quite frankly, we don't get the cooperation of the stores," complains Walter J. Lewis, Jr. of the New York Intelligence Division of the Police Force. "They realize the problem exists, but they don't want us to tell others about it. 'Don't rock the boat' seems to be their attitude."

That attitude seems the easy way to handle things. Do nothing. And hope that the situation will cure itself.

It won't.

Chapter *IX*

Cheating
in the
Schools

Did you ever cheat on a test in school? Ever look over the shoulder of the boy or girl in front of you to peek at the answer to a hard question?

Ever copied 500 words on air pollution or over-population straight from an obscure library text?

Ever copied the homework done by a friend, changing one or two answers to disguise your dishonesty? Ever paid $10 or so for someone else's term paper and turned it in as your own?

If you answered yes to any one of these questions, the following comments on corruption in the American educational system will have particular importance to you. They will be especially significant if you have children of your own of school age, from kindergarten to university. Cheating—like stealing—is a habit that many learn at an early age. Like all habits it's hard to break.

Two mutually contradictory public images of American youth have been projected during the 1960's and '70's. The unflattering one consists of references to drug-abuse, sexual irresponsibility, lack of attention to personal cleanliness, and either political apathy or radicalism. The flattering image concentrates on youth's idealism, its social courage in confronting a materialistic establishment, its rejection of phony adult values and pretensions, its emphasis on love rather than war, and its charitable concern for unfortunate minorities. Both images are rooted in reality. Neither comprises a complete picture. What is relevant here is that young people should not assume that they are unaffected by the corruption and ethical breakdown to which they are so sensitive in their elders. The fact is that cheating is prevalent in American schools, at all levels. A few examples:

Ten students at a prominent California university were given "disciplinary F's" for cheating in an English literature course by plagiarizing a standard reference work in reviewing Henry James' *Portrait of a Lady*.

An Indiana professor's survey shows that 57% of the students questioned had cheated at some point in their college careers; nearly 75% of the seniors had done so. Not only was cheating common, it was not strongly condemned by other students. Only 13% thought that the student who cheats is "basically dishonest."

According to a survey by *The New York Times*, cheating occurs on nearly all levels of academic excellence. Slow students cheat to get passing grades, passing students cheat to get better grades. Bright students cheat to raise a mark in the 80's to one in the 90's. *One principal said that brighter students are more inclined to cheat on examinations than slower ones, the latter often taking a "who cares?" attitude.*

A Boston psychiatrist, writing in the *Annals* of the American Academy of Political Science, says: "We must face the unpleasant reality that a society that condones income tax evasion and political graft, and admires the one who 'gets away with it,' is far from creating the atmosphere of respect for individual needs and for authority that is vital for the prevention and control of delinquency in the young."

Television station KNXT in Los Angeles in December, 1976, took a survey of 3,651 students in 12 elementary schools, six junior high schools, and six high schools. Reporter Connie Chung stated that in the fourth, fifth, and sixth grades, 43% of the youngsters owned up to having cheated.

In the seventh grade, the figure climbed to 65%. And by the tenth grade, it had reached an astounding 88%!

The cheaters showed little remorse. "I was doing my spelling test," said one nine-year-old girl. "I was sitting down here and I didn't know this really hard answer, so I looked over at Christie's. I copied her and I got it all right."

In a third-grade class the experienced TV reporter was shocked when 25 children out of a total of 27 confessed to having cheated at least once during their limited school careers. By the time these same youngsters reach junior and senior high schools, most likely 100% will have cheated and the techniques will have become more sophisticated and ingenious than merely copying answers from someone else's paper.

One student in junior high school told reporter Chung how a member of her class had stolen a copy of a geometry test to be given later in the term. The test had been worked by the brightest girl in the class, and then others memorized the answers. A boy admitted freely that he had a way to tape notes to the inside of his coat pocket, where they could be easily glimpsed as he reached for a fresh pencil. A girl revealed how she could "telegraph" answers to friends across the aisle by tapping a thoughtful finger against her cheek.

In another interview a high school senior told how he had capitalized on his intellectual powers, earning $60 each time he took college aptitude tests for less knowledgeable students. "It started," he explained, "when a friend couldn't get into UCLA ... I decided to help him out and took the test for him. Soon after, he became sort of my agent. He'd arrange deals for me with very desperate students."

Some college students have turned cheating into an organized business venture. They buy and sell lecture notes, purchase term papers from ghost writers and companies that specialize in providing them, and collect commissions for hiring specialists in various subjects to take exams for lazy pupils.

For the paltry sum of less than $10, students can buy photocopy booklets of lecture notes on any course in their college—and usually can find such notes available for sale at the college bookstore. In other words, a wily student can register, say, for "The History of Western Civilization," never show up in class, skip the lectures on Greece, Rome and all the rest—and still, by memorizing the notes someone else has put together, pass the examinations.

At UCLA, it has been found, some professors who market their own lecture notes earn considerable royalties from the practice. Small wonder that cheating and plagiarism are rife on the campus, especially at the graduate level, according to Byron Atkinson, dean of students. One graduate student was caught when she turned in to her professor, as her own, a copy of a Ph.D. thesis she had purchased from someone else. The thesis had been written years before by the professor himself.

The operations that specialize in reselling old term papers and theses are called "mills." Though they've been repeatedly hit by legislation restricting their activity, a great many still flourish. In West Los Angeles, a company called Research Assistance, Inc. says that it does nothing illegal in marketing the work of others, since any student buying one of its papers must initial a form that says the material will be used for research only—and not for academic credit. Once the student has the term paper in his hands, however, there is nothing to prevent him from retyping it with his name at the top, perhaps with slight revision, and turning it in as his own work.

This particular form of corruption is almost impossible to police; a student who sets out to buy a paper that he will submit as his own is not likely to hesitate when asked to sign a form saying he has no intention of doing precisely that!

The mills flourish, though not because their merchandise is always of high quality. For the KNXT survey two student interns at the station purchased for $30 a term paper guaranteed to get a good grade. When a journalism professor was asked to evaluate the paper, he said that he might give a high mark for the research that went into it, but that the writing was so poor it barely deserved a grade of C. Another investigative student paid $50 to a group that promised professional research and writing service on any subject. Several weeks later the mailman brought him a bundle of paragraphs clipped from numerous articles in magazines and newspapers. "All you have to do," read the accompanying instructions, "is glue the words together."

Looking into the spread of ghost-written papers the *Los Angeles Times* uncovered a nationwide operation. Robert E. Dallos described how a young man at Boston College had purchased a five-page essay, "The Boston Police Strike of 1919," for $12.50. Interviewed in the office of the company selling the paper, the student was asked if he had any sense of doing wrong.

"Of course," he said. "I never thought I'd bring myself here. This is degrading." But he bought the paper.

George May, president of Term Papers, Unlimited, a Southern California subsidiary of the Boston company that sold the police-strike essay, told Dallos that some 4,000 papers had been marketed to students at California colleges in a period of two-and-one-half years.

The practice grows despite increasingly severe punishment and warnings from administrators. At Harvard University the penalty for submitting ghost-written material can be expulsion—which is precisely what happened recently to two students unlucky enough to hand in the same paper to the instructor in a course on British History. When news of the expulsions got out, an undergraduate confessed to the dean of students that he had worked as a ghost-writer for the mill that sold the paper. He, too, was expelled.

Said Archie Epps, dean of students, "These term-paper firms are a blot on the conscience of American institutions of higher learning. This generation of students is so outraged about hypocrisy in the war in Vietnam and the nation's racial problems. Yet some of the same generation is being hypocritical about its college work."

The offending companies are not staffed by over-40 types whose greed is corrupting otherwise innocent youth. Dallos identified one of the leading entrepreneurs in the industry as 22-year-old Ward Warren, "a self-made millionaire" only six months after he graduated from college. He founded Term Papers, Unlimited while he was still a student at Boston's Babson Institute, selling a snack-bar he owned to get $25,000 for the new venture.

Within a short time he had franchised offices in 50 cities throughout the country and was headed toward first-year sales of about $1.8 million. Warren was quoted as saying he thought sales would eventually climb to $5 million or $10 million, and was thinking of selling stock in his operation.

Speaking freely to the interviewer, Warren disclosed that one of the more fascinating aspects of this business is the range of anonymous writers he employs: graduate students, out-of-work scientists and engineers, psychiatrists, college instructors, and professors on every subject. One favorite writer, said the young ghost-chaser, has a Ph.D., teaches at a college in the Boston area at night, and—during the busy end-of-term period—can turn out one term paper a day!

Undoubtedly one of the most brazen customers of Warren's firm was a freshman at the Massachusetts Institute of Technology who turned in a ghost-written five-page essay to his English professor. The paper's title: "Why I Would Not Use a Professional Term-Paper Writing Service."

More states are putting laws onto the books to make it a crime or misdemeanor if an individual uses fraud to obtain a degree. Sections 224 and 225 of the New York State Education Law, for example, say that persons convicted in such cases can be fined $500 and sent to prison for up to three years. Prosecuting persons suspected of plagiarism in term papers and dissertations, however, is difficult, particularly in light of the fact that one student's direct copying is another student's "legitimate research."

In one case that made headlines recently, it was not a student who was involved but the Dean of Business, Andres Bermudez, at World University in San Juan, Puerto Rico. Bermudez, who had received a doctoral degree from Kent State University and served as executive vice president of a Puerto Rican cement company, came under investigation when it was discovered that he had paid the expenses for ten business professors who visited Puerto Rico. In addition several professors admitted that they had received presents— top-quality island rum and cash in amounts ranging from $200 to $1,000—for services labeled by Bermudez as "lecturing" or "consulting."

In the course of its investigation the inquiry committee

concluded that Bermudez had "received preferential treatment in the form of improper waivers, substitutions, and transfer credits in the course of his academic career at Kent State." As the study continued, it was discovered that some 71 pages of the doctoral dissertation submitted by Bermudez had been copied from previously published materials. Among the sources from which Bermudez had drawn inspiration—and exact wording, in numerous cases—was an article written by a New York City tax lawyer, a paper by the former director of the Office of Industrial Tax Exemption in Puerto Rico, and the work of the president of a private consulting firm in P.R. The university trustees early in 1978 were studying the question as to whether Bermudez' degree should be rescinded.

Are there any answers to the growing problem of cheating in the schools? Many concerned citizens argue that it is not a problem for the schools to worry about, it is a problem for parents. Morals are supposedly inculcated and nurtured at home. Others say that the solution is to get tough in the schools. If a student cheats and is caught he or she should be prosecuted by special committees on ethics and conduct. And, if found guilty, the offender should be given a punishment more severe than being ordered to write 100 times, "I promise never to cheat again."

The problem is complicated by the extent to which our society tolerates cheating on the adult level.

Corruption in education—God help us—exists everywhere—from the lowliest student on the brink of failure to the prestigious educator.

The New York Post recently revealed that seven school principals had been fired over a three-year period after an investigative body found them unfit to serve in the posts they had held for years. One of the men who looked into the principals' qualifications for their positions labeled the seven as "illiterate." The job of an eighth was also reported to be in jeopardy. Few details were provided on how the principals had risen through the educational ranks, but it is likely that records were modified—or falsified—somewhere along the way.

Consider the school lunch program. Could anything

seem less likely to be corrupted? How could anyone turn the laudable goal of providing low-cost lunches for a city's underprivileged youngsters into a profit-making scheme?

Somehow people could—as a major investigation into the New York lunch program revealed. More than half the food delivered to lunch rooms was being thrown out or appropriated by groups other than the children!

A school breakfast program was initiated, after parents filled out questionnaires in English and Spanish to state that they were financially unable to provide their children a healthy breakfast. But the kids themselves did not go for the idea—failing to show up to consume thousands of cartons of milk and bowlfuls of cereal each day. Did the schools stop buying the food? Of course not. Six-year contracts had been signed with the suppliers.

The educational system in our nation suffers from a hoarding instinct that can partly be blamed on bureaucracy, but in which corruption also frequently plays a part. In one fascinating example the board of education of a large Eastern city was discovered—at a time when it was pleading poverty and reducing the educational curriculum—to have stockpiled a 40-year supply of postcards, enough to last until the year 2007! It also had a six-year inventory of new desks and a three-year backlog of chairs. Did some businessman make a killing, wondered one television reporter who looked into the massive stocks of material, when he sold 20,000 chairs to the city? Why did the order go to one particular company, *without competitive bidding?*

Other questions arose when the discovery was made that school janitors with seniority were earning between $50,000 and $75,000 a year by holding official custodial positions at more than one public school. Was there no one who noticed this kind of dishonesty or was someone higher-up getting a piece of the action?

Despite the many abuses, education is such an important part of the quality of American life that authorities diligently make the effort to improve it. A blue-ribbon panel of educators, foundation officials, and administrators recently spent $600,000 to try to learn why college entrance scores had declined from 1952 to 1977. Their report cited "leniency in the nation's high schools (easier grading, increased absenteeism, simpler textbooks, less homework)," and also listed a number of sociological factors. Among these were the growing number of broken homes that led to reduced parental supervision, increased watching of television, the general trauma related to the Vietnam War, "domestic unrest and the assassination of national leaders."

Interestingly the panel made no mention of the fact that widespread cheating might have helped *boost* the more recent high-school averages, despite knowledge that plagiarism, term-paper mills, and other corrupt practices are on the increase. No one asked the question: if students have been learning less, is it partly because they have been cheating more?

An optimist might take heart from a recent Associated Press dispatch from Cambridge, Mass. A preliminary survey at Harvard, Radcliffe, and two other colleges indicated that college students today are showing less "drive to achieve" than they did 15 years ago. For someone interested in the growing amount of cheating on campus, this reduced drive could in the future mean reduction in the incidence of cheating.

Looking for an explanation, Dr. Dean K. Whitla, head of Harvard's Office of Instructional Research and Evaluation, says, "It is conceivable that young people have become more skeptical about the chances of accomplishment and, as a result, student scores were low and there was no gain from freshman to final year." The researchers found that students showed an increase in the ability to learn and to reason, but there was no increase in "one's need for achievement."

No one wants to see our intelligent young people—the ones who will be leading this nation tomorrow—lose the desire to improve their lot and that of those around them.

There has to be a degree to which our young men and women want to reach the top but reach it honestly, where the fear of failing does not justify using immoral methods to gain success, and where today's cheating youngster realizes that he or she might be the parent of the child cheating tomorrow.

Chapter **X**

The Ethics of Show Biz

Several months ago, after William Friedkin, one of Hollywood's most talented young directors, had returned from Boston and the filming of *The Brinks Job*, Jayne and I had dinner with him. During our purely social conversation he made casual reference to the fact that he had met some actual criminals in the process of facilitating certain on-location production details. By mid-December, 1978 the federal government was investigating the matter. Gerald McDowell, head of the New England Organized Crime Task Force, confirmed that there was substance to an NBC-TV news allegation that the film's producers sought help from underworld boss Ralph LaMattina. The network, in a three-part report, stated that pictures surreptitiously taken by authorities while the film was in production show crew members with one Joseph "Joe Shoes" Cammaratta, an associate of LaMattina.

"Police say the film company made payments to Joe Shoes," the NBC report continued, "and other reputed mobsters to help persuade residents of the North End to cooperate with the movie people."

Also under investigation, according to NBC, was the role of the Teamsters Union in the film's production. An Associated Press report of December 14 added, "NBC said the movie company was forced to hire almost twice as many Teamster drivers as it needed, some Teamsters falsified their work records, and many Teamster jobs on the movie set were given to men with long criminal records."

Part II of the series, aired the evening of December 14, referred to lawyer Sidney Korshak, who, according to state and federal authorities on the subject of organized crime, is "the key link between the mob and show business in Hollywood." The third part of the series dealt with the 1978 efforts on the part of the Teamsters to organize members of the Producers Guild of America and other film-production groups.

Does information of the sort revealed by the NBC news investigation indicate simply a rare occurrence? I wish it were so. Connections between organized crime and the world of entertainment were common in the 1920's. They're even more common now.

This is not, of course, to say that if every Las Vegas or Beverly Hills syndicate hoodlum were jailed, show-business would therefore become a model of ethical behavior.

Mario Puzo, author of *The Godfather* and other popular films, is powerful enough to speak with total frankness. Motion pictures, he has said, are "the most crooked business that I've ever had any experience with. You can get a better shake in Vegas that you can get in Hollywood."

As much as I'd like to be able to gloss over the evils within the industry most familiar to me, as much as I'd love to think that people with whom I'm in close contact are incorruptible, the headlines would make me look like a dummy if I did so.

For centuries the theatre has had a questionable moral reputation, long before pornography was at issue. Although the entertainment media from the days of ancient Greece have provided an outlet for artistic expression, true art has always been in short supply. Show-business, for the most part, is primarily a *business*, with the general morals of the marketplace.

The entertainment world is not exempt from the pervasive corruption that pollutes the nation. The industry has always had its share of charlatans and double-dealers. The world of entertainment has long been peopled by gypsies, wandering minstrels, free-souls, sharpsters, smooth operators and connivers of all kinds. One could make the assumption that the combination of ages-old irresponsibility and the development of modern techniques of corruption might even cause the entertaimnent industry to be *more* unethical than some others.

A strong statement, but I work in a strange world, one that is almost a separate nation, with its own unique culture, with a language that is different, where morals, ethics, and customs are diffcrent. The creative people are usually honest. But they comprise a small part of the show-biz population.

Let's start, as in other chapters, by looking at some relatively minor instances of wrongdoing—then work our way up to the multimillion-dollar thefts.

If you read fan magazines you've seen the ads for phony talent agencies that promise to find work for newcomers in pictures or in television. Or the "songwriter's service" that will take your lyrics, put them to music, and record songs so that you can become rich and famous overnight. These rackets have been around since the 1930's and have been exposed again and again. But the gullible continue to send sizable sums of money. And they end up with a stack of phonograph records in a basement or a pile of eight-by-ten photographs in a closet. No jobs, no recording contracts.

If the bastards involved were Soaking The Rich maybe you could put a sort of Robin Hood slant on the situation, but in fact almost all victims hit by the racket come from the unemployed, families with young children, or the black and Spanish-speaking communities.

For those newcomers who do survive, another rich rip-off vein is the field of personal management. There were always a few managers who were thieves at heart, but the explosive expansion in rock music has greatly increased their number. They spot a promising but unknown singer, musician or composer, flash a contract and require him to sign away important rights. Sometimes they work hand-in-hand with record producers or executives of record companies. If the newcomers never succeed, the managers have lost nothing, but if they make it big the rock stars make the unhappy discovery that staggering percentages of their concert income—or royalties from their songs or records—are the property of the managers.

A few years ago my wife Jayne and I had a personal experience that says something about the recording industry when a group of about 80 people—mostly in the record-distribution business—came to our home for a social event which I will not identify for fear of embarrassing the principals. I should explain that our home, like that of some other celebrities—not all, alas—is occasionally used as a site for fund-raising purposes. People who ought to send, say, a 25- or 50-dollar check to some worthy organization often will not do so unless they personally are given an inducement— tickets to a Broadway show at reduced prices, chances on a raffle or something of the sort. Attendance at a fund-raising luncheon or other meeting can be increased if the gathering takes place in the home of one prominent entertainer or another. In the perhaps 30 instances in the last 20 years when we have opened our home for such a purpose we have not been inordinately inconvenienced as a result. But in the case to which I refer the results were incredible. A priceless and irreplaceable gift—a handmade, antique silver fish that had once been part of the royal Egyptian collection—was stolen, along with assorted ashtrays, plants, napkins, vases, etc. Most of the thefts did not come to our attention till later but one woman, quite drunk, was observed picking up a large, heavy potted plant from the front of our home and walking toward her car with it. As it happened one of my sons, David—who was at the time 16—was standing nearby and said, "Where are you going with that plant?"

"What's it to you?" the woman answered belligerently.

"It's not your property," David said.

"You can go to hell," was the woman's response as she continued toward her car.

Only when David threatened to take her license number and report her did she rethink the matter. One such incident, even though it involved a group, does not make a nationwide survey, but if there is any field of American enterprise that has a more questionable ethical reputation than that of the record business I frankly don't know what it might be.

On a visit to Philadelphia in October of 1977, British rock star Elton John delivered himself of a few observations about corruption in the record industry: "I've never been ripped off in the way most rock stars get ripped off," he said. "I shudder at some of the people who are making a great deal of money now. The record industry has been taken over by hideous people like lawyers and accountants. They're making all the wrong moves for the artists and all the right moves for themselves. We've had artists on our label and our relationships with them have been ruined by pushy solicitors and accountants. The record industry at the moment is grotesque."

Another show-business racket is perpetrated by certain agents who serve as go-betweens in bringing together sponsors who wish to hire celebrities to do radio or television commercials, and the entertainers willing to accept such assignments. I've personally been victimized by this ripoff and have a great deal of company, believe me. The racket works like this: the agent calls or writes to an entertainer and says "Jones Brothers Cough Syrup would like you to do some commercials. It'll only take one afternoon of your time and they're willing to pay $25,000."

If the price is acceptable the deal is shortly agreed to. How, you might ask, can there be any chicanery involved? Very simple. What the entertainer isn't told is that the client has earlier gone to the agent and said "Listen, I want some prominent actor to do my commercials and I'm willing to pay $35,000. Can you get me somebody important for that amount?" By this simple process the go-between, with little trouble to himself, steals $10,000 from the entertainer. But he does even better than that for himself because, in addition to the $10,000, he also takes a 10% commission— $2,500—off the $25,000 he pays out. He therefore pockets $12,500. The entertainer earns a fee of only $10,000 more. It's happened to me, at least, for the last time, since my business manager now insists on dealing directly with the true employer.

Another crime, though one concerning which the public usually hears nothing, is committed by business managers who manage the affairs of wealthy entertainment-world clients, but to benefit themselves. I've often wondered why even more of this sort of thing doesn't go on—assuming it doesn't—because the situation provides a maximum of temptation and practically no opportunity for overseeing the activities of the tempted. The average successful entertainer makes enormous amounts of money, is rarely especially gifted at the management of it, and is generally too busy to pay much attention to bookkeeping, accounting and tax matters. Almost everyone in the industry, therefore, is forced to depend on a business manager. The term—like many in show-business—is a misnomer in that very few of these gentlemen actually have any thing to do with the management of the entertainer's businesses, if any. They are chiefly accountants who receive the entertainer's checks, keep accurate books, handle the payment of taxes, and perhaps in rare instances recommend a business proposition or two.

At the end of the year the entertainer is presented with state and federal tax forms to sign and, unless he calls in an outside auditor, he has little or no opportunity to evaluate the accuracy of these and other documents prepared. I have heard that Red Skelton, Henry Mancini, Kirk Douglas and Rita Hayworth have suffered seriously at the hands of those supposedly managing their business affairs. In my own case, through a combination of dishonesty and stupidity on the part of a former business manager, I suffered a loss of $500,000 early in the 1960's. Perhaps some of my actor friends, reading this chapter, will write to tell me if they have been so victimized. If any appreciable number have, there might be a bigger story here than either the media or law enforcement agencies have suspected.

As for the picture companies, they have no way of knowing how many theatre-owners are robbing them. On January 11, 1972 the *Hollywood Reporter* revealed that in four different parts of the country—New

York, Chicago, Rosebud, Texas and Taylor, Michigan—major distributors for Columbia, MGM, Paramount, Universal, Warner, United Artists and other Hollywood studios had filed actions against theatre owners and operators for fraudulent box-office statements, fraudulent gross-admission receipts, and failure to produce books and records requested by distributors. The law-suits brought to a head a long-simmering period of suspicion on the part of film studios that the theatre-owners were robbing them of earnings from motion pictures.

The studios do know the methods employed in cheating. Since profits are related to attendance figures, a dishonest theatre operator will contrive to under-report daily receipts. When you go into a theatre, a man at the door tears your ticket in two, gives you half the ticket and throws the other half into a box. The torn halves are available later for counting. But the man at the door will frequently simply palm half the ticket you gave him. The next man in line gives him a complete ticket and receives in return half of yours. Eventually 25 or 40 whole tickets are simply returned to the box-office, where they are sold to new customers. I noticed recently that Jack Valenti, addressing the Motion Picture Association of America, said that under-reporting is a "national problem of some magnitude." He doesn't know the half of it.

The motion picture theatre business has never been noted for adhering to Sunday-School standards of morality, but in recent years the amount of dishonesty on the part of theatre employees has been enough to cause management unusual concern. The Continental Protective Service, Inc., with headquarters in Lake Success, New York, not long ago ran an advertisement in *Daily Variety* and other entertainment world tradepapers headed, "How much did your employees steal today?" Below the attention-demanding headlines was a reproduction of a signed confession by a theatre employee which read as follows:

Dear Sir:
My name is _____. I live at _____. I have been employed at the above theatre for the past ten

months, as a cashier. After about two months I was approached by Mr._____, a manager of the theatre, and asked to resell about $5 worth of tickets. This happened on several occasions. These amounts totaled about $30. On one occasion Mr._____printed up tickets on white paper and had me sell them. These were to be used for a drawing at a Kiddie Matinee. He said he was going to use the money, which came to about $35, for a plane ticket to Florida. I never received any of this money.

When Mrs._____, the new manager, came to the theatre, she propositioned me to resell tickets, and I am sure she did the same with other cashiers. At first I told her no, but she persuaded me. I usually sold what tickets she gave me. But sometimes I ripped some of them up, because she gave me so many. Over two months I resold about 75 tickets each week for her for $2 a ticket, for a total of $1200 for two months. I got about $75 for this. I realize I was wrong. You have been good to me. I will try to repay you. If you allow me to stay, I not only will not steal again, but I will watch others to prevent this kind of thing.

Sincerely, _____

A story in the February 6, 1969 edition of the *Hollywood Reporter* related complaints by the Texas Drive-In Theatre Association that drive-in theatres throughout the nation had become twice as vulnerable to dishonesty as other motion picture theatres, and that theatres generally were suffering 20 percent greater losses from *employee* theft than any other segment of American business. The most common method resorted to by thieves masquerading as employees is the fake head or vehicle count, combined with the pocketing of receipts.

Talk to some theatre operators, though, and they'll probably tell you that holding back on some of the money that comes their way is the only way they can make any profit at all—because the film producers and distributors force them to pay such high prices for the pictures they show. As Hollywood has turned out fewer and fewer pictures each year—perhaps 100 a year currently vs. 300 or 400 during the 1940's and 1950's—theatres have been compelled to bid ever higher amounts on each film. The theatre operators gripe that they must pay huge sums in advance— sometimes without having even seen the film they're bidding on—and then, if the picture bombs, they're left holding an empty bag. Where the studios and distributors once would settle for 30 percent of the box-office take as their rental fee, on some pictures they now demand 80 or 90 percent.

They make other demands, too. Not long ago the Justice Department kicked off an investigation into an illegal practice called "block booking." Under the practice, a theatre owner is required to show an inferior or less popular movie for several weeks if he wants to get a popular film, such as *Star Wars*. Owners of 25 theatres in New England had provided the Justice Department with documents that they contended showed they had been forced by 20th Century-Fox to play *The Other Side of Midnight* if they wanted *Star Wars*. Supposedly a consent decree signed by Fox in 1951 has barred this kind of deal.

A handful of states have outlawed the practice of "blind bidding," where theatre owners agree to put up money for pictures they have not seen. The producers and distributors argue that in many instances they have to set the release patterns on the films long before the final picture is edited and ready for audiences to view—but theatre owners who paid huge sums for pictures such as *The Exorcist—Part II* or *Sorcerer*, and saw them die at the box office, claim they cannot afford to be stung repeatedly and stay in business. The answer of the studios? States which passed laws against blind bidding would simply be bypassed when the sales departments began to accept bids on upcoming pictures, meaning that audiences in those states would not get to see new films as quickly as audiences elsewhere.

In dealing with the studios, "theatre owners are at a disadvantage," states John H. Shenefield, chief of the antitrust division of the Justice Department. There might be some comfort in the theatre owners knowing that they are not alone. Things are seldom any better for the authors, directors, composers, and performers whose earnest toil goes into making the films that earn millions for the studios and distributors.

One of the most indignant artists to complain publicly about the injustice of the all-powerful studio system is Alan Jay Lerner, lyricist of *My Fair Lady, Gigi,* and *Paint Your Wagon*, and a multiple-winner at numerous Academy Award ceremonies. In a recent autobiography Lerner recounts what happened after he wrote *Gigi* for MGM. The picture, he says, cost $3 million to make and brought the studio some $16 million in rental fees. A $13 million profit, you figure? Not at all, says Lerner.

In Hollywood bookkeeping, he explains, the cost of the "negative" (as a finished picture is called) is multiplied by *250 percent* to cover the costs of advertising, prints for the numerous theatres, and distribution. This cost then becomes the "official" cost of the film. So, with *Gigi* costing $3 million initially, it went into the books at MGM as really costing $7.5 million.

Lerner comments that "no matter how much the film may have cost, the advertising rates are stable: so much per line, so much per half page or full page." Moreover, he says, "The factory that manufactures duplicates of the negative charges the same per foot if there are two people on the film or two hundred thousand." So why use the arbitrary figure of 250 percent? Why not just compute exactly how much the advertising and duplication of prints costs?

He does not profess to know, and I don't either. But the computation of distribution costs is an even stranger thing. In Chicago, say, a film company will have an office whose job it is to sell its pictures to theatres in the area. The office has an overhead—salaries, rent, telephones, heat, light and so on. But, Lerner points out, if the office has five films to distribute in the area, does each film pay one-fifth of the total overhead? Not at all. *Each film is charged with the entire overhead.*

"Well, then, you say [writes Lerner], where goeth the extra four salaries, four rents, etcetera? Into whose pocket do they fall? The answer . . . can only be found in the I Ching Division of the motion picture company's accounting department. I say the answers *can* be found, not that they will be found. . . . The purpose, however, is simplistically clear. It is to reduce the profit—on paper, that is—thereby trimming the taxes and reducing to the shadiest possible minimum the money that is owed to those who have any percentage of the film's profits."

In another example of accounting wizardry, the lyricist details how he and his partner, composer Frederick Loewe, were denied any share of profits from the motion picture version of *Camelot*. A financial statement from the producer, Warner Bros., detailed the cost of the picture, with the usual charges for advertising, distribution, and additional prints. But it had another item that seemed a bit unusual: "Miscellaneous—$2 million." The studio, Lerner relates, "adds 25 percent to the cost of each film for the use of its facilities. So the $2 million became $2.5 million. When it was multiplied by 250 percent, it became $6.25 million. Ergo, no profits. . . ."

Other voices have been raised recently to criticize what they say are decades of cheating by the studios. Double-billing and the invention of expenses, say a number of filmmakers, are so common as to warrant little attention. Norman Lear, producer of *All in the Family, Maude, Sanford and Son* and other hit TV shows, was quoted as saying: "If a major distributor has four pictures being produced in Europe and sends a representative to check them out, chances are that the cost of the entire trip will be charged to each production." And I wish to be quoted as saying that any executive who authorizes such bookkeeping devices is a thief.

In the same *New York Times* report, actor Tony Curtis contended that studio executives sometimes include their own personal expenses in production costs. "A producer goes to Acapulco to talk to another producer about a movie, but in reality he takes 14 little 'chicklets' along with him."

Robert Evans, formerly head of production at Paramount Pictures, made an adventure film called *Black Sunday*, and was supposed to get *36 percent of the gross*. After the amount of the gross was balanced against all the expenses, he said, his percentage was "not quite worth a ticket to the movies." He similarly did not expect to see any profit from *Marathon Man*, which cost $8 million to make and took in $35 million for Paramount!

Two major stars—Sean Connery and Michael Caine— upset about a deal with Allied Artists Pictures Corp., took the company to court, claiming they were cheated out of earnings from *The Man Who Would Be King*. After six months of wrangling, an "amicable settlement" was reached, out of court. "You have to fight to get what's legally yours," said Connery, who won fame as James Bond. "And all the time you're chasing to get the money to which you're entitled, the studio has the use of it."

It seems an incredible situation, doesn't it? Companies with hundreds of millions of dollars at their disposal, bickering with the creative talent they need so desperately—over relatively small sums. But it is happening more and more in the private world that is Hollywood.

I sat in one of New York's better restaurants recently, with one of the brighter representatives of the world's largest theatrical agency, and heard him say, "Two of the major film studios are now taking a frankly criminal position toward people they owe large sums of money to."

"What do you mean?"

"Well, _____ studios owes one of my clients $200,000. We went to talk to them the other day and, as well as I thought I knew this business, I was shocked to hear the top executive of the studio say, 'Look, we're just not going to give you the $200,000. You have two alternatives. Either you accept 50¢ on the dollar—with no dickering—or we'll meet you in court.' "

"What did your client do?"

"He settled for half."

"Why?"

"It was never a close decision and they knew it wouldn't be. They knew it could cost him thousands of dollars, and years of his time, to even get the case into court. Even then there would be no certainty that he'd win it. Since he needed the money now rather than two or three years into the future, he had to accept their proposition."

"But morally that's exactly the same as sticking a gun in a man's gut and stealing a hundred thousand dollars from him."

"Exactly. And the studio isn't the only company doing it."

Apparently not, according to Richard Brooks, director of *Looking for Mr. Goodbar* and other profitable pictures. "The new attitude out here seems to be, 'Go ahead, sue. Take us to court.' The studios know it's going to take two or three years to get on a docket, and they can lend your money out at 18 percent meanwhile." Accounting practices in Hollywood now are "intolerable," adds Sean Connery. "I'm talking about millions of dollars. And every actor, producer and director in this town knows what I'm talking about."

Such policies and patterns are set at the top levels of studio management. They do not evolve naturally by the manipulations of small-time sharpies in the accounting departments. Nor are they confined to the film industry alone. Seated with the talent agent and myself at the restaurant table was a successful record producer. "Wow," he said, "I thought only the record business was that dishonest."

"Have you gotten robbed, too?" I said.

"Are you kidding? It's almost impossible to get a fair shake in this industry, or even to know when you're getting one."

"Why is that?"

"Because of the nature of the record business. Who the hell has any way of knowing how many records of yours the manufacturer has sold? You can't check out all the record shops, department stores, drug stores, and novelty shops—thousands and thousands of them—that sell the albums. And returns don't come in all at once the way they do in an election; they come in over a period of weeks, months, years. To really check whether or not the manufacturer is being honest about how many copies he's sold, you'd have to hire a team of accountants and go through warehouses full of paper. You might be legally entitled to do that, but you know that you never will—'cause the record company would never give you another assignment. And if word got around that you were some kind of 'honesty freak,' pretty soon nobody in the business would hire you."

The fourth man at the table was a composer and lyricist with several rock hits to his credit.

"It's the same with music publishers," he said. "That's why most of us set up our own publishing companies as fast as we can. You know that if you have a flop song you won't have much bread coming in anyway. And you know that if you have a big hit, you can count on a fair piece of change. But as to how much you have coming, there's no way of knowing. All you can do is take the word of the publisher— and I'm sorry to say the word of the average publisher isn't worth shit."

I was puzzled. "Does this represent some new degree of deterioration?"

"I don't know," the songwriter replied. "I remember that years ago, when I was just breaking into the business, one of the old-timers told me an industry joke that he said dated back to the 1930's. At that time two of the biggest publishing houses were E. B. Marks and Mills Music. The saying was that 'Marks pays off in mills, and Mills pays off in marks.'

"Some publishers are more honest than others," he added, "but in most cases I don't think they even feel any guilt about what they do. I guess they just figure that's the way the whole business is run, so they personally would be shmucks if they became completely honest."

As in almost any other industry that has been charged with corruption, there are those in the entertainment business who feel the blame is to be laid elsewhere. Norman Lear says: "How surprised should we be in an age when the aircraft industry pays off foreign governments? Cheating in colleges across the country is of epidemic proportions. We're not talking about the motion picture business but about the country. Who is making out an income tax this year and not doing the same thing?" Max E. Youngstein, a former executive of United Artists Corp., contends that if and when payoffs and bribes take place in the movie business, they are part of business in general.

"I've had plenty of opportunities to take money or other things, but I always refused," Youngstein recently was quoted as saying. "There were offers from people, whose names I won't go into, to approve a deal. My approval was important as to whether the producer got a sizable amount of money. They offered me money, automobiles, or to build a new wing on my house."

That is the way a number of deals are made—offering an executive a little extra for himself if he okays a production budget for the producer. In one case a producer who needed $4 million to get a movie made told the studio head that one scene of the picture would have to be shot on a tennis court. "Why don't we build a court at your house, and you'd have the use of it after the scene was shot?" suggested the producer. It's difficult, for some, to dismiss that kind of logic. After all the scene will have to be shot on *some* tennis court—and if there is an allocation for building a court in the $4 million budget, well . . .

Tom Laughlin, who created the *Billy Jack* film character, puts it flatly: "The industry is *built* on cheating; it's corrupt *all down the line.*"

Which brings us to the headline-making case of David Begelman, former head of the motion picture and television operations of Columbia Pictures. For four years after he took over at the studio, he was looked on as something of a wizard who helped the company avert bankruptcy by turning out a series of hits, including the blockbuster *Close Encounters of the Third Kind.* A likable 56-year-old—he was once my agent—Begelman earned salary and bonuses worth $400,000 a year and spent a lot of it on lavish parties, a Rolls-Royce, and other extravagant purchases.

Begelman's troubles came to light when actor Cliff Robertson, making out his 1976 income tax, discovered that he apparently had been paid $10,000 by Columbia Pictures for some work in a film during the year. The problem was that the actor didn't remember having worked for the studio at all. He asked his secretary to check with the studio. Had some other "Cliff Robertson" gotten a check for $10,000?

Rather than a routine call from a studio accountant, back came a call from the head of the studio, Begelman himself. It was all a mistake, the executive explained. A young man at the studio had forged a check and cashed it at the Wells Fargo Bank, but later had confessed stealing Columbia's $10,000 and promised to repay the money. The whole matter could be forgotten. Begelman even invited Robertson to lunch with him at some point in the future. "It's been too long, Cliff," he said.

Robertson later realized that he had better have a copy of the forged check, in case the IRS wanted to know why he did not declare $10,000 in income on his tax form. He called the bank to get the copy, talked to the teller who had cashed it and discovered "the young man" was actually David Begelman. Irate, the actor suggested that his lawyer talk to the police and district attorney to find out what in hell was going on. But he hesitated to make out a formal complaint. In the small world of Hollywood, he knew that charging the head of a major studio with forgery was not what an actor does if he wants to work in pictures again.

The Beverly Hills police department began contacting Columbia executives, including Alan Hirschfield, head of the studio's parent company in New York. When Hirschfield asked Begelman about the $10,000 check, the studio head pleaded that it had been a momentary aberration—one of those once-in-a-lifetime missteps. Then Columbia auditors reported that they had found another forged check—one for $25,000, made out to a public relations man at one of Begelman's favorite Los Angeles restaurants.

More checks showed up. The auditors discovered that the studio had been overbilled some $22,000 for Begelman's travel and limousine expenses, and that $20,000 of the company's money had gone to build additions on Begelman's home in Beverly Hills. The situation began to resemble one at CBS, Inc., a few years ago, when the head of the company's hugely profitable record division was discovered to have spent $80,000 in company funds on his son's bar mitzvah. The record executive had been dismissed promptly, even though he had agreed to pay back the money from his huge annual salary. It seemed inconceivable that Begelman—a forger caught red-handed several times over—could remain in his job.

But Hollywood is Hollywood. The Columbia board suspended Begelman for several months, then reinstated him after he agreed to pay back more than $61,000 (the amount of the various forged checks) and $23,000 in disputed expense account payments. Oh, yes, he agreed to pay interest on the "loans" as well. Hirschfield opposed putting an admitted forger back as head of Columbia Pictures, but his objections were overruled by the board.

Probably, if it had not been for the massive publicity that the whole affair received, that would have been the end of it. Until that time a tight lid of security had been kept on the situation. Few outside of Hollywood knew that anything more was going on other than some accounting discrepancies. But Robertson, seeing that a man who had stolen thousands of dollars from his company was once more in a position where he could steal thousands more, talked to the *Washington Post*. Suddenly, everyone in the media began looking into poor Begelman's past. I so describe him because I truly feel sorry for him.

Interesting new charges were aired in a *New West* article by Jeanie Kasindorf who had talked to Sid Luft, who had long been married to Judy Garland and who had been her manager. Judy's agent in the early 1960's had been young Begelman. According to Luft, Begelman had regularly made out checks on the Judy Garland account to "cash," then had cashed them himself at the Sahara and Dunes hotels in Las Vegas. An investigation revealed how much was being drained from the singer's account, but Luft says that when he told her about it, she had a quick reply:

"Look, suppose he did steal $200,000 to $300,000; sweep it under the rug now. I'm going to make $20 million on the television shows his agency set up for me. What's $300,000?" The same kind of thinking 14 years later won Begelman his reinstatement as president of Columbia Pictures. After all, you can't fire a man who has made millions for his company, and who has only stolen thousands, can you?

But the publicity and the institution of criminal charges against Begelman did the job the board could not do. He "resigned" to become an independent producer who will make pictures for the studio, and his lawyers kept him from going to jail. In a final bit of irony, Alan Hirschfield—the man who had opposed Begelman's reinstatement—lost *his* job at the top of the Columbia ladder.

Hirschfield, a financial wizard from Wall Street, had been given his assignment a few years earlier and had worked diligently to stave off financial collapse at Columbia. "But he wasn't a Hollywood' type," says a motion picture executive at another film company, "and in opposing Begelman he went against the Hollywood establishment. That just isn't done; they protect their own kind. So they took the first opportunity to get rid of 'the outsider.' "

What worried Hollywood most was that the national spotlight of publicity that focused on the Begelman case might spark a series of government investigations into movie business dishonesty. Such a look-see might turn over a lot of rocks. At a stockholders meeting of MCA Inc., for example, a question was raised about a payment of $242,349 to Lorraine Gary, the less-than-major actress who played the wife of the police chief in *Jaws* and *Jaws 2*. As salaries go in Hollywood these days, the amount is not overly large—but it was questioned because Ms. Gary happens to be the wife of Sidney J. Sheinberg.

And who is Sidney J. Sheinberg? Merely the president and chief operating officer of MCA, which owns Universal Pictures, the company that made the films.

Another area into which an investigation is warranted, says Tom Patterson, who heads an organization of independent theatre owners, is collusion between the film studios and some of the big movie chains. Patterson contends that the distributors make secret deals with the chains, taking money to get their new films into major theatres all across the country at one time—and effectively blocking the little guy who owns a single theatre from getting good pictures. "From all we can tell, it all goes back to the head office— that's where the decisions are made and that's where the money goes," says Patterson. *"The only people who can survive are people who become dishonest."*

Strong words. But there's evidence to back them up. But, as stated back a few thousand words, dishonesty exists in virtually every part of the entertainment industry.

Chapter *XI*

Corruption Is Old in New Jersey

I have stated earlier that this book will not deal directly with the problem of Organized Crime. But it is, of course, impossible entirely to omit references to syndicate racketeering in any study of American corruption simply because the activities of syndicate criminals mesh gears with those of crooked politicians, policemen, merchants and business executives. In certain areas, such as New Jersey, the pattern of corruption is so pervasive that is is impossible to draw a line between Mafia-dominated crime on the one hand and corrupt business and political practice on the other. The entire state of New Jersey, in fact, is so notorious that it is known, in the words of journalist Hank Greenspun of Las Vegas, as "the *home* of Organized Crime."

The New Jersey predicament is aptly described by Andrew F. Phelan, Director of the State Investigation Commission. "No one is immune," he says, "Organized crime has affected the lives of every man, woman and child in New Jersey." Syndicate leaders in that state have bought and paid for police officials, magistrates, union leaders and business executives, not just in one or two cities, but in every part of the state.

Naturally such a state of affairs did not mushroom over-night. The history of Organized Crime has been importantly interwoven with that of the state of New Jersey at least since the days of Prohibition when Abner "Longy" Zwillman, one of the nation's leading bootleggers, established control over the previously disorganized rum-running activities in the area. A few years later Zwillman joined forces with top-level criminals from New York areas—Vito Genovese, Joe Adonis, Anthony (Tony Bender) Strolla, Albert Anastasia and Frank Erickson—all of whom had been discouraged, if not put out of business, by the vigorous Thomas E. Dewey, then making a national reputation by prosecuting Mafia and non-Italian criminal elements in Manhattan. The New York hoodlums immediately established in New Jersey the same rackets that had been so successful for them in New York: loan-sharking, heroin selling, gambling and labor-union racketeering.

Needless to say, they also brought with them the mil-lions of dollars necessary to buy police protection. With typical business efficiency the racketeers wasted little time in dealing with beat-level officers. *Political leaders and chiefs of police were purchased. Even the governor's state-house was not immune. The Governor's aide was paid more than a quarter of a million dollars for his cooperation in criminal activities.*

Such public pressure as had been brought to bear by the 1960's, along with new federal legislation permitting wire-taps, enabled the FBI to listen in on the telephone conversa-tions of New Jersey Mafia executives such as Angelo Bruno, Angelo De Carlo, Gerardo Catena and Sam "The Plumber" de Cavalcante. From such overheard conferences a great deal was learned about top-level criminality in the Garden State. Some garden.

In August, 1971, the former Mayor of Jersey City, Thomas J. Whelan, was sentenced to 15 years in prison, having been convicted of extorting money from con-tractors who did business with the city. In sentencing Whelan and Jersey City Council President Thomas Flaherty, United States District Judge Robert Shaw called the Hudson County Democratic organization, "the rotten system whose sole function is to enrich itself." Pouring out of the seven-week trial came daily admissions of shakedowns of contractors, murder threats, and other sordid trivia of the corrupt. Ex-Mayor Whelan and Flaherty went to jail but had nest eggs waiting in Florida when they got out, having deposited $1.2 million in a bank there. The news must have been comforting to the thousands in Jersey City living on inadequate pensions or in slums on welfare. Convicted with Whelan and Flaherty were:

Walter Wolfe, former Hudson County Democratic Chairman.

Former Jersey City Purchasing Agent, Bernard Murphy, described by Shaw as "a potential menace to the community." 15 years in prison.

Former Port of New York Authority Commissioner William A. Sternkopf, whom Shaw identified as "a messenger-boy for the organization." Ten years in prison, and a $20,000 fine.

Former Hudson County Treasurer, Joseph Stapleton. He was banned from taking part in politics for the rest of his life and sentenced to 6 months in jail with a 3-year period of probation.

Former Hudson County Chief of Police, Fred Kopke, described by Shaw as a "tool of the organization." Sentence: 5 years.

Former Jersey City Business administrator Phillip Kunz. Six months in jail, three years probation.

"It really taxes the imagination to try and imagine the amounts of money that seeped down by corrupt practices over a ten-year period," Shaw said in sentencing. He was particularly critical of Whelan, Mayor of Jersey City from 1963 to 1971, and closely linked to Lefty Larchitto, a gambling figure. During the seven-week trial there was testimony not only about shake-downs of contractors but of phony records, death threats and the usual collaboration with underworld elements.

In 1970 Newark, New Jersey Mayor Hugh Addonizio and four co-defendants were found guilty of extortion. The conviction was a rare experience for the

United States government which, with varying degrees of zeal, had tried for years to publicly expose what was a matter of common knowledge in New Jersey, the close personal connection between city and state officials on the one hand and Mafia gangsters on the other. When Addonizio and his cohorts were indicted in December, 1969, on 66 counts of extortion and conspiracy, U.S. Attorney Frederick Lacey said that the government would establish that the defendants had extorted $253,000 from an engineering company and that Addonizio personally had collaborated with the Mafia to set up a phony corporation in a conspiracy to conceal $1,400,000 in kick-backs for government contracts.

"It's a fact of life in Newark that anyone wanting to do business with the city must kick back 10%," Lacey explained. Mafia boss Anthony Boiardo was the mob's top representative in the shake-down scheme. One of the most effective witnesses against Newark's corrupt officials was Irving Kantor, a man extremely ill with a rare nerve disease, who testified from a rolled-in hospital bed that, at the instructions of one of the defendants, Mafioso Joseph Biancone, he had set up a check-cashing service, the device used to pass kick-back money from contractors to Newark City officials. He identified checks totaling $928,726 as kick-back payments from contractors that eventually wound up in City Hall.

The plain fact is that practically every contract signed with the state, county or municipal governments is inflated by from 5% to 15% to allow for a kick-back or "tariff," to use the term common among the racketeers. Head of the clan of crooked politicians in Hudson County was 77-year old John V. Kenny, the long-time political boss who was indicted by the same grand jury that called Mayor Whelan of Jersey City and ten other public officials to account.

Lest the reader think that his personal distance from New Jersey makes the scandal none of his business, it should be appreciated that corruption involved *federal* as well as local money. Consider the case of the $40,000,000 postal complex constructed in Hudson County. The "design contract" was awarded to a Jersey City firm which had made large campaign contributions to Hudson County politicians. The tip-off—as is often the case when unethical business is being conducted—is that the award was made *without competitive bidding*. The building contractor who got the gravy was A. J. Sarubbi, the Mayor of North Bergen and a lieutenant of boss John V. Kenny. The electrical contracting went to a firm employing "one of the boys," Anthony Boiardo—Valentine Electric Company.

The situation was equally as bad in Atlantic City, New Jersey, where "The Organization" has long been under the management of Republican State Senator Frank Farley, in charge since 1940, *after his two predecessors in office had gone to jail*. Even after all the recent exposés it was still the case that no judge or prosecutor was named in Atlantic City without Farley's personal approval. *Readers Digest* investigators revealed what was common knowledge locally, that the city's Board of Commissioners was no more than Farley's personal rubber stamp. To make sure he would have a tight control over the spending of the taxpayers' money, Farley saw to it that he was named treasurer of Atlantic County.

Police in the area justifiably complain that they are permitted to enforce the law only against small fry, not major racketeers and gamblers. The rackets as of the early 1970's were controlled by Angelo Bruno and Herman Orlin, one of the few non-Mafia hoodlums operative in the state. The Public Safety Commissioner, according to *Readers Digest*, met regularly with ex-convict Paul Amato, whose 500 Club was known by federal agents as local headquarters for Angelo Bruno's Mafia family.

Like most old-line experts in corruption, State Senator Farley is an expert at putting on an innocent face. "If the voters object," one of his lieutenants has said, "they can vote us out." But Farley is in considerably less danger from infuriated voters than would be the case in other parts of the country since vote-fraud is a highly developed art form in the state of New Jersey. The Organization has had long experience at producing votes from boarded-up tenement buildings, empty lots, and winos who will sell a vote for the price of their next bottle. Mental patients from the Atlantic County Home have had absentee ballots cast in their names.

One of the richest sources of crooked money for The Organization—the point must be repeated—

is the community of merchants and contractors who do business with city and county governments. One contractor who admits kicking back under-the-table money says, "It's the only way to get a contract. You want the business, you pay 10% to The Organization."

Another effective government witness was Paul Rigo, a 45-year old contractor who, though he knew he was risking his life by testifying against the Mafia—revealed the entire process that had started when his engineering company, Constad, Inc., secured a contract for a Newark, New Jersey sewer project. *Newark's director of Public Works, Anthony La Morte, at once set up a meeting with Boiardo, telling Rigo, "You're going to meet the real boss of Newark, the man who runs this town."*

Boiardo, Rigo explained, instructed him that he would have to kick back 10% of his fees from the city. When Rigo protested that he couldn't make a profit on that basis, Boiardo said, "You'll pay, and in cash. Everybody in Newark pays 10%—or he doesn't work in Newark. There are a lot of mouths to feed in City Hall."

Rigo testified that at a later point he complained to Mayor Addonizio personally that the city was slow in paying for a construction assignment, at which Addonizio told him he would have to work out the details with Boiardo! At the same meeting Rigo reported that he happened to ask Addonizio why he left Congress to become Mayor of Newark. "It's simple," he quoted the Mayor, *"you can make a million bucks as Mayor of Newark."*

When Rigo had the meeting with Boiardo that Addonizio had advised, the Mafia leader told him, "You'll pay 10% or I'll break both your legs." Feeling he had no recourse, Rigo later put $30,000 in a brown paper-bag and gave it to Ralph Vacarro, another defendant, known to New Jersey police as a muscleman for Boiardo.

At one point during Rigo's testimony one of the defendants, former councilman James Callaghan, suddenly interrupted the proceedings to change his "not guilty" plea to guilty when a $5,000 bank check made out to him was admitted into evidence. Another defendant, Phillip Gordon, formerly New York corporation counsel, at least had enough decency left to concede his feeling of shame when it was revealed that he had accepted $4,000 from Rigo.

A dramatic sidelight on the trial came when Judge Barlow revoked Boiardo's $50,000 bail and had him jailed because *police had received information that Mafia "hit men" were plotting against the lives of prominent attorneys and witnesses!* For many years a common method that Mafia criminals have employed to escape conviction is the murder or intimidation of prosecution witnesses. Indeed in this trial two witnesses did die in mysterious auto accidents. Paul Anderson, elderly bank vice-president who had planned to testify regarding his authorization for treasurer's checks for almost a million dollars withdrawn from a banking account in the name of an imaginary supply company, was killed in an accident while driving alone, two miles from the spot where defendant Mario Gallo had been killed in a similar accident while driving alone after a secret meeting with government investigators.

Although there could not have been many street-wise 12-year-old children in Newark who didn't suspect that Addonizio was a crook, it reveals a great deal about the moral and ethical climate of that community that *Newark's Police Benevolent Association overwhelmingly endorsed the mayor during his campaign against Kenneth Gibson*, who was subsequently elected.

A great deal of evidence about Jersey City, N.J. police corruption was obtained by the FBI in their wire-taps on various Mafiosi of the area. In one of the recordings made of a conversation with Angelo "Ray" De Carlo of Mountainside, New Jersey, a subordinate asks, "Ray, who's been winning all the money in the numbers business?"

"The detectives. The ice," De Carlo answered. An FBI memo on De Carlo's phone-tap describes the racketeers' complaints:

"De Carlo said that everybody is trying to make a connection, and as a result you have to pay so much for it that you can't make any money." He cited Hudson County as an example, and said, "Bayonne Joe [Zicarelli] ruined Hudson

County. Ray claimed that formerly protection in the county cost $500 a month, until Zicarelli started paying everyone and now the price is $1,000 a month, and keeps you from making any money."

Murray Kempton, writing in the December, 1970, issue of *Playboy*, observes that similar problems had come to plague New York City Mafia elements. "New York City," Kempton observed, "is priced out of the market, demanding, as it does, the care and feeding of 7,000 policemen. The FBI recordings have De Carlo saying, '*You'll have every sergeant in that precinct calling you up.*' As regards the community of Perth Amboy, New Jersey, De Carlo complained that it was too big. 'You'd have 50 cops and all the detectives coming around to get on the payroll. You got to have a *little* town like Carteret, with about ten or fifteen cops. You put about 10 of them on the payroll for a sawbuck a week, you can handle them.'" (Italics supplied.)

De Carlo was furious, however, about the going rate for police protection in New Brunswick, New Jersey. "$2,500 a month, and you don't even know if you can get a crap-game started down there. People who are handling these things are asking enormous prices, so you can't get no money at them. Who's going to open for them? Now, you know you got to pay the state [troopers?] at least $1,500 a month. You guys are crazy if you think you can't lose money on a crap-game."

As Kempton notes, "All in all, the New Jersey police seem never to have been better at enforcing the law than when their greed forced the price of their favors too high for the law-makers to meet. For Ray De Carlo the 1960's were a continuous confrontation with the agony and delusions of power: In 1962 he thought he had purchased a state-police official (by 1963 the policeman was only a bitter thought):

De Carlo: Do you know what this [man] wants?

Louis Percello: He wants $1,000 [a month] for Long Branch and $1,000 per month for Asbury.

Carmine Persico: For each town?

De Carlo: Yeah. Each town. And for the whole county he wants a different price ... no good. He knows every racket guy in the state. We'd have been better off with a dumb guy.

"The Mafia in New Jersey nevertheless has long known who its friends were in power. The FBI tapes have De Carlo saying, in 1961, 'If Hughes [Governor Richard Hughes] gets elected, we're all right.' In 1962, the tapes revealed, De Carlo raised a great deal of money for Addonizio's first mayoralty campaign. As a result, De Carlo was able to boast—entirely accurately—'I guarantee, we'll own him.' When an associate inquired, 'How the hell are we going to get to Kenny?' [Democratic boss John V. Kenny of Hudson County] De Carlo answered, 'Tell him I sent you. Tell him ... Hughey [Addonizio] has helped us along. He'll give us the city!'

"The tapes also include De Carlo's disgust with Carmine DeSapio, who was for years the Democratic leader of New York County but was convicted in December of 1969 of bribery-conspiracy charges. 'The organization,' De Carlo grumbles, 'must have gave over half a million to DeSapio and he probably stuck a couple of hundred thousand right in his pocket.'"

It is not possible in this book to give more than a faint suggestion of the scope of Mafia-influenced corruption in the Garden State. The cast of characters is simply too large, and the details of their dishonesty too numerous. A few additional examples will nevertheless give an idea of the situation. Christopher S. Wren and Margaret English's "Murder New Jersey Style" in the March 10th, 1970 issue of *Look* told of the murder of numbers racketeer Gabriel Franco, who operated in Paterson, New Jersey. *An actor in the drama was county investigator Joe Moccio, who had been mayor in 1946 of West Paterson, New Jersey, when Mafia leaders Joe Adonis and Willie Moretti had run an important gambling room in the township.* Moccio owed his subsequent success, such as it was, to an important leader in Passaic County Republican politics, Joseph Bozzo. Bozzo had been summoned by the Kefauver Crime Committee in 1951 to explain his close friendships with the likes of Joe Adonis, Willie Moretti, James Cerce and Abner Zwillman. That same year *Bozzo placed Moccio as an investigator in the Passaic County prosecutor's office.* Moccio worked hand-in-glove with local gamblers, even though he secured an assignment on the county gambling squad.

In time he rose to be the *Republican leader of West Paterson,* maintained two comfortable homes, a Cadillac and a mahogany speedboat, all on his modest investigator's salary.

Believe it or not, *Moccio was put in charge of the investigation into the murder of Franco by Passaic County prosecutor John Thevos, who passed over a dozen qualified, police-trained county detectives in making his choice.*

Detective Sergeant John De Groot, who had investigated the related murder of Clifton, New Jersey, housewife Judy Cavanaugh, wisely refused, in January, 1967, to turn over to Moccio the name of a federal informer in another case. Moccio was furious. "I run this county," he told De Groot. "I'm the boss here and I'll tell you what to do. I'll get you if it's the last thing I do." Nine months later, Moccio made good on his threat. De Groot found *himself* indicted for the Franco murder and was actually sent to jail!

There is not space here to tell the entire story of the case, but the statement of F. Lee Bailey who was called in to it makes an apt moral. Bailey, angered by what he had unearthed, wrote to every legislator in the state of New Jersey to demand an investigation, saying, *"I have never, in a state or federal court, seen abuses of justice, legal ethics and constitutional rights such as this case has involved."* The result of Bailey's complaint: No investigation followed, but Bailey's own right to appear in New Jersey courts was revoked!

William Schulz, reporting in the February, 1972, *Readers Digest,* on "The Mobs' Grip on New Jersey," refers to a typical instance of extortion. "When a group of developers in Union County announced plans to build a 702-unit apartment complex, they were visited by a 'labor consultant,' Mafia boss Nick Delmore, who offered his assistance in the event of labor problems. Within weeks, pickets from *a Cosa Nostra-controlled union* had shut down the entire project, and Delmore was offering to settle the strike for a 'piece of the action.' The developers forked over $10,000. Then Delmore died and his partner, Sam Decavalcante, demanded and received another $25,000.

"Nowhere is Mafia authority more complete," Schulz reveals, "than in Port Newark, the sprawling waterfront complex where 67-year-old *Jerry Cetana exercises undisputed control through lieutenants who are officers of the International Longshoremen's Association. There are gambling and loan-sharking on the docks, and straight theft. With 9 billion dollars worth of goods moving into Port Newark each year losses from Mafia hi-jackers run into tens of millions a year.* 'There's nothing they won't steal,' says one waterfront expert, talking of recent syndicate heists: Sewing machine parts ($18,000), coffee ($35,000), whiskey ($60,000), radios ($80,000), 'They've got a market for anything.'" (Italics added.)

Again the point must be underlined that such stolen merchandise is not sold to professional criminals. It is distributed to average citizens, most of whom have a clear idea about the origin of the merchandise they are being offered. In some cases "legitimate" storekeepers become the outlet for the stolen merchandise, knowing its source.

The situation in New Jersey unions is so outrageous it may quite literally be hopeless. *At least 25 unions throughout the state are under mob influence.* One example would be *Teamster Local 97*, which "serves" about 10,000 maintenance and factory workers. These workers receive scant benefits from the union, although they pay it over $500,000 a year in dues.

As of February, 1972, three of the union's officials were under federal indictment for embezzling large amounts of money from the union's treasury. They were in business with Mafia member Thomas Pecora. Pecora, through a business front, the All-Purpose Chemical Company, marketed an inferior but high-priced cleaning fluid called *Poly-Clean*. Employers were urged to purchase great quantities of it by assurances that by doing so they were buying "labor peace"—which meant low wages for workers and no work-stoppages.

Another corrupt local is *Local 170 of the Hotel and Restaurant Employees*, in Camden, New Jersey. It was taken over in 1966 by Bucky Baldino and Andrew Chalako, who told one employer, "You have 7 days to come across with $5,000. Otherwise we'll shut down your place tight as a drum." Other employees were threatened with physical harm. One bar-owner who resisted Chalako's threats was bombed. One of his employees lost a leg in the explosion. Rank-and-file members of Local 170 who tried to criticize the corrupt leadership in union meetings were threatened by strong-arm goons. This is a time-honored method employed by crooked union leadership to perpetuate itself in power. Decent workingmen who buck the system may be killed, beaten, threatened, kept from better employment, or intimidated in other ways.

It happens in the land of the free and the home of the brave, but in New Jersey crooks have more freedom than straight-arrows and acting too brave can get you killed.

Chapter *XII*

Corrupting a Labor Union – It Doesn't Take Much Work

The time is 1926. We're in the heart of the garment district in New York City, watching groups of sign-carrying pickets march back and forth in front of their respective places of employment. For some days now, as more and more workers—many unschooled, unskilled immigrants—have grown angry at the long hours and low pay that are part of their jobs, the picket lines have grown longer. A number of newly formed labor unions are just beginning to flex their muscles.

Down the street come several large trucks, engines growling. From the pickets, a roar goes up. "Scabs!" The pickets bunch together, trying to form a barricade against the trucks and their occupants—dozens of new workers to man the sewing machines and garment racks. The newcomers are mostly hungry Puerto Ricans, even more unskilled and unschooled than those they intend to replace. As the sign-wielding pickets try to prevent them from entering the factories, a fight breaks out. Chaos erupts.

From the trucks leap several dozen rough-looking men armed with crowbars and billy clubs. They hurl themselves violently into the crowd of pickets, swinging their weapons to split skulls and break bones. Before the police can arrive, scores have been injured. Wounded men are lying in the street, writhing in pain, retching uncontrollably as their blood trickles along the gutters. Soon the air is filled with the sound of ambulance sirens.

The next day, a group of those men and women gather in the plush mid-Manhattan office of Arnold Rothstein, the gambler who has strong influence in both labor and politics. The garment union officials plead with Rothstein to use his influence to call off the thugs hired by the garment manufacturers to rout the strikers. Rothstein is reminded that his father was one of the most respected men in the garment industry.

"Right," says the mobster, picking up the telephone. "It's no problem." He places a call to the notorious "Legs" Diamond. "Legs," he says, "how about keeping your guys out of the garment district. Instead of knocking heads together there, I'd rather have 'em down on the docks looking after the whiskey I've got coming in from overseas." He hangs up the phone, and the pleased union leaders leave.

A few days later they are back. This time they tell Rothstein that they have hired a gang of toughs of their own to battle the scabs and harass the miserly employers.

Later peace is restored in the garment district, but the hired ruffians refuse to go. Unless they are kept on the union payroll, they threaten, some of the officials may themselves suffer bodily harm. Can Rothstein help? Nodding, he picks up the phone again and talks to one Augie Orgen, who gets orders to pull his men out of the garment district and find them work elsewhere.

As Rothstein turns to them, grinning, the leaders of the strike look at each other with a sudden revelation. The two opposing armies on the front lines of this particular labor battle, they understand, are both working directly or indirectly under the jurisdiction of Organized Crime in the person of Arnold Rothstein.

The unique situation is one of the first instances of the mob having a measure of control in the American labor movement. Today in many instances the gangster is an integral part of the movement—so much so that where the saying used to be that gangsters work for the unions, it is now said that the unions work for the gangsters. Such is not the case in *every* union, but recent history helps to explain how and why professional criminals have achieved a wide measure of control in many.

As American society in the late 19th century created the factory system and put an increasing number of workers under the control of individual employers, the lines between labor and management became ever more clearly defined. There were unions in the late 1800's—the American Federation of Labor was formed in 1887, and the United Mine Workers in 1890—but it was the advent of assemblyline techniques after the turn of the century that brought about a sharp division between ownership of expensive machinery and blue-collar workers.

The original ideals behind the creation of labor unions were high-minded. The goal was to improve the worker's wages and conditions of employment. Few dreamed that in striving to achieve a balance of power between business and labor, the union movement would become one of the nation's largest social institutions. With the passage of the Wagner Act in 1935, the New Deal of President Franklin D. Roosevelt provided an impetus to industrial unionism.

The growth in membership, power, and affluence of the unions became both a boon and at times a curse to the large body of workers who flocked to them. Labor leaders came to sit side-by-side with company presidents and high-level politicians. Then, as the men who had reached powerful positions sought to increase their influence, a spreading bureaucracy appeared. Men such as John L. Lewis, for several decades leader of the United Mine Workers, ruled their unions with iron fists and tolerated no opposition from within the ranks.

With the passage of time it became obvious that a Machiavellian code of ethics was subscribed to by various labor leaders to ensure their authority. In addition men who had organized and led a movement of the working class found that as they broke bread with corporation presidents and politicians they became part of an elite *nouveau riche*.

Strains developed between union leaders and the rank and file, as the workers began to wonder just how well they could be represented by leaders who increasingly seemed to be on equal social terms with management. In time leaders resorted to unethical means to consolidate their power.

When the McClellan Committee was formed in 1957 to investigate corruption in the ranks of labor and management, no one knew the full extent of the disease. It was generally thought to be confined to a few locals in isolated regions of the country. With each investigation, however, a pattern emerged that showed the depth of the problem had been greatly underestimated. The late Robert Kennedy worked tirelessly to reveal that labor corruption in some industries had grown to cancerous proportions.

The investigative spotlight soon came to focus on the dim figure of the "labor influence peddler," who serves as middleman and courier to the two powerful camps of labor and management. While the crooked labor leader and racketeer are generally regarded as the focal point of most studies of corruption, it is actually the middlemen who are responsible for much serious illegal activity. These crooks serve both management in industry and union leadership at the expense of the worker. One of their devices is the "sweetheart deal."

A sweetheart deal is one that is favorable to management and sometimes crippling to labor. One of the most infamous of those who put such deals together was the unsavory Nathan Shefferman. Shefferman's largest "customer," it appears, was Dave Beck, former president of the powerful Teamsters Union, and the first of a long list of labor leaders to run afoul of the law. For Beck and some 90 other labor leaders and management executives, Shefferman is estimated to have contracted for nearly $2.5 million worth of business for himself in arranging corrupt contracts over a seven-year period.

His operation involved agreements with union leaders who settled on substandard contracts for their workers—in return for favors that industry management would channel to them through Shefferman. In Chicago he ran a firm called Labor Relations Associates; a chief client was the country's leading retailer, Sears, Roebuck & Co. Sears helped Shefferman ingratiate himself with labor leaders by providing access to goods at a token price—goods which the middleman then bestowed on influential labor leaders and others as a sign of his "friendship."

When automobile and electric appliance distributors were confronted with a growing movement toward unionization, they contacted Shefferman to ask what could be done to keep unions out. There was a standard fee, they learned, for this kind of service: $100 monthly for an indefinite period, plus $2,000 for "entertainment expenses" that would go for Super Bowl tickets and Canadian fishing trips for union leaders. To employers faced with sizable pay increases for newly organized workers, such ripoffs were minor. The money was paid—and the unions promptly removed their pickets from in front of the offending companies.

The continuing investigation revealed that a great deal of the annual profit of Shefferman's firm came from businesses willing to pay small but regular sums to keep the unions at bay. The victim, of course, was the worker struggling to support a family. The triangular system of corruption prompted Sen. McClellan to remark: "It looks to me like we are developing a pattern of what amounts to payoffs to union officials to have them disregard the rights of the working man; to be reluctant, if not to refuse entirely, to press any drive for unionization."

There are other means of cheating the workers. At times the labor ranks are infiltrated by undercover "labor relations" people who suggest conflicting proposals to create confusion and disrupt employee unity. This was the technique used by Shefferman when Sears, Roebuck employees voted to affiliate their independent union with the Retail Clerks International. After the three-to-one vote was taken, a "public relations" official was brought in to help smooth the changeover. With him came a group of about 20 who ostensibly would work with the Sears employees, but were actually ordered to gather files on the most dissident workers and try to "brainwash" them on the supposed disadvantages of membership in the larger union organization. The chief disadvantage, of course, was to the employer, who might be required to increase pay scales.

When results where slow in coming, Shefferman's undercover squad tried to disrupt the union organization plan with a program of sabotage! Employees found their cars destroyed, their homes damaged. There were threats of physical violence. The extreme acts served to turn employee sentiment against the union because of the underlying belief that a criminal element was in favor of the unionization. The "reverse psychology" operation, like the earlier effort, eventually failed to pay off—but it slowed the orderly process by which ethical management and labor relationships are formed.

When it becomes apparent that unions cannot be kept out altogether, steps can be taken to see that their influence is minimized. Such a situation was brought to Shefferman by the Englander Co., a New Jersey manufacturer of mattresses. Most of the company's employees were women who belonged to a local of the Retail Clerks Union, whose leader was a close business friend of Shefferman, and who was wined and dined accordingly. The mattress company officials were not at all unhappy with the work of the union— and for good reason: its women employees were making 60 cents per hour less than the average throughout the industry. For his help in keeping wages low Shefferman received payments totalling $76,400 over a period of four years.

There are counterparts to Shefferman in many cities; their hands stretch out for payment in all directions. Most would consider themselves merely "consultants" or "advisors"—a far cry from the underworld figures that infest the labor movement. If pinned down, of course, they would have to admit that often their "legal" activities make it possible for flagrant racketeers to operate freely within the union, using it as a power base.

Such was the case when criminals Bernard Adelstein and Vincent Squillante bought their way into several New York garbage-collection companies. In New York City, Nassau County, and Westchester County a total of several hundred sanitation companies split some $50 million annually paid by restaurants, private citizens, and business to have their refuse hauled away. With funds supplied from the upper echelons of organized crime, Adelstein and Squillante moved in and promptly began warning competitors to stay out of their territories. Threats against their drivers, vehicles, families and their lives forced several independent garbage collectors to sell their routes to the mobsters' growing operation.

The next step was predictable enough. Customers received word from "street soldiers" that the cost of garbage collection was henceforth double what it had been. If anyone balked and looked for service from another firm, he promptly learned that—in order to keep his business running smoothly and without "trouble" it would be best to stay with the union firms under the control of the underworld.

When the owner of a Safeway grocery in Westchester County refused to listen and hired an independent contractor, all garbage-collection service to other Safeway stores in the area was discontinued *under union orders*. Within days, officials at the chain's headquarters advised the local store to accept the union terms.

As men like Adelstein and Squillante showed off their power and encouraged other mob figures to step into the lucrative business, a whole new set of rules was developed. One was that there was to be no competition among companies working in the same union. Each firm would have its own routes, its own customers. Another rule concerned competitive bidding. One man would be designated to make an appropriately high bid for each customer, and no one would be allowed to underbid him. Thus profits were kept at maximum levels.

More often than not the customers of the garbage-collection firms were not large chain operations like Safeway but small, family-owned stores. Many operated on profit margins barely large enough to eke out a living. Artificially inflated rates for sanitation service proved a severe hardship and forced some out of business. Similarly small garbage-collection operators found that they could not compete with the gangland rivals: if they bid low to get a customer's business, there was always a union man present to underbid them—and once the rival was forced out of business, the union man was free to raise his rates sky-high.

Such is the basic vicious pattern of mob control in the labor rackets. The idea is to gain control of a few locals in a union, then change a legitimate business into a monopoly situation controlled by a ring of insiders. When underworld figures with minimal labor influence wish to extend their range, or want to spread across states from a base of one or two cities, it is not difficult to do so. A phone call that feeds into a central network of underworld labor power is often all that is necessary.

Most often the call is made to a public labor figure of great influence, a man who also serves as a type of "ambassador" to organized crime and who can offer a side door into the unions. The most notorious of this type was Teamster head Jimmy Hoffa, who would go to any length to help out his buddies from "the Syndicate."

When, for example, hoodlum Johnny Dio wanted to set up Teamsters locals in New York, Hoffa handed them to him with no serious questions asked. To Hoffa, Dio was reputable; never mind that his friend would later be convicted for selling "protection" *against* union organization and would go to jail for extortion.

In another instance Paul Ricca, one of the most powerful men in what had been the Chicago Capone operation, needed $150,000 to flee the country before Federal prosecutors came down on him. Ricca got the money within hours of his request to Hoffa, who supplied the funds from two locals he controlled in Detroit! In exchange the Teamsters were given half-title to Ricca's estate in Indiana, complete with swimming pool and tennis courts. During an investigation Hoffa defended the deal as one that provided the union with a structure that could be turned into a business school.

Hoffa's misdeeds were blatant, scornful of outside authority. In much the same way he had aided Johnny Dio, the tough-talking union boss helped another racketeer named Shorty Feldman obtain a charter for a restaurant local in Philadelphia. Even though the police monitored incriminating phone calls they were powerless to bring charges against Hoffa that would stick.

At the height of his power Hoffa's influence extended far beyond the Teamsters Union, already the world's largest and most affluent labor organization. Because of the organizational ability of the Teamsters, and the fact that many other unions depend on them for their support in strike actions, Hoffa was able to offer the underworld its strongest connection into the labor world. By controlling the nation's highways, Hoffa could refuse to move goods unless industry management played by his rules. Often he got his way.

He did, for example, when the Distillery Workers Union demanded that a group of Eastern distilleries give them recognition. The companies refused. They refused, that is, until the union leaders turned to Hoffa for help. When Hoffa began passing word to distillery employees that they should join the union, management reluctantly agreed to permit the contract—out of fear that the Teamsters would refuse to move their liquor.

While there is evidence that Hoffa manipulated union funds for his own gains, and that he wielded his influence to the detriment of the public and many of the workers within his union, such misdeeds were difficult to prove in a court of law. He was eventually convicted for paying a spy to infiltrate the committee that was investigating his corrupt empire and still did his best to run his union from a prison cell.

So successfully did he manage to operate from behind bars that it took considerable effort on the part of Frank Fitzsimmons—whom Hoffa himself put into power—to keep his predecessor from regaining control of the Teamsters once he was released from prison. It is widely believed that a Presidential pardon from the Nixon White House for Hoffa was blocked only after Fitzsimmons promised that the Teamsters would endorse Nixon in the 1972 election. Whether or not Fitzsimmons made his own connections in the underworld during the time that Hoffa was incarcerated is open to speculation. All that is known is that when Hoffa was freed and tried to take up the reins of power, he was killed.

The emergence on the union scene of such a powerful man as Hoffa was prefigured by other men of almost equal repute in prior years. In labor union annals the name of Joe Fay virtually symbolizes corruption. Fay was the president of the International Union of Operating Engineers, which had power far greater than a membership of only 280,000 workers would indicate. The members drove the tractors, earth-moving equipment, cranes and other machines that are vital to the construction industry, and consequently held a primary position at bargaining tables. The sitdown of a single operator of a huge construction crane could immobilize 1,000 other workers on a building job.

Like Hoffa, Fay ran a totalitarian union. Any opposition was instantly snuffed out. The rank-and-file members were kept in total ignorance of what happened to their dues money, and if any became overly inquisitive about who was spending what, they were kept in line by Fay's "soldiers." Bosses in the local unions would regularly extract "strike insurance" from contractors. Or they would give choice jobs to friends in the contracting business by pressuring builders under the threat of a possible walkout of workers—which would mean costly delays on a job. Naturally, the friends would frequently kick back part of their revenue from the jobs. In some instances the bosses of the locals had business sidelines of their own—operation of contracting companies to which they could funnel lucrative building jobs. Fay himself ran such a sideline, making very generous deals between himself as an employer of construction workers and his alter ego as a labor leader. He was aided in his maneuvering by friends on local labor boards who played large parts in making high-level policy decisions.

How is this for audacity? When he was brought to trial on the charge of having extorted $370,000 from several contractors, Fay indignantly said that he was innocent of extortion. The money, he claimed, had been freely offered and—at most—he was guilty of having taken bribes!

Like Hoffa Fay continued to try to run his union from a prison cell. His appointed successor, William Maloney, continued the strongarm tactics that had become so much a part of the basic operation and managed to do all right for himself in the process. Over a six-year period, estimated McClellan Committee investigators, Maloney's income totalled more than $700,000. When his shabby dealings were exposed, he resigned as union president on a pension of a modest $50,000 a year!

As is the case with corruption in so many other areas, it appears that the repeated incidents of labor ripoffs have served to make the American public callous rather than concerned. It took such a brutal and violent episode as the murder of union leader Jock Yablonski, along with his wife and daughter, to shock us into a more sober view of the problem. But with each day the killings recede further into memory, and there is danger that the apathy of the past will surface once more. To prevent that from happening, it is necessary to reexamine the Yablonski case in some detail— and to remember it.

After Tony Boyle became president of the United Mine Workers, he was overlord of what John L. Lewis had proudly called the "greatest union in the country." Like Hoffa and Fay, Boyle ran a tight ship; any mutineers were promptly thrown to the sharks. To hell with the American ideal of Democracy. Following a practice begun by Lewis, Boyle placed relatives and friends in positions of power. He also made generous loans of union funds to locals and officials that he favored. Although the majority of union officials rely on their union's trade papers to further their causes and help keep themselves in power, Boyle was much more obvious in this manipulation of a favorite public relations tool.

Trying to shape himself in the Lewis mould—as a crusader who cared only about the welfare of the workers in his union's ranks—Boyle grossly misused union funds, and went so far as to establish a secret trust fund for his own use and a few other high-level executives. When records of such transactions began to surface, Ralph Nader accused Boyle of misrepresenting the mine workers. The UMW, said Nader, should find itself a new leader.

The criticism reached the ears of Yablonski, who long had been a Boyle supporter and had praised the union leader at national conventions. When a grass-roots movement against the dictatorial rule of Boyle began to develop, however, Yablonski began to fret about the welfare of the membership—a concern that increased as more evidence of

Boyle's lack of integrity was uncovered. Beginning to speak for himself, rather than for Boyle, Yablonski found that he was getting strong support to run for the leadership of the union at the 1969 convention. For a man such as Boyle, there seemed to be only one way to hang onto his position of power: Yablonski must be eliminated.

There is evidence that several attempts to kill Yablonski were made before the election took place, but that they failed for various reasons. It should have been evident to anyone with an understanding of the bureaucracy within the UMW that the upstart rival had no chance of beating Boyle for the presidency. To ensure his victory, Boyle refused to have a certified ballot company supervise the voting. For a membership that totalled 193,000, he printed 275,000 ballots—and got 225,000 of them into the mail before he was blocked by a court order! Officials at various locals brought the entire membership together at one time and made sure that they voted for Boyle by showing them exactly how the ballot should be marked.

Even though reelected, the vicious Boyle went ahead with his plan to eliminate Yablonski. Possibly he thought that a random crime against a man who had lost the election would seem to be without motivation—at least so far as the victor was concerned.

Yablonski had demanded a full investigation of the way that the election had been carried out, and stood a good chance of getting a rerun. Even if he did not, there was the certainty that the rival would continue to chip away at Boyle's iron-fisted rule from within the union's ranks. This was more than Boyle could tolerate.

Yablonski had to die. The price offered by Albert Pass, one of the union leader's right hand men, was $10,000. For the fee he found a taker in one Silious Huddleston, who knew several small-time crooks from Cleveland who agreed to do the job. It was a careless job, a messy one, clearly not the work of professional hit men. The killers were apprehended and sentenced to jail.

Fretting behind bars, Huddleston began to sing. The money paid to Yablonski's killers via Pass had come from union funds, and the man who had access to such funds was

Tony Boyle. A stunned public watched first Pass and then Boyle become the highest labor leaders ever convicted of a capital crime.

It seems almost incomprehensible that much of the American public has become so accustomed to hearing about misdeeds within the ranks of labor that it takes an instance as serious as the Yablonski murders to make an impression. One can only hope that there will be few similar cases in the future, although it has been demonstrated all too frequently what can happen to workers who oppose the dictatorial rule of union leaders. Meanwhile, outright corruption among high union officials—including the illegal manipulation of union funds—continues to run rampant. Consider one example from recent history.

Al Bramlet, one of the most powerful men in the state of Nevada, left his office one evening—and disappeared. As president of the Nevada chapter of the AFL-CIO and secretary-treasurer of the Culinary and Bartenders Union, Bramlet was in control of about 22,000 members working in the hotels and restaurants of Las Vegas. The union is particularly powerful in that it has shown in the past that by calling a strike against the hotel operators, it can effectively close down the city's immensely profitable gambling casinos.

Shortly after his disappearance, Bramlet turned up. Rather, his body turned up—in a shallow grave forty miles northwest of the city, riddled with bullets. Investigation revealed that, as a union trustee of the local's pension fund, he had made loans totalling *an incredible $31 million* to Morris Shenker, a real estate operator who also had casino interests. The sum, by the way, was out of the fund's total amount of $42 million. Subsidies of $500,000 a month were being paid to support two Shenker companies which were in financial distress and delinquent in payments owed on other loans. Moreover, Shenker's companies had accrued approximately $3.2 million in unpaid interest and had returned only $1.2 million.

Worried about the serious depletion of the union's assets, the U.S. Labor Department entered the picture and filed suit to demand restitution for any money unlawfully paid from the fund. The sudden and mysterious death of Bramlet, however, seems likely to disrupt any real investigation of how and where the money was used. All that does seem certain at this point is that the pension funds that thousands of workers thought were secure have partly melted away beneath the hot Nevada sun.

Is there no hope, no bright ray in the gloomy sky of union corruption? Well, recent findings of the U.S. Labor Department indicate that while corruption in the unions continues there are citizens working to reduce it. For instance, an agreement was reached between the Labor Department and the Teamsters' Ohio Highway Drivers for a revision of their welfare plan. This involved the restoration of some $560,000 to the union fund by Robert Kree, Jr., the fund administrator. Kree had been charged with having received unreasonable amounts of money for his services. As part of the agreement Kree resigned, as did the entire board of trustees.

The Labor Department went on to file suit against Frank Fitzsimmons and eighteen other Teamster officials to recover losses resulting from imprudent loans made from the union's Central States Pension Fund. Four vice presidents—Robert Holmes, Ray Williams, Joseph Morgan, and Jackie Presser—were charged with violating their obligations to manage the fund properly. In the suit, the Labor Department noted that the fund had been used as the source of *at least $125 million in bad loans*, and the amount was said to be only representative, not all-inclusive.

One of the most satisfying catches in the history of the war against union corruption came with the arrest and conviction of Anthony Provenzano, one of the most powerful union leaders in the country. A former close friend of Jimmy Hoffa, Provenzano was thought to be involved in that labor leader's disappearance—but while the investigators pressed for the murder conviction that was recently obtained against "Tony Pro," they got him on a less serious charge: conspiracy to arrange a $300,000 kickback on a loan of $2.4 million from a Teamsters pension fund. Proving such a relatively mild charge took the work of undercover agents and a court order permitting wiretaps. Only when a big fish is involved can investigators devote the time and energy required to produce a semblance of justice.

What, then, can be done about the numerous lesser instances of corruption within the labor movement? How can we remain a democratic society when the trade unions that are an integral part of our social fabric harden into a totalitarian bureaucratic mold? In searching for a way to restore the moral authority that characterized the labor movement in its early years, one should be aware that since the 1800's, periods of idealism have often surfaced within the movement—usually to sink as a new encrustation of bureaucracy arose, reappearing after each economic disaster.

Hopefully it will not take a disaster of national proportions to produce a new idealism in the ranks of labor. It is easy to say that one answer might be to give control of the unions back to the members. But can this be done? Federal rulings have found that unions such as the Teamsters and Operating Engineers have unlawful constitutions, and the unions have been ordered to restore democratic elections and keep careful records of all union funds. But the group in control usually has the means to stay in control, orders from outside or not. Besides, if new leaders are selected from the rank and file, what assurance is there that they will be immune to the bureaucratic tendency toward corruption? One answer, it seems to this concerned citizen, is a system of checks and balances within the union itself—perhaps stemming from the creation of some kind of a two-party system. At present, the constitutions of many unions prohibit dual-unionism, but if allowed, it might provide the necessary measures to prevent dictatorial control by corrupt officials.

The most obvious examples of thievery occur in highly fragmented industries—trucking, longshoring, hotel and restaurant operation, and construction, to name a few—where small operators and employers are always looking for deals that give them a competitive edge. Unions largely reflect the industries they have organized, and it is in these fields where organized crime makes its infiltration most easily. It is here where sweetheart deals, payoffs, and extortion predominate.

To show how easily things are done in just one of these

industries we have only to look at how Fred R. Field, Jr., general organizer of the International Longshoremen's Association, was alleged to have shaken down United Brands Co., and its predecessor, United Fruit Co., for nearly $125,000. The story was detailed in full in a *Wall Street Journal* series. The indictments handed down by a Federal grand jury charged Field with basically having demanded money to keep United's bananas moving during three strikes in the 1968–1971 period. Moreover, it was claimed that cash payments to Field produced a three-year period of labor peace starting in 1974.

B. K. Hachmann, United Brands director of labor relations, said that he made the payments to Field upon demand. The payments were in $50 and $100 denominations and were made at Field's Manhattan apartment. One, of $15,000, was made—after a hospital benefit dinner for Field—at a midtown hotel.

Another United Brands official testified that he gave authority to make the payments because he was Hachmann's superior. The cash was provided by the controller of the company, and came in packets of $2,500 each on United Fruit ocean vessels from Panama. Because such voyages sometimes took weeks, the controller temporarily drew on corporate funds in Boston. This practice enabled Field's attorney to allege that the United Brands executives themselves were taking the cash and trying to blame the dock leader.

The case against Fields was set forth by a series of government witnesses testifying under immunity from prosecution in the payoff situation, but not immune from being cited for lying. The kind of corruption they charged was taking place had been largely avoided in the major consolidated industries—steel, aluminum, autos, rubber, coal, foundries, and manufacturing industries. This does not mean that they are pure. There is corruption in these industries, too, but it is likely to be on a local basis rather than national.

Such leaders as Walter Reuther and George Meany have long endeavored to run their organizations honestly, and have been active in trying to root out corruption and labor racketeering. It is the Hoffas and Boyles who have tarnished the movement. Those who have not yet turned into Hoffas or Boyles must be encouraged to hold on to their ideals and principles. It is not easy. For a man to remain incorruptible in an operation where individuals are given great power to deal with businessmen who frequently are themselves dishonest requires a tremendous amount of moral fortitude.

Chapter *XIII*

Moral Rot in the Military Service

In January of 1979 Jayne and I had the pleasure of entertaining an audience of cadets at the U.S. Military Academy at West Point, New York. While there we naturally took the occasion to see a bit of the area. The young students on campus are indeed our nation's finest. As one meets them individually or en masse it is difficult to believe that, barring the occasional moments of human weakness to which we are all prone, they could possibly be part of the large sobering picture of corruption I have sketched out. The fact is, nevertheless, that the moral rot in our society has even touched West Point.

In a career spanning four decades of military service Lieutenant General Andrew J. Goodpaster has probably faced no challenge more difficult than the one he faces today. Called out of retirement in 1977 in the wake of the worst cheating scandal in the history of the West Point military academy, Gen. Goodpaster is trying to eliminate what many senior officers believe is a "moral rot" that has infested the U.S. Army in recent years.

A soldier-scholar who has served as deputy commander

of the American forces in Vietnam, defense liaison officer, secretary to President Eisenhower, and as a professor at the Citadel, the military college in Charleston, S.C., Gen. Goodpaster traces the deterioration among Army personnel to Vietnam with its "phony reports on resources and readiness." Others believe that a decline in discipline can be traced to the character of the war itself, particularly the turbulence in the officer corps that involved field commanders "getting their tickets punched" by serving six months with a field command, then returning to the United States or to staff duty in Saigon. Drew Middleton, in a *New York Times* report, stated that senior officers now believe the "ticket punching" system was a mistake, and that continuity of command—particularly at company and battalion levels— would have reduced the number of desertions, attacks on officers by enlisted men, and refusals to obey orders.

I would guess, however, that the military's present problems have deeper roots. One recent study, *Crisis in Command*, by officers Richard Gabriel and Paul Savage, lays the blame at the doorstep of Robert S. McNamara, the former Secretary of Defense. In trying to run the Army and all the services as an enormous business, the authors state, McNamara substituted the values of business enterprise for those of the old Army. And, as several other chapters in this compilation of corruption indicate, the values of business are seldom based on largely ethical considerations.

Machiavelli would have wondered if it is possible to run such a huge complex as the modern military machine on an ethical basis of any kind. Consider: The Army, Navy, Marine Corps and Air Force have approximately 2.5 million men and women on active duty, and a similar number in the reserve components. Add another one million civil employees in the Defense department. Then fund the entire operation with one quarter of the total federal budget.

It is an enormous machine, certainly, and one in need of repair. For decades since the end of World War II, but growing louder in the post-Vietnam years, there have been angry cries from the public and Congress over evils within the system. Is there excessive and unnecessary spending? What about close ties and under-the-table deals between defense contractors and the military? Are some new members of the armed forces treated unjustly by sadistic officers? Have the abuses that led to cheating scandals at West Point and the Air Force academy in Colorado been corrected? The list of questions goes on and rightfully so.

One of the areas that has come under scrutiny of late is "double dipping." The term applies to hundreds of thousands of veterans who collect pension checks and other retirement benefits from the armed services at the same time that they receive regular wages from civilian jobs. A career soldier may retire after 20 years of service, on a pension of 50% of his salary, and accept a lucrative job in private industry as well. In 1978 pensions paid to veterans cost the taxpayer $9.8 billion. The figure is expected to rise to $28 billion by the year 2000. Is the cost really necessary?

No, says Charles Zwick, chairman of the Military Compensation Board. "The system can no longer by justified," he adds, noting that it involves a great and dangerous abuse of the taxpayer's money. In addition to present regulations that allow the 20-year veteran to collect 50% of his base salary upon retirement, a proposed plan involves even greater cost: It would let a 30-year veteran retire at the age of 55 and collect a pension equal to three-fourths of base pay.

To call such systems corrupt, of course, might be a gross exaggeration. They grow more from poor planning by well-intentioned men, or from plans that may be reasonable at one moment but not as conditions change. A similar situation has grown up around occupational courses for military personnel. According to one alert member of the House of Representatives, the Defense department has recently wasted millions while spending about $3.5 billion a year on the courses.

It was not the first time, of course, that the department has been charged with unnecessary spending. Some of the most stringent—and well-supported—attacks came during the late 1960's from investigations by Sen. William Proxmire's Joint Economic Committee's Subcommittee on Economy in Government. Heeding Pres. Eisenhower's warning of "unwarranted influence, whether sought or unsought, by the military industrial complex," Proxmire investigated some abuses within the system. It was not that the Senator debated the rationale for a strong military and munitions industry; rather he did not feel that such an industry could justify the development of inefficient or defective weapons, expensive cost overrides, and costly publicity campaigns on behalf of new weapons systems.

The information that Proxmire presented to Congress in the spring of 1969 was alarming. *More than 2,000 retired military officers, he revealed, were employed by the leading 100 defense contractors. Among them, these companies held more than $26 billion worth of prime military contracts, or some 67 per cent of the total defense budget.* Among the major defense contractors involved in producing key components of our anti-ballistic missile system, nine employed 465 retired officers. The Senator did not go so far as to imply any sort of conspiracy between the military and the defense contractors, but pointed to the dangers of a relationship between the two.

When former high-ranking officers have ready entrée to the Pentagon, it is not difficult to see how favoritism can influence decisions, how the armed forces can be cajoled into overlooking cost overruns, how "unacceptable" weapons can be accepted, and so on. In a world where prime military weapons can be produced under contracts that generally exceed their estimates by 100 to 200 per cent, it does not take an expert to guess that something might be askew.

One of the most controversial instances of undue influence possibly affecting a Defense department decision was that of the award of a contract to build the F-111 fighter-bomber in 1962. Today, more than 15 years later, the decision to choose General Dynamics rather than Boeing for the project is still a matter of discussion. Since billions of taxpayers' dollars are involved, it might be instructive to recall some of the points of contention.

Although the conception and procurement of the F-111 was perhaps the proudest accomplishment of Robert McNamara during his tenure as Secretary of Defense, others consider it a mammoth boondoggle. I. F. Stone, for example, in an article entitled *Nixon and the Arms Race*, raised the question of "improper influence" playing a role in the selection. Stone notes that when the award was made, "McNamara was wrong in giving the F-111 contract to General Dynamics instead of Boeing, in having the same plane be adapted for the diverse needs of the Air Force and the Navy, and in surrendering to the pressure of the Air Force for a new bomber and the Navy for a new missile weapons system to meet a non-existent Soviet bomber threat."

As evidence, he offers some interesting revelations:

In 1960, General Dynamics had suffered a loss of over $20 million—and the award to build the new fighter-bomber was "the company's only hope of being saved" from collapse.

"The major law firm of Cravath, Swaine and Moore became counsel for General Dynamics in the late 1950's. Roswell Gilpatric, Under Secretary of the Air Force from 1951 to 1953, and No. 2 man to McNamara from 1961 to 1964, was also a lawyer with Cravath, Swaine and Moore. Gilpatric played a major role in awarding the F-111 contract. General Dynamics had other close ties to the military. The company's president in the 1950's was former Secretary of the Army Frank Pace. Fred Korth, who was made Secretary of the Navy by the Kennedy administration, was a Fort Worth banker, and past president of Continental Bank, which had loaned money to General Dynamics."

Stone ends his analysis of the situation by concluding that General Dynamics won the contract because the military "didn't want the weaker of the two companies to go down the drain. General Dynamics was based in Texas, which traditionally has been known as a 'swing state' with 24 electoral votes, and its biggest contractor on the F-111 was in New York with 45 votes. Boeing would have produced the plane in Kansas, which has only eight electoral votes, and in Washington state with only nine votes."

In other words, "commonality" played a role in the decision. "What is best for General Dynamics," says Stone, "is best for the country."

It would be an error to say that the strong personal ties between men involved in the F-111 decisions fostered corruption of any sort, but still the question must be asked: Even if there was no chicanery, what about other parties in similar situations? In matters where billions of dollars are involved, where the survival of the nation is perhaps at stake, is there room for the slightest taint of profiteering? Can the country afford the chance of even one person acting primarily to line his own pocket?

In dealing with the military's decisions a "civilian" (who is automatically an "outsider," someone who will not understand) must endeavor to comprehend the military mind. A key part of the training of any man or woman in the armed forces involves discipline. Orders are given, and are to be obeyed. No questions are to be asked, no answers need be given. Under such a system it is easy for an individual with corrupt intentions to force others to do his bidding.

The files of the services are filled with cases of black marketeering, traffic in narcotics, misappropriation of government funds and material, and numerous other crimes. Often they were the work of men and women who claimed the "system" had destroyed them as individuals, had turned them into ciphers, faceless soldiers who had lost concern for their fellows. In such an existence, they ask, is it wrong to turn to petty crime?

If the reader has any doubt that the military can be a brutalizing experience for some individuals, recall the clamor that arose around Presidio Camp roughly a decade ago. Presidio was a penal camp for military prisoners in California. It hit the headlines after 27 soldiers broke formation in the work line one morning to demand attention from the press and higher military authorities. Conditions at the camp, they charged, bordered on the horrendous and inhuman.

The men—or boys, in some instances, since the average age was 19—were charged with mutiny, the most serious of all charges under the Military Code of Justice and one seldom used in modern times. Three of the 27 fled to Canada before a courts martial hearing could be held; charges against two were eventually reduced to the lesser crime of disobeying an order. The others underwent a full hearing that produced some sobering facts.

At the time of the sitdown in the Presidio, it was revealed, 120 men were held in confinement in a space meant to hold only 88. With 140 prisoners in the camp, there were only four toilets. The facility was rat-infested, and medical attention was slow in coming—even to the prisoners who made suicide attempts. *There were 52 such attempts in 1968*, said inmates, including attempts by hanging, drinking of lye, and slitting of throats and wrists. Said one attorney for the defense: "The whole incident was an effort—a misguided, perhaps foolish appeal—to beseech the properly constituted authorities to recognize that grievances existed, and that those grievances had a real basis in fact. There were sadistic prison guards and inferior food and living conditions." The 22 soldiers nevertheless were convicted of mutiny.

According to Robert Sherrill, author of *Military Justice Is to Justice as Military Music Is to Music*, "to bring about these convictions, the Army spent a half-million dollars for investigators, court costs, attorneys' salaries, public relations campaigns, and travel." Speaking of the mutiny, a prosecuting attorney stated: "It is the attack on the system . . . that is important. . . . That's all we are concerned about."

In such a milieu, one in which men are dehumanized and—presumably—made into fighting machines, it is perhaps not unusual to spend a half-million dollars of taxpayers' money to resist an "attack on the system." But what is the meaning of democracy if the system cannot be questioned?

Is the military system then partly corrupt in itself? Answers might be found in the "cheating scandal" that rocked the United States Military Academy at West Point just a few years ago. On April 22, 1976, officials announced that the cadet honor boards had found 50 third-term cadets guilty of cheating on an engineering examination. The board had acquitted 49 other cadets; two more had resigned before charges could be pressed against them. A conviction under the cadet honor code entailed expulsion, and in the case of third- and fourth-year students could mean two years service in the Army as an enlisted man. Despite the threat of such severe punishment, more than 100 men had taken the risk. One cadet casually tossed off the danger, saying: "There is a lot of hypocrisy; this sort of thing goes on all the time."

Less than a month later Lieut. Gen. Sidney Berry, the

Academy's superintendent, reported that cheating was even more widespread than had previously been believed. An internal review panel of officers and cadets began conducting some 70 to 90 investigations of cases of suspected cheating. By September, 65 cadets had given sworn statements to several Congressmen that *some 700 of their classmates had engaged in practices that violated the honor code.*

Despite the contention of Secretary of the Army Marvin Hoffman that "the overwhelming majority of violators" in the scandal had already been uncovered, the investigations continued to turn up new names. Soon, however, a different form of corruption was at issue. Some of the accused cadets and Army lawyers charged that the Academy itself was limiting prosecutions in order to minimize the scandal. The charge was later supported by prosecutors in some of the honor code cases.

Lending credence to the idea that higher-ups were "soft-pedalling" the whole matter was the statement by Hoffman in January that 150 cadets who had been implicated in the scandal would be readmitted to the Academy. He also noted that the honor code which made expulsion mandatory for any violation would be altered in its language. The new wording would read that "A cadet will *normally* be separated for a violation."

To illustrate how the officers supposedly looking for violations of the ethics code themselves appeared to violate decent ethics, some cadets said they were forced to testify against themselves. An informal Congressional hearing was told by Army defense lawyers that their superiors had taken a dim view of their zealous efforts. Captain Daniel H. Sharpan, for example, told some 40 members of the House of Representatives that derogatory remarks had been entered in his personal file, and Captain Bunk E. Bishop said that he had been denied a transfer that ordinarily would have been granted as a matter of routine.

Gen. Goodpaster has perceived the true roots of the problem in saying that it lies not only with the individuals involved, or with the Army, *but with the entire society in which they live before entering the Academy.* The plebes who enter the school each year, he contends, are the product of a permissive society that teaches and preaches, "you scratch my back and I'll scratch yours." He believes that one way to overcome this kind of thinking is by requiring all first-year students to take two courses in ethics, and one course each year afterwards. He is right.

For West Point, it is a new kind of thinking. Previously the honor code that says, "A cadet will not lie, cheat, or steal, nor tolerate those who do," was considered sufficient. Now, says Gen. Goodpaster, it seems necessary to teach the cadets that committing such acts not only damages the moral fiber of the man or woman who lies or cheats, but also of the person who tolerates it—and, in time, the moral quality of the entire army.

In the ethics course, explains the Academy superintendent, "We put the problems on the tables. The cadets get a chance to talk them through and to come to grips with the consequences of cheating or lying or plagiarism." And, he adds, if a young junior officer finds himself faced with a situation in which he believes a superior is ordering him to do something that he feels is corrupt, his way out of the moral dilemma is simple: "All he has to do is ask his senior officer, 'Sir, are you asking me to send a false report?' That will do it," concludes Gen. Goodpaster.

There will still be complications, of course. The ultimate commander of the military forces is the President of the United States, and recent history attests that morality in that high office has not been all that it should be. If a young soldier cannot find the proper kind of leadership in the higher echelons of the military, he may conclude that he has no one to turn to in the event that he decides to disobey an order on ethical grounds.

It is hoped that the teaching of ethics in structured courses brings about a lessening of corruption at the lowest levels of a military officer's career—but a nagging question occurs: Will a scandal break about students cheating to pass their courses in ethics?

Meanwhile, in many parts of the nation the problem grows. Among the scandals presently troubling the Navy is a fraud-and-kickback system allegedly operating at the Naval Oceans Systems Center in San Diego, California, which became the target of a federal grand jury investigation in late 1978. According to the *San Diego Tribune* suspicion centered on four senior civil servants employed at the Systems Center and the president of a San Diego defense contracting firm. Indictments appeared to involve diversion of navy funds by means of dummy research projects.

Pressure to keep up with recruitment averages apparently led to the 1978 scandal in which the Alabama National Guard—according to a report by U.S. Army Major Francis J. Cummings—issued orders to its officials to work as recruiters on dates already in the past. The orders were backdated as part of a fraudulent collection of federal money for allegedly full days of recruiting service. Colonel William Cole of the Alabama Guard is suing Cummings on the ground that his constitutional rights were violated by actions that resulted in his being fired as a state personnel officer.

Chapter

Foul Balls and Errors in the Great American Games

"Say it ain't so, Joe."

Any student of the history of sports—and, particularly, of that great American pastime, baseball—knows the source of those words. According to legend they were spoken by a young street fan, to one of the players accused of taking part in the infamous Chicago "Black Sox" scandal of 1919. Tearful, hoping that some mistake had been made and the players were innocent, the youngster asked his impassioned question. He did not get the answer he wanted.

It is hard to believe that in the sixty years that have ensued since first baseman Chick Gandil persuaded seven other players to join him in rigging the outcome of several games, such naive young fans have not gone the way of the nickel hotdog. At the time the scandal disrupted the sportsworld, it was easy for the players and their lawyers to come up with excuses. Club owner Charles Comiskey, it was noted, was both tyrannical and stingy with his players. The team was wracked with dissension, with enmity among the players. And when a profitable offer came from gambling figures—well, why not? Take the money and run—or *don't* run too fast around the bases—was the attitude. It was a shock, all right. But in the overly-media'd world of today, six-year-old boys who follow sports know that tyrannical managers and teams torn by dissension are commonplace. So why should fixes, payoffs and corruption be anything other than usual?

There was a trial in 1921. The players involved were barred from the sport; the gamblers got off scot-free. Far from being the end of corruption in sports, the most famous "fix" of all time was only the beginning. Today almost every game—football, basketball, soccer, boxing, hockey, tennis— is big business and big money, and that means the profits from illicit endeavors can be bigger, too.

The probability of swindles in sports now is so widespread that few are above suspicion. Players can be bribed to lose games or "shave" points off the final score so that gamblers come out ahead. The growing ranks of agents and lawyers who work for the athletes are not unfamiliar with "deal-making." Team owners are subject to tempting offers from businessmen who want to see a big-league franchise in their locale. Even the television networks, whose initial responsibility was merely to cover the sporting events arranged by others, now are heavily into the business of promoting games and matches—a practice that has led to charges of cheating fans and viewers, and in turn, to the resignation of a network president.

With reports of such dishonesty almost routine, can fans of any age remember the line, "Say it ain't so, Joe," without shaking their heads? Today a similar situation might be greeted with a derisive question: "Hey, Joe, how much d' you get, 'n can you cut me in for a piece?"

That was the kind of question faced by 37-year-old Richard Sorkin, agent for a number of professional athletes. More than 50 hockey and basketball players were among Sorkin's clients. Perhaps "victims" would be a better word, since the trusted agent was charged with having misappropriated as much as $1.2 million worth of the players' funds. The case, which surfaced recently, began in 1959 when the youthful Sorkin got a job with a Long Island, N.Y., newspaper as a sports reporter. He quickly became friendly with players on the teams he covered, and, says a former colleague, "talked about money a lot."

After a few years Sorkin opened a public relations and advertising office. When his brother-in-law acquired a New York franchise in the World Hockey Association, the young entrepreneur strengthened his contacts with players. Then he discovered the Western Canada Hockey League and soon was dividing up players with a second agent—reputedly by paying $5,000 kickback fees to management who steered team members their way. Sorkin's responsibilities were to negotiate contracts, advise on financial matters and check the players' tax forms, in return for a 5½% cut of the players' earnings, a figure later increased to 7½.

Basketball stars came to Sorkin, too. A number of players granted him power-of-attorney, virtually giving him rights to spend their money as he saw fit. Few knew that he had lost his newspaper job a few years earlier because he had been reported conducting financial dealings with jockeys at various tracks.

With free access to the players' money, Sorkin plunged into the stock market. He also gambled away as much as $100,000 a week on horses, baseball games, and football parlays. His ties to gambling interests were not tenuous.

A Bronx bookmaker, Dominick Gentile, allegedly invested nearly $10,000 in Sports Worldwide, Inc., a small company established by Sorkin to market board games endorsed by such stars as tennis champion Bjorn Borg and others. Another bookmaker reportedly helped arrange for an $80,000 mortgage on Sorkin's Long Island home.

One of the first players to suspect something was wrong—after Sorkin repeatedly made him wait for funds that should have been in his bank balance—in 1976 hired a lawyer. His demand for an accounting produced a chain reaction. Other players sought proof that their funds were safe, but failed to get it. One lost $27,000 he thought was in a savings account, and discovered that his widowed mother's savings were gone as well. Others found that a total of $600,000 had vanished at the race track and $300,000 more had gone into stock market losses.

An isolated instance? Commissioner Larry F. O'Brien of

the National Basketball Association warned in a *New York Times* article that, sooner or later, "someone is going to realize that there are people walking around with briefcases in sports whom nobody knows and who are accountable to no one." Dennis Dillon, the Nassau County District Attorney who prosecuted Sorkin, agrees and has called for careful scrutiny of agents. There are calls for the licensing and bonding of agents who supervise multimillion-dollar salaries.

As for boxing, tales of crooked managers go back almost to the beginnings of the sport itself. Hollywood and writers of sports fiction have poured out countless tales of fighters' managers betting against their own clients, ordering them to "take a dive." Heavyweight contender Georges Carpentier was surprisingly candid: "I always took a dive when I felt I could not win. It is easy to make your nose bleed, you know."

Although the disreputable fight manager has become almost a cliche figure, few expected the television networks to get suckered in on a massive boxing fraud against the American public. At least the networks contend that they were suckered in, themselves defrauded.

ABC-TV, in 1976, made an exclusive deal with Sugar Ray Leonard, the Olympic light-welterweight champion. The fighter agreed to put three 1977 bouts on ABC for $120,000, and three more in 1978 for $200,000. The young folk-hero had chalked up a record of 145 wins in 150 amateur bouts, but now here he was on network television—on a network that had a great financial stake in his future. It would not do—would it?—to have him get knocked cold in the early bouts. So Leonard won.

But in December, 1977, just two weeks before the fighter was to climb into the ring with an opponent named Hector Diaz, ABC associate producer Alex Wallau made an interesting discovery. In looking over Diaz' record, he saw that the last five victories listed for him had never occurred. He brought his discovery to the network—which promptly cancelled the telecast, although the fight went on. Leonard won easily, and still collected his money from ABC.

For his services as an expert, Wallau was given $10,000 by the network—a payment it later had to deny was a silencing fee paid by Roone Arledge, president of ABC News and Sports. Still, there was evidence that Wallau had filed lengthy memoranda criticizing ABC for its projected series of U.S. Boxing Championship telecasts. Wallau complained that less than half of 56 fighters in the contests were "qualified" and 14 were "disgraces." The entire event was eventually suspended by the network after rumors of kickbacks, payoff, and unethical behavior.

NBC-TV, too, has had its problems with boxing. In a drive to improve its ratings, the network aligned itself with boxing promoter Don King. So? Well, King had been the guiding force behind the U.S. Boxing Championship on ABC. His relationship with that network brought ABC so much embarrassment, that the network hired an investigator to look into how the tournament was put together. The man they chose was Michael Armstrong, an attorney who had headed up New York's investigation into police corruption after the "Serpico" charges. Armstrong put together a force of ten attorneys, five law students, and private detectives. The result was a report 327 pages long. As a *Newsweek* editorialist put it, "The report describes enough nefarious goings-on to keep Charlie's Angels busy for a couple of years."

The conclusion of one investigator: "If Don King Productions must rely on people who have been shown to have been involved in irregular or unethical conduct in connection with the Tournament, or upon persons whose primary business is to manage or book fighters, then we believe that DKP cannot be relied upon to produce a national tournament that can meet the standards set by ABC."

Newsweek's William Leggett commented: "If King's operation was not good enough to meet ABC's standards last spring, it is hard to believe that it now measures up for NBC's telecast this week (*A Night With the Heavyweights*) or for the ABC presentation of the King-promoted Norton-Young fight scheduled for Nov. 5. The suspicion is that ethical considerations may have had little weight in NBC's or ABC's decisions to put on these fights. Once again, ratings may have taken precedence. The numbers show that fans are fascinated by boxing, and the networks want to cash in. . . ."

If cashing-in means working with people who are suspect—or worse—well, so be it. "Before we bought *A Night With the Heavyweights* from King," says Al Rush, executive vice president for NBC Sports, "we thought it over very carefully. Our conclusion was that, while there were all sorts of allegations against King, he has not been found guilty of anything."

Perhaps not, but the investigators who put together the Armstrong report had no subpoena powers—and so could not amass all the evidence they wanted.

CBS did not get involved with King, but two of the network's executives found themselves on the hot seat anyway after they signed an exclusive deal with Howard Davis, winner of a lightweight Olympic medal in 1976. Davis was to get between $1.3 million and $1.6 million to let CBS-TV broadcast 12 or 13 of his fights, over a three-year period. What aroused the ire of the House Subcommittee on Communications—was that Davis' contract allowed him to pay his opponents "some or all" of the $200,000 the network would give him for each fight. Davis would really have had to be punch-drunk, the Congressmen concluded, to pay his opponent the entire sum. In fact, they reasoned, the tendency would be for the fighter to find the cheapest possible opponent—maybe a worn-out has-been or an inexperienced kid with no record at all. The result might be fine for Davis, who could keep the bulk of the two-hundred grand, but the television audience might be subjected to some god-awful fights.

The Washington inquiry into the television and boxing connection raised fascinating questions. Are some fighters considered too good for some popular opponents, and so kept out of major TV bouts so that the public won't see its heroes defeated? Does a tie between a network and a boxer raise the suspicion that a fight has been fixed in favor of the TV "star?"

As reporter Sally Bedell noted in *TV Guide*, "In at least one case, the viewer was misled." She was talking about a Davis fight in which his opponent was described as "tough" and "dangerous"—adjectives that were applied to his opponents in five other bouts, as well. This time, Davis was up against one Jose Resto, who was repeatedly characterized on the air by announcer Tom Brookshier as "a tough little fighter." Resto, Brookshier told millions of viewers, "has been in the ring at least 100 times." Then, he added, "We're not even sure what is his record." A glance into any of several boxing reference books might have helped the announcer out. Resto had lost six times straight in one year, and had fought only 68 professional fights—*out of which he had lost 49.*

The Congressional committee asked questions of Barry Frank, then senior vice president for programming at CBS Sports, and Robert Wussler, then president of CBS Sports and later president of the television network for a brief time. The time was brief because, in the wake of a second sports scandal, Wussler first moved back to his old job and then out of CBS altogether.

Another questionable situation involved tennis, a sport which historically has been considered one of the most gentlemanly. Long played by the money-and-manners set, tennis began to attract major TV interest after the famous match that saw Billie Jean King defeat Bobby Riggs. Attendance figures soared with the increasing success of such superstars as Jimmy Connors, Ilie Nastase, Bjorn Borg and Chris Evert.

When CBS decided to offer viewers a series of matches featuring top players in a "World Heavyweight Tennis Championship" elimination, somebody within the organization decided that more viewers would tune in if the matches had an extra little fillip: They would be billed as "winner take all," meaning that one player might come out of the contest with several hundred thousand dollars—and the other would come out with nothing but aches and pains. Viewers were so advised in ads and on the air. Then it was learned that the matches were not "winner take all."

In every case the loser stood to go home with tens of thousands of dollars. In three matches, found the Federal

Communications Commission, there was no prize money at all. Each player was working for a prearranged fee. Still, the "winner take all" publicity drums kept beating.

Unfortunately for CBS the investigation into the arrangements behind the matches uncovered some other infractions of FCC rules. The Las Vegas hotel and casino, Caesars Palace, that served as the site for three matches got numerous plugs on the air—without anyone bothering to tell viewers that the mentions were in exchange for free rooms, meals, and other favors given by the hotel to the TV crews and announcers. Under FCC regulations put into effect after the scandals involving rigged quiz shows and payola, all programs that get "freebies" from hotels or airlines are obliged to announce the fact.

When Wussler testified in the inquiry over the "winner take all" matches, he evidently did not come as clean as some FCC members wished he might. Therefore, while the commission was weighing the kind of punishment it should mete out, the network brass decided to replace Wussler as president and had him step back into his old job as head of the sports division. When that failed to affect the FCC deliberations, Wussler resigned to become an independent producer.

The *New York Times* noted that Wussler's decision—made while the FCC jury was still out—had nothing to do with any scandal, or so said the new network president. "It's unfair to draw any implications from that," he said. "Bob [Wussler] and I have been talking for quite a long time about his becoming an independent producer. His background with the network has been as a producer, and he has a lot of very good ideas." And so the career of a top network executive came to an end at CBS, after 21 years there and at a time when he was on the verge of moving even higher at the parent corporation.

The players that took part in the phony "winner take all" matches were not chastised. Were they any more ethical than the network? But perhaps they were still looked on as *tennis players*, a different breed of athlete from money-hungry baseball players, football players or prizefighters.

There was a blow-up in tennis circles recently when two

leading players, Bjorn Borg and Guillermo Vilas, decided not to participate in a couple of late matches during a Grand Prix Masters tournament sponsored by Colgate-Palmolive Co. The "round robin" style of tournament is a promoter's dream because it guarantees that spectators will see every player meet every other player at least once, and so tickets can be sold far in advance and all the big names advertised. Scoring is done on the basis of games won and lost over the entire tournament, but the contestants in the final matches get to select their opponents under a complex statistical arrangement. The system produces a risk: a player can lose an earlier match deliberately in order to gain the advantage of selecting an easier opponent in the semifinals. The process is called "tanking."

In the Borg and Vilas affair, neither player set out to lose intentionally. But each decided not to play their scheduled matches against challengers, pleading illness or exhaustion, and losing by default. In Borg's case, the "loss" caused him to wind up second in the rankings in his group of players—and, under the rules, that meant he would be paired off against the No. 1 player in the opposing group. That put Borg against Vilas in the semifinals, rather than against Jimmy Connors—whom he would have faced had he won the defaulted match. Borg had beaten Vilas 11 out of 15 times, whereas he had lost to Connors 7 out of 10 times in previous matches.

The move may seem a smart one. No one was harmed—unless it was the spectators who laid out as much as $20 a ticket to see the matches. They travelled many miles, some of them, to get to Madison Square Garden, arranged for babysitters and cancelled other engagements. And they wound up watching some relatively unknown players putting on a hastily-arranged exhibition.

David R. Foster, Colgate's chairman of the board, contended that the public was not cheated. He compared the situation to one where someone buys a ticket to a Broadway show and then finds the star is out sick and the understudy is taking his place. Is it the same? Why can't tennis players operate under the same rules as Olympic athletes—who, if they pull a hamstring or otherwise get injured in an earlier match, either must withdraw from later matches or tape up their injuries and compete?

Then there's the sport of horse racing, where fixing races has gone on for centuries. Consider the "ringer" scandal that recently rocked tracks on two continents and put a veterinarian from Long Island, N.Y., in a position where he faced two years imprisonment.

The tale of deception began when a horse named Lebon, a long shot, scored an impressive and surprising victory in a race at Belmont Park. When pictures of the horse appeared in a newspaper in Uruguay, racing experts there were puzzled. The horse in the photographs resembled another South American horse, Cinzano, a big-money winner that supposedly had been destroyed after he became injured in an accident.

An investigation revealed that both horses had been purchased by Dr. Mark Girard, a veterinarian familiar with racetrack procedures. Actually, as Girard testified, Cinzano was purchased for one Joseph Taub, a New Jersey horse owner, and Lebon was purchased by another man—but both animals wound up on the vet's farm. There, after suffering a fractured skull when he reared and struck his head on a door in his stall, Cinzano had to be destroyed. An insurance company paid Taub, the "owner," $150,000 for his loss. Then it turned out that a mistake had taken place. The horse that was destroyed appears to have been Lebon, a $9,500 nag. And then Cinzano, renamed Lebon, was entered in the Belmont race.

In repeated trips to the $50 window, Gerard wagered $1,300 on Lebon. He collected winnings of $77,000 after the 57-to-1 shot came flying down the stretch. Not bad for a few days' work.

In a two-week trial, Gerard presented as his defense the contention that the switch of horses had been done without his knowledge by his estranged wife, Alice. Mrs. Gerard testified that she had gone to South America on a horse-hunting expedition, and after seeing Cinzano had purposely sought out a "garbage" horse with similar markings. The jury deliberated for 10 hours before it found Gerard guilty of two counts of "entering a horse in a contest of speed under a false name."

During the investigation of Gerard, it appeared that the Cinzano-Lebon case was not the only time that the vet was suspected of shady maneuvering. He purchased a horse named As De Pique II in 1975 in Argentina, and was believed to have bought a faster thoroughbred, Enchumao, shortly afterwards. Enchumao was supposed to have died in Florida, but officials wondered if a similar switch had not taken place. They knew for certain that the long-shot, As De Pique II, came in first in two races, paying $85 in one and $42 in the other for a $2 bet.

Gerard's name surfaced in another "horse sale swindle" as well, this time involving a businessman named Marvin Kraut. Kraut sued trainer Mervin Marks, who introduced him to Gerard, who had a horse named Pomeroy for sale for $30,000. Pomeroy, originally a prize in a $2 raffle in Argentina, had been purchased by Gerard for $15,000. When Kraut decided not to buy the horse, Gerard sold him to a California woman for $75,000 with the assurance that the animal was a winner. Two years later, the horse had not won a race and the owner was claiming that she had been "royally gypped."

Meanwhile trainer Marks promised to get another horse for Kraut for his $30,000. A few weeks later he phoned from Kentucky to say he had found one, Ole Bob Lehmann, on the famous Golden Chance Farm, and that it was a bargain at the price. Kraut wrote out a check to Golden Chance and took possession of the horse—which failed to win a race after a few weeks of starts. Noting that Marks had failed to give him a bill of sale on Ole Bob Lehmann, Kraut phoned the farm and discovered that the records there showed a surprising fact: that he had purchased *two* horses on the same day, Ole Bob Lehmann for $15,000 and a horse named Double Command for another $15,000. He was sent notarized bills of sale on both horses and promptly went to the Belmont Park officials to complain that Marks had "stolen" a horse from him.

An inquiry revealed that Marks had looked at Double

Command on the same day he found Ole Bob Lehmann for Kraut, but the trainer said he was interested in Double Command as a purchase for another friend, Dan Marentette. Marentette bought the horse, said Marks, then sold it after a few weeks to Mrs. Albert Katz in California. Three weeks later, the horse was returned to him in New York, where it was raced in his wife's name, Sheila Marentette. The Marks then sold a half-interest in Double Command to a Mr. A. Marks (no relation) in Houston, Tex. And then a few months later the horse was claimed for $18,000 by another trainer, José Martin.

While judges and juries try to untangle that situation, officials at other tracks are wrestling with a series of charges by those closest to the horses, the jockeys. A female rider named Debby Hicks rocked Hazel Park Race Track in Pontiac, Mich., with complaints of fixed races and widespread corruption. She said that most jockeys "hold horses" so they could cash bets on them, and also charged that there was widespread use of electrical devices—known as "batteries" or "buzzers"—to give a lagging horse a jolt that would spur him on to the finish wire. A few days after she made the charges, the 23-year-old woman found herself arrested after someone complained that she had written checks with insufficient funds.

"I can't trust jockeys and even other owners or trainers," she said.

It's hard not to think of the title of Johnny Carson's old afternoon game show, *Who Do You Trust?*, when the subject of sports corruption comes up.

The agents, players, managers? But wait a minute. How about the landlords, the people who own the stadiums where the events take place? Aren't they far enough removed from the sometimes illegal goings-on down on the field and at the betting windows to deserve a reputation for honesty?

Not always, if the recent situation involving New York City's Yankee Stadium is any example. The office of John F. Keenan, a special prosecutor for the state, was looking into

possible corruption by city officials in the awarding of contracts and the approval of minority-controlled subcontracting companies for the $55 million modernization of the
stadium. One of the key questions was: had there been
kickbacks or collusion on the stadium's plumbing contract?
The original low bidder for the work, the B.L. & A. Construction Co., was allowed to drop out of the bidding after
the bids were opened—but then was quietly awarded a
$342,000 subcontract by the company that replaced it.

Suspicions were raised when it was learned that the
kind of work B.L. & A. was to do—excavation and installation of piping—is normally *not* subcontracted. Then it was
determined that the obscure Bronx company had been approved by city officials as being especially worthy of getting
subcontracting jobs because it is run by "minorities," although *it had no black or Hispanic officers.* There also was a
"significant" financial relationship between B.L. & A. and a
rare coin firm in Westchester County suspected of being
dominated by organized crime.

While city officials came under fire, the Yankees themselves found that they were on the receiving end of some
serious charges of wrongdoing. In 1976, for example, the
Yankees were supposed to pay the city $800,000 in rent on
the stadium. Instead, the city paid *them* $10,000. In 1977,
instead of paying $1 million in rent, the team paid only
$170,000. Maintenance costs, which are deductible from
rent, made the difference, the Yankees claimed.

Arousing doubts, however, were the ways the Yankees
figured their maintenance costs. It was shown that part of
the cost of a television commercial made by Catfish Hunter,
Yankee pitcher, was charged off to the city as a maintenance
cost. A similar instance occurred when former Yankee great
Joe DiMaggio made a TV commercial. And, it turned out, no
city agency had been given the task of looking over the
$800,000 worth of maintenance-cost vouchers the Yankees
submitted each year, to see if they were correct.

"It seems certain," said an official of the comptroller's
office, "that we will have to go behind the scenes and check
with the companies that issued the bills to the Yankees for
maintenance work. We have bills from the Yankees. But

looking at the bills is not enough. So you have a bill. You still don't know if the charges are correct."

How about amateur sports? Well, the world of amateur athletics would seem as greedy as the professional one. The picture was summed up once by John Smith, world record holder in the 440-yard dash. "I've always spelled amateur m-o-n-e-y," he said.

Some of the hypocrisy that covers up much of the illicit dealings in the amateur environment was dispelled recently when Dwight Stones, two-time Olympic medalist in the high jump, filed a lawsuit against the Amateur Athletic Union. He charged the AAU with anti-trust violations, fraud, unfair competition and involuntary servitude, complained that he had been blackmailed, enslaved, and conspired against by a dictatorial monopoly. At the heart of his charges was the fact that the AAU had barred Stones from competition on the grounds that he had improperly diverted money in violation of regulations. Stones and three women athletes—Francie Larrieu, Jane Frederick, and Kate Schmidt—were banned for life after they competed on ABC-TV's *Superstars* program and earned a total of $58,000. They did not take the cash, the AAU acknowledges, but had the money go to their respective local track clubs. Stones' Desert Oasis Track Club got $33,400, and the women's Pacific Coast Club got $24,600.

Stones' resultant suit unearthed some of the abuses that are part of the amateur sports scene. "For years," wrote Judson Klinger in *New West* magazine, "track stars have received 'under the table' expenses and generous appearance fees from meet promoters. The knowledge of these payoffs is so widespread that the IRS last year opened investigations into the personal finances of many top American competitors."

Klinger quotes Steve Smith, former world record holder in the pole vault, as saying, "The word 'amateur' is a joke. I know people who are making $100,000 and more as amateurs." Former 1968 Olympic champion Bob Seagren agrees: "There's not a top amateur today in existence who's not taking money under the table ... If you're a name athlete and there's two track meets the same night in different cities, you can just barter back and forth with the meet promoters. You name your price. You can make a nice living off it."

Seagren, noting that prices probably are higher today, admits that he received "on the average, probably around $2,000 per meet" in the late 1960s.

No one would argue that the amateur taking money is something new. Early in the century Olympic champion Jim Thorpe was stripped of his medals simply because he had played semiprofessional baseball before his Olympic victories. In the 1950s, after he accepted double air fare as his "expenses" from a promoter, miler Wes Santee was barred from competition for life. What drives the athletes up the wall is the selective way the AAU seems to apply its punishment. Frequently, it is charged, the organization uses its sanctions to stomp out competition. In the case of Stones and the others who appeared with him on *Superstars*, the athletes ran afoul of a dispute between the AAU and a rival organization, the International Amateur Athletic Federation. The international group convinced Stones that it had jurisdiction over the program, which is more an entertainment event than a true athletic competition, and that a contribution to his track club was legal. The AAU ruled otherwise. An initial request by Stones for an order that would allow him to compete while his court case drags on was denied. Months and possibly years will pass before the case is resolved.

In the sports world—whether amateur or professional— the idea evidently is that everyone should get his (or hers, in recognition of the increasing role of the female athlete). And more and more, it appears, the only person who is not being cut in on the financial pie is the fan—the man or woman who turns out to watch the big money players who are backed by the big money owners and the big money gamblers. When we talk deceit and fraud, it cheers us to see that others are starting to recognize that perhaps it is the fan who is being made into a victim.

One of the primary culprits in this unhappy state of affairs is television. The people who run the TV networks think nothing of taking advantage of the spectators who show up to watch events in person. Take what happened at the Grand Slam of Tennis competition at Boca Raton, Florida, for example. Thousands of fans had bought tickets for the event, which was scheduled to start at 1 P.M. Unfortunately, to accommodate the TV taping schedule, the starting time had been moved up to 12:30. When the fans arrived— late—they found they could not get to their seats until an hour after the matches began, and down the drain went their money. A similar thing happened when fans turned out for a 15-round featherweight title fight in Oklahoma City. The World Boxing Association refused to sanction the bout, and NBC subsequently cancelled its telecast. The promoters then had to call off the fight, despite the fact that tickets had been sold to fight fans anxious to see the bout—sanctioned or not.

The "corporatizing" of sport, as Ralph Nader and Peter Gruenstein called it in a *Playboy* article, is benefiting everyone but the fan. Those ticketbuyers—some 300 million strong—will pay about $2 billion this year to witness sports events in person. Some 40 million will subscribe to sports magazines. The TV networks will spend more than $350 million to broadcast about 1,200 hours of sports events. And a lot of people—players, gamblers, owners, but not the ordinary fan—will grow rich.

Consider the case of Robert Short and the baseball team that was the Washington Senators of 1969. Short, who had grown rich from his hotel and trucking company businesses in Minneapolis, bought the team that year for $9 million. But he actually laid out only $1,000 in cash, according to a study made in 1971 by two economists working with the Brookings Institution. They found that Short had made a complicated series of loans involving himself and his other businesses, and that he was entitled to depreciate most of the full purchase price of the team over a five-year period. By using his paper losses, Short could put income from his other businesses under a tax-shelter arrangement that would give him $500,000 a year in tax savings. "In comparison," said the *Playboy* article authors, "an average investor would need about $6 million to ensure such a return."

Short promptly instituted the highest ticket prices in

the American League, then sold a number of promising young ballplayers for operating cash. But after two years, deciding that baseball wasn't for him, he put the club up for sale for $12 million. When no one bit, he sought permission from the rest of the league to move to Texas, midway between Fort Worth and Dallas. Texas interests, anxious to have big-league ball in their state, arranged for a number of sweetheart deals, including an advance of $7.5 million from several banks to be loaned against future broadcast revenues. This allowed the club owner to pay off most of the loans he had taken out.

In two years, he had converted $1,000 into a paid-off franchise and still had three years left to make use of the tax shelter. So he cheerfully sold off 90 per cent of his interest in the ball club for $8.3 million. It was all possible, of course, because baseball has been a legally sanctioned monopoly since 1922, when the Supreme Court ruled that the game did not constitute interstate commerce. This ruling came down despite the fact that teams move freely from state to state to play each other, and fans in one state can readily purchase tickets to watch teams play in another state. The ruling (and a similar antitrust exemption for football recently voted by Congress) allow the owners of teams to do just about anything they want: Move entire teams to other cities, charge whatever they want to, and take advantage of their fans if they so choose.

When hit by complaints that such teams as the Washington Redskins charge up to $20 for a ticket to a football game and the New York Knicks get $12.50 for a basketball game, the owners cite rising costs as the reason for what looks like gouging. But the Brookings study contended that the real villain is profit maximization; that is, the owners' desire to charge as much as the traffic will bear. "Prices tend to be positively correlated with attendance, which indicates that team owners respond to higher demand by *raising* prices," said the Brookings economists.

Fans, too, end up paying through the nose in their role as taxpayers. New York City was on the verge of bankruptcy when it spent $100 million—more than four times the original estimate—to modernize Yankee Stadium. The Houston

Astrodome cost the city $43 million in 1965, and the New Orleans Superdome came in at a whopping $173 million. As if that isn't enough, most teams require season-ticket buyers to put up their money for seats several months before the players take the field. That way, the owners collect interest on their customers' money. Then there's the question of fans being deluded by TV and radio announcers who actually are hired by the team owner. To help correct these and many other abuses, Nader and Gruenstein set up an organization called F.A.N.S., for Fight to Advance the Nation's Sports. It is supposed to represent the interests of fans before various government bodies, the leagues, owners, and the broadcast media.

"It is time for fans to stop being spectators," say an angry Nader and Gruenstein, as they raise a cry for the abolition of any number of abuses that are part of today's sporting scene. They would like artificial turf eliminated, for example, along with announcers hired by the teams whose games they broadcast. They would like "wholesome, reasonably priced food" sold at sporting events. They want fans polled regularly on pressing issues—rule changes, night games, and the like—before arbitrary decisions are made. And they want operating costs and profits on the teams made public so that fans and sportswriters could evaluate the need for ticket price increases and taxpayer support.

All that. And membership only costs $9 per year. I hope Nader has as much luck here as he did with the Corvette.

Chapter **XV**

Let the Buyer Beware— of Dishonest Ads

It was a simple two-line ad placed in the classified sections of hundreds of newspapers across the country. "Last chance to send your dollar to Box 214, in care of this newspaper!" But the results were phenomenal. According to court records more than 140,000 people—not knowing why they were responding, not knowing what they were supposed to get for their money—placed a dollar bill in an envelope and mailed it to the post office box. And what did they get?

Nothing. What else?

The only one who got something from his advertising scheme was the shrewd mail-order clerk at a novelty company who had observed how eagerly people entrust money to the mails—and who proved that a clever ad could entice thousands to part with their hard-earned cash. In court it was shown that he had broken no law. He had not failed to make good on any promises, since he had made none. He got off scot-free.

Thousands also have bit in recent years on another ad that offers a sure-fire "roach killer" for a buck or two. *No chemicals!* says the ad. *No sprays. No dangerous poisons. Safe to use even with small children around. Never misses. Sure-fire!* What do they get? Two blocks of wood fastened to the ends of a short length of string. And a sheet of instructions that tell you to catch a roach, place it on one of the wood blocks—and crush it with the other.

A joke? Perhaps, but thousands were sold to unsuspecting victims. Such frauds ripped off millions of Americans for some 514 million dollars in 1977, a 25% increase over the year before. And postal authorities say that only about 5% of dissatisfied customers ever bother to complain.

Mail fraud is only a small part of the crooked system employed by advertisers to deceive the public. Because the con usually involves a direct appeal for money in exchange for a promised product or service, it is relatively simple to bring legal action against those who take the money and run. As consumers, state and city governments, and the federal authorities have all found, it is not so easy to get back at those who perpetrate another kind of fraud: These are some of the nation's largest corporations which sometimes use deceitful and even downright false advertising to sell products. In many instances, the products draw hundreds of millions of dollars out of the pockets of gullible consumers and prove to be—if not patently dangerous, as in the case of Firestone's much-publicized self-destructing tires—at least less than their advertising claims make them out to be. And, in some case, they are worthless.

Edward Buxton, advertising writer for 20 years and publisher of a trade paper called *Ad Daily*, listed in a book entitled *Promise Them Anything* the names of some of the prestigious companies "caught in lies, misrepresentations, misleading claims, spurious demonstrations, half-truths, false testimonials, and contrived picturizations." Among his examples: American Home Products, Bristol-Myers, Campbell Soup, Coca-Cola, Colgate-Palmolive, Carter-Wallace, the aforementioned Firestone Tire, Lever Brothers, Mattel Toys, Philip Morris, Sterling Drug, and J. B. Williams. These and others, Buxton says, "have been called to account for advertising action that, if not actually illegal, has been sufficiently questionable to be cited by the Federal Trade Commission or the Food and Drug Administration."

There is little doubt that Madison Avenue has no respect for the intelligence of the American consumer. But some of the stunts that admen have pulled to prove the superiority of the products they advertise have been so blatant one wonders. Take the case of the automobile window in which a television commercial demonstrated how clear the glass was in comparison to the window of a rival car. "Look," said the announcer. "Our glass shows no reflections, no streaks, and you can see through it almost as if it wasn't there at all."

A convincing on-camera demonstration. The only problem—as the FTC pointed out to the advertising agency involved—was that when the commercial had been photographed, the car window had been rolled down. The glass wasn't there at all! In its defense the agency claimed that the window glass was every bit as clear and transparent as it said—but that the large numbers of floodlights used in the TV studio made it impossible to shoot the window without reflections.

The same kind of "defense" was offered by one of the world's largest ad agencies when the FTC challenged a commercial for Campbell's Soup. The vegetable broth appeared to be thick with peas, carrots, and other tempting morsels—far more, a rival soup manufacturer complained, that were contained in the typical can of Campbell's. The ensuing investigation brought out that the director of the commercial had not actually loaded his on-camera bowl of soup with more vegetables than it should have had; but he had dropped some clear glass marbles into a bowl, then carefully poured the soup and vegetable bits on top of the marbles. The idea, he explained, was to let the viewers see the vegetables floating on the surface of the soup. Without the marbles, they tended to sink.

The director, agency, and client—need it be said?—thought that nothing wrong had taken place. And Campbell's sold millions of cans of soup.

Such efforts to bend the truth were more common not

long ago. Colgate-Palmolive's agency, to demonstrate that a shaving cream could soften a man's beard more effectively than competing brands, came up with the infamous "sandpaper" demonstration. In the commercial the cream was spread on a piece of sandpaper and made it so soft that one swipe of a safety razor actually "shaved" the sand off the paper. If it could work like that on sandpaper, said the announcer, imagine how well it works on your beard!

The problem—as the FTC found out—was that the sandpaper used in the demonstration wasn't the usual kind. It was a sheet of plexiglass that had been dusted with sand. Again the agency's defense was that studio heat and lights made it impossible to use actual sandpaper in the demonstration, but that the cream really did the job the commercial said it did. The commission ordered the agency to use no more "mock-ups" in the future.

The same kind of ruling was handed down in a case that charged the makers of Chevron gasoline with deception. In a TV commercial the exhaust gases from two cars—one running on Chevron, the other on a rival brand—were collected inside two clear plastic balloons hooked over the exhaust pipes. The gas from the car using the rival brand was inky black; the Chevron exhaust was virtually clear. How was it done? Simply by making sure, said the FTC, that the motor of the car running on the rival brand was "unusually dirty." The commission was also unhappy about another bit of deception used in the commercial. The test took place in front of an impressive building that bore a large sign reading *Research Center*. The building actually was a city hall in a small town that had been borrowed for the afternoon.

Such instances have spurred government and citizens' watchdog groups to militancy. New regulations and restrictions have been passed with such frequency that Madison Avenue worried that it would be put out of business, since all ads might have to carry so many footnotes and clarifying clauses that they would be unreadable. Sure, the government said, you can say that a slice of Profile has fewer calories than a slice of a rival bread, but you must explain that it's because Profile is sliced thinner. Sure, you can say that Bufferin gets into the bloodstream faster than a competing analgesic, but you must point out that a few seconds' difference in reaching the bloodstream has nothing to do with how fast a user gets relief from pain of a headache, and that such relief in any event is still six to ten minutes away. If you're going to say, "Six out of ten medical men prefer . . ." make sure the men you show in the commercial who are wearing white coats are actually doctors and not just a bunch of actors dressed up.

Today the commercials turned out by every major agency are approved not only by the client but by a battery of lawyers. Nothing gets to the public, the agencies claim, that is not honest and realistic. You would think that they would indeed try to make sure, because the government has recently come up with a new kind of punishment for companies that employ deceptive ads. The punishment is referred to as "corrective advertising," which means that the offender must run ads that refute what was said in the past. Most recently, for example, the makers of Listerine mouthwash and antiseptic were ordered to run a series of corrective ads saying that, despite years of earlier claims, Listerine does not prevent colds or sore throats.

Corrective advertising has been proposed in few cases thus far, and of course by the time they are called for, the damage has been done. Hundreds of millions of bottles of Listerine have been sold over the years, and all the corrective ads in the world will not un-sell them.

Obtaining such rulings is an expensive and time-consuming task for the government (and, remember, the money comes from you). Highly-paid lawyers for corporations that spend millions on advertising know how to stall prosecution for years. Indeed in most of the cases where a company is charged with a deceptive ad campaign, a decision is not reached until long after the campaign itself is off the air or out of magazines and newspapers. And then the judgment usually handed down simply orders the advertiser to stop using the campaign!

To illustrate how effectively an advertiser can tie a government investigation in knots, the makers of a laxative long known as Carter's Little Liver Pills were ordered by the FTC to take the word "Liver" out of the product name.

The reason: the product had absolutely no effect on the human liver. The manufacturer, Carter Products Inc., fought the order for an incredible *16 years* before it complied with the ruling. Nearly a decade later, *New York Times* columnist James Reston reported how firmly the product name had stuck in people's minds: During the 1976 Presidential election campaign, said Reston, most people in the West thought Carter was "a liver pill." There is no way to calculate how many people spent how many millions of dollars on this product—and are still spending it. And there is no way to calculate how many thousands of people suffering with a liver ailment put off seeing a doctor because they believed that Carter's Little Liver Pills were doing them some good.

The advertising industry, worried about stricter regulations, works with the Better Business Bureau to police advertising, but BBB action is usually too little and too late.

Anyone who has ever tried taking a complaint to the Bureau will know what I mean. The typical local agency has no police authority to get your money back from the phoney storm-window salesman or used-car dealer who has gypped you. If it gets enough complaints it can withdraw whatever "certificate of good practice" it has given a local merchant. A lot of good that does those who have been defrauded.

In the advertising watchdog operation set up by the Council of Better Business Bureaus, a National Advertising Review Board looks into complaints brought against *major* advertisers. But by the time the NARB studies the complaints to see if they are worthy of further consideration, and by the time it calls a panel together to make some kind of ruling, the ads usually have run their course. Nevertheless, the watchdog continues to bark. It seldom, however, bites.

In the seven years since it was formed in 1971, the NARB has received a total of 1,380 complaints. (Although it receives complaints from BBB offices throughout the country, a pre-screening service weeds out many that do not deal with national advertising or which are not considered worthy of study.) What happened to the complaints it agreed to investigate? 530 were dismissed when advertisers provided "adequate substantiation" for their claims. Nearly 300 were marked "case closed" because of various administrative procedures. About 65 were still pending as this is written. 474 were settled after the advertiser agreed to modify the ad or discontinue it altogether. In the majority of "discontinue" rulings, of course, the ads long since were out of the picture.

In one case the Procter & Gamble Co. was accused of saying its Bold detergent would wash clothes "brighter" than any other detergent on the market. A majority of panel members rejected the complaint, saying that use of the word "brighter" was not specific enough for a ruling. But dissenting panel members held that the commercial misled substantial numbers of consumers. These consumers, they argued, had been falsely convinced that if they wanted to buy a detergent with "brighteners," they would have to buy Bold. P&G, of course, went right on using the commercial.

Block Drug Co., manufacturer of the sleep-aid product Nytol, did not do so well in another case. One of its ads suggested that the results of a medical study showed that other sleep-aid products contained a harmful ingredient. Nytol, without the ingredient, was said to be safe and superior. The NARB panel decided that the ad made misleading use of the medical study and Block Drug agreed to drop it. It did not admit to having made any mistake or to having had any intent to delude the public, however. Instead the company issued a statement in which it sought to clarify the situation: The medical study, it contended, had mentioned three products by their trade names as having the harmful ingredient—but Nytol itself had not even been included in the study. Therefore, the advertiser and its agency contended, the ad in question was the result of an error or some confusion. Obviously, there had been nothing intentionally deceptive on anyone's part. Uh-uh. Nothing at all.

There was no intent to fool anyone, either, when Zenith Radio Corp. ran ads for its television sets saying they were "U.S.-made by Americans," even though nearly 15% of the components in the sets were foreign. And Allen Products Co., the maker of Alpo dogfood, had nothing deceptive in mind when they claimed that Alpo Beef Chunks Dinner was an "all meat product"—even though they knew it contained soy flour.

Of course not.

In the last-cited cases, advertisers agreed to modify their

claims in future commercials. But no one said anything about giving money back. To force such an action would have taken years in the courts and an expenditure of many hundreds of thousands of dollars, a factor that encourages advertisers to be loose with their claims and extremely casual in their regard for the public. They know that in most instances it's a case of locking the barn door long after the horse has been stolen—and the advertiser who promises "never to make that claim again" is all too likely to make another claim, one just as insubstantial as the first, in his future ads.

It is difficult to understand how the current generation of Americans, brought up with a television medium that bombards them with ads day and night, can fail to be skeptical. And yet the majority of young men and women I meet appear to be trusting, willing to part with their money if a TV spot is colorful enough, a magazine ad headlined intriguingly enough, or a brochure in the mailbox plaintive enough. Writers Steve Lawrence and Karl Lauby, in the New York *Sunday News Magazine*, told the story of a number of young people who were taken in by all sorts of deceptive ads.

Louis Collins, 18, was one. He fell for a pitch that began with an unsolicited invitation that asked him and his parents to attend a dinner to learn about a retirement village called Rio Rancho in Albuquerque, N.M. "We went to this swell dinner," Collins said, "and when our bellies were full and our minds were lax, they gave us this pitch about land in New Mexico." Collins signed a contract, got a loan for part of the money, then worked nights and taught part time at drug treatment centers to make enough for the payments. When the entire Rio Rancho operation turned out to be a fraud, he was out $3,000. And he was bitter: "The bastards got the money: there's nothing on that land and never will be. You work your butt off and believe in people, and look what you get."

A main ingredient in getting ripped off by mail, say Lawrence and Lauby, is an ad that looks foolproof simply because it says "guaranteed" or "no risk, money back if not satisfied." (One scam artist who was caught explained, "I meant I'd give the money back if *I* wasn't satisfied, and I am.") A Brooklyn promoter came up with a scheme that most intelligent people would think laughable, but he collected nearly $300,000 with it. He simply ran an ad for a new weight-loss program called Grapho-Therapeutics. People were asked to send $7.95 and a sample of their handwriting to get a diet prepared exclusively for their use by a graphologist who could distinguish their personality traits from the loops and swirls in the handwriting sample. The guy who pulled it off went to jail on 18 counts of mail fraud, but made no refunds.

The sharpsters who clean up quickly with fraudulent advertising are often those who jump in on new "fads" at the beginning. In Chicago, for instance, when digital watches were still selling for $100 and up, a company called Teltronics Ltd. began offering watches for $16.95 each. It even promised to toss in a free calculator if a customer ordered two watches. The ads in *Parade, TV Guide,* and small town newspapers pulled more than 100,000 orders totalling almost $1.7 million!

There were no watches. No calculators, either. And Dennis L. Roberts, who headed Teltronics, knew it. He started his scheme by duping a national credit-rating agency into giving his company a favorable report, then hired a Chicago advertising agency to place his ads. When orders for the watches came in, he hired women to type labels and mail customers a note saying that a parcel service strike was holding up delivery of the watches. Meanwhile he was wiring hundreds of thousands of dollars to himself at various banks in Mexico City.

A spokesman for *TV Guide* insisted that the magazine had satisfied itself that the Teltronics ads were on the up-and-up. A representative visited the company's offices, was shown sample watches, and learned that the ads were prepared by a reputable agency. Roberts traded on the reputation of the publication, said a member of the Chicago Attorney General's office. "Most of the responses came from kids, from convicts, from people who wanted to give their parents a Christmas gift," he stated. "The appeal was to people of lesser means, and it looked to be a straightforward deal."

Roberts' scheme was chicken-feed compared with a Brooklyn operation called Rack Shops International. This scam was begun in the early 1970's by a shrewd wheeler-dealer, Stanley Fuchs, in partnership with a friend, Andrew Montero. A clever series of ads promised investors that they could get in on the ground-floor of a new Avon-type of sales operation known as Susan Roberts Cosmetics. An investment of $2,800 could return at least $624 a month; Then the value of a distributorship would grow until it could be sold for many times the original investment. The promoters said the business was booming to such an extent that the factory "was working night and day" to satisfy the "incredible demand" for the new cosmetics line.

The pair took in $2,800 each from 160 people—investors who grew nervous when the products failed to materialize. When they notified the authorities, Fuchs and Montero merely closed down Rack Shops International and began running ads for a new company, Cope Enterprises. Now the eye-catching ads, run in the "business opportunities" sections of the New York papers, promised that people who invested and worked only part time could earn $700 a month. Full-time workers could make ten times as much. And all it took to get in on this goldmine was an investment of $2,800.

"Make the American Dream a reality for yourself," the copy said. "Be in your own business ... no selling ... secured investment ... public company has outstanding success record since 1945." Would anyone fall for it? Some 300 people did. People like Albert Bradley, a half-blind man from the Bronx who was waiting for a cataract operation and who poured half his life savings into Cope Enterprises.

Small potatoes, though, compared to the Rio Rancho swindle—which began for thousands of unfortunate investors with a dinner invitation like the one that went to the young Collins boy. "This month Rio Rancho Estates celebrates the new season with a series of gala holiday banquets," said the card. "You are invited to attend as our complimentary guest without any obligation." What none of the "lucky" guests knew, of course, and had no way of telling from the expensively printed brochures that later came their way, was that Rio Rancho estates was the brainchild of four men running something called Amrep Corp. on West 61st Street in Manhattan.

Over a period of 15 years the four had purchased 92,000 acres of desert near Albuquerque at $180 or so per acre. Cutting the property into building-size plots, Amrep began promoting Rio Rancho Estates as the perfect place to build a vacation home—at just $3,200 for an entire acre. People were told that they were buying a "guaranteed and protected investment," that fast-growing Albuquerque was expanding toward the area and already most of the lots were sold out, and that there would be roads, water, and sewers in Rio Rancho shortly.

It was all there in the brochures and pamphlets the operation handed out, but it was all lies and the promoters knew it. They knew the Albuquerque City Planning Commission had said, as far back as 1964, that the city limits would probably never reach the Rio Rancho area. And there were no plans to provide sewers, water, and paved roads to more than 2% of the lots. No, the promoters had almost nothing—except money, for 45,000 investors in 37 states and overseas gave them $170 million. The partners made more, too, by selling stock that they owned in Amrep. One bought his original shares for $1,200 and sold them for $1.8 million. Another did even better, selling for $2.7 million shares that cost him $1,800 initially.

And when it all fell in on them, what did they get? Are you ready? Six months in jail although the maximum penalty was five years! But, by God, *you* steal 20 dollars from a delicatessen and see what your sentence is! Oh, yes, there was a fine of $45,000 for Amrep. And, of course, the four men who were accused of having commiteed "no less than a massive robbery of the public" were let free on bail pending an appeal.

One of the problems in penalizing the sharpers who pull this kind of swindle is that they usually have to be tried for using the mails to defraud, rather than for false advertising. Yes, they use the mails, but that is an incidental part of the whole operation. It's the ad—the first crooked ad—that starts to separate the sucker from his money. But, on both federal, state, and local levels, the laws against false advertising are extremely vague. And the penalties for using false advertising to get rich are almost nonexistent. Who is keeping those laws lax? Why? What are they afraid of? What Congressmen do they influence?

The Federal Trade Commission set out to kick the big corporations that use fraudulent advertising right in the pocketbook. Until recently the governmental body had to face up to an obvious fact: the rewards for advertising deception were so great and the penalties so slight (especially when discounted against the remote likelihood of detection and prosecution) that it was almost inevitable that advertisers would make false claims.

Even if they were caught—as Prof. Robert Pitofsky of the Georgetown University Law Center put it in *Issues of Advertising*—"successfully prosecuted violations resulted in a 'cease and desist' order that directed the advertiser not to engage in similar future frauds. Violations of these orders could result in prosecutions (extremely rare in practice) leading to fines of $5,000 per day per violation. Since most advertising campaign themes run for a year or less, and most commission advertising enforcement proceedings span periods of two to five years—with one horrible example running to 16 years—the effect of any order was usually to direct the advertiser to discontinue an advertising campaign that had long since disappeared. Thus the major risk that an advertiser ran in disseminating a false claim was that the litigation expenses necessary to delay enforcement might exceed the value to the advertiser of the business advantage generated by the deception."

That was why, in 1970, prodded by Ralph Nader's organization and a number of consumer groups, the FTC latched onto the sound idea of corrective ads. If the fraudulent advertiser had to run ads that would correct his earlier misleading ones, that would cost him, plenty! And, it would be better than fining him the same amount since the corrective ads might cut into his future sales and punish him even more. How much might it cost?

$24 million was the amount of Anacin ads that would

have to be run by American Home Products Corp., the maker of Anacin, recently ruled Judge Montgomery K. Hyun of the Federal Trade Commission. And each ad would have to state: "Anacin is not a tension reliever." The product was advertised as just that—in ads that ran for five years before the FTC got through the case and the judge handed down a verdict. Even the judge, who presumably has sat in dozens of similar cases, seemed surprised at the boldness with which the advertiser had set out to defraud the public:

"American Home has represented [said a UPI report on the case] that Anacin contains more pain-dulling ingredients than any other over-the-counter internal analgesic, that its analgesic ingredient is unusual, special, and stronger than aspirin, and that the product contains twice as much of its analgesic ingredient as other marketed products," said Hyun.

"These representations are false," he said. "Anacin's analgesic ingredient is not unusual, special, or stronger than aspirin, since it is nothing other than aspirin."

The judge took issue with another claim that a product known as Arthritis Pain Formula would cause gastric discomfort less frequently than any other over-the-counter analgesic. The claim, he said, "is false . . . Moreover, there existed a substantial question recognized by experts . . . as to the validity of the representation." He was not finished. Hyun also held, contrary to claims, that Anacin does not relieve nervousness, tension, stress, fatigue or depression, nor will it enable persons to cope with the stresses of everyday life.

In pleading that something—and, hopefully, something drastic—be done about the ripoff artists who twist our language into a manipulative mess, I must make the point that the governments can't look for fraud in every headline or block of copy. Some zealots have lashed out, damning all advertising as worthless. There are plenty of good, responsible commercials that inform or educate, and do a good selling job, too. But because there are so many that are poorly conceived and appear to oversell or which are deliberately designed to defraud, it is perhaps understandable that the finger-pointers see danger everywhere.

The FTC, for example, is said to have been investigating

an ad for a novelty "money-making" machine. The device was illustrated in an ad that appeared in a comic book. It consists of two rollers mounted on a wooden frame with a piece of frabric wrapped around the rollers. If you put a dollar bill on one roller and twist the handle, it disappears inside the fabric. Then, if a blank piece of paper is put on the other roller, as the handle turns, the blank sheet goes inside the machine and the dollar comes out. It looks—to a child, at least—as if the blank paper was being "printed" into a dollar. The device sells for less than two dollars, but the FTC has on file a letter from an angry parent stating that his child read the ad and believed that it could actually print money.

I find it hard to believe that FTC's regional office spent 154 manhours working on a proposal to get government money to investigate and study the complaint. In its request, the commission noted that the ad was one of a series that "if developed into a case . . . might establish the precedent that comic book publishers are responsible for advertising that is 'clearly deceptive' on its face." The commission had another ad in the series that also was patently of interest only to the very young. This one said, "Drive a spike through metal with your hands."

How many of the taxpayers' dollars are expended in efforts to root out every word that may be misleading none of us will ever know. But others are concerned about it. Prof. Wesley J. Liebeler of the University of California at Los Angeles, also in *Issues in Advertising*, pooh-poohed the FTC investigation of whether Dry Ban was really as dry as its advertisements said it was. "I would have supposed that interested customers could have tested this claim by the ready expedient of buying a can of Dry Ban, spraying it on some appropriate part of their body, and observing whether it was dry," said the professor. "Even if it was not totally dry, they could presumably use the rest of the can. Barring allergies or extreme dissatisfaction with the product, the purchase price would not be totally lost. The consumer loss from ads of this type cannot conceivably be large enough to justify the expensive attentions of a federal agency."

There is another consideration to be made when we start looking to the government to solve the false-advertising problem. It costs us money, yes, but it also tends to make us lazy—and that is dangerous. If we think that the FTC, the Justice Department or some other agency is going to take care of cleansing the airwaves, the print media and the mails of false or misleading ads—won't we tend to accept the ads we see as honest ones? Won't we start thinking, "If this ad has been checked by ad agency lawyers and the company lawyers and media lawyers, and if the government hasn't called anyone to task for it, it must be okay"? When we ask the government to hit out at anything that looks just the slightest bit suspicious, aren't we asking for tacit approval of everything else?

None of us can afford it. None of us should take any ad for granted. Every word has to be scrutinized—and sometimes those words show up quite small. Take the case of Löwenbräu beer, for example, currently getting a onceover from the FTC. Everyone knows Löwenbräu, the great imported beer. But a new brand, Löwenbräu Light, is marked "Brewed in the U.S.A." on its label and in its ads. The question is how an imported beer can be made in America.

Anyone can be fooled. The smartest consumer as well as the least educated, the elderly as well as children. Recently, however, several groups of watchdogs have charged that children—being naive—have to be protected, and they have demanded a complete ban on all television ads aimed at the youngsters. It is true that kids are bombarded with TV pitches for toys, cereals, candies, and dozens of other products—but I'm not so sure that it is wise to legislate such ads off the air entirely. According to a group called Action for Children's Television, children are too young and trusting to understand that TV ads are trying to sell them something. In other words the kids do not understand the *purpose* of advertising, and that makes the ads inherently deceptive. And, because the government has control over deceptive advertising, it can ban such ads outright.

I have given the subject a lot of thought as the battle has gone on within the halls of various courts and government agencies. And it seems to me that a basic mistake is being made. In this media-governed world that we live in, the sooner a youngster is educated to the dangers of false advertising, the better off he or she will be. If a child sees a TV commercial for a cereal that is said to taste good and contain so many vitamins that whoever eats it will fly like Superman; and if, after eating it (because the kid demands that mom and dad buy it), the child cannot fly—well, a valuable lesson has been learned. The child will be a little less trustful of the next ad he or she is confronted with.

Authors Lawrence and Lauby list a number of steps to take to make sure that you do not get taken in by false advertising, but some of the suggestions are fairly simplistic, it seems to me. They say, for example, that you should not buy mail-order merchandise on impulse, but should take the time to shop around locally for the item and compare prices. Also, if you have never heard of the mail-order company, write for a catalog and buy an inexpensive item first to test their delivery and quality. Ignore almost every ad that promises you can "earn easy money" or a "guaranteed income." If there are such claims write the company and ask that it back up the offer—and, say the authors, "chances are that you'll never hear from them."

Even if this is all followed faithfully, you—and thousands of people just like you—can still get stuck. If you think you've been ripped off, don't waste money on a phone call to the company; you'll just be shunted around and eventually told "somebody will look into it." Instead write a complaint letter that gives all the pertinent facts—item ordered, how much you lost, where you saw or heard the ad, and your name and address. If the company hasn't made good on their promises in two weeks, write your local postal inspector, the Better Business Bureau, Federal Trade Commission, the Direct Mail/Marketing Assn. headquarters in New York City, and the newspaper, radio station, magazine, or TV station that was the source of the original ad. Keep copies of your complaint letter to the company, and enclose them with follow-up letters.

It's a lot of work, and if a small amount of money is involved, it may not be worth the effort. A better answer is needed, but so far no one has come up with a simple and workable solution.

Chapter *XVI*

Who's Got
the Solution?

It's a cliché to observe that it is not enough to decry a problem, one must suggest a solution. There is no one answer to the problem of the corruption of America. Rather there are a thousand-and-one separate factors of solution. No one individual, however morally determined, can attend to all of them. But each of us can do something. The following specifics certainly do not exhaust the possibilities.

*An incredible amount of money is spent each year in the U. S. for the purchase of merchandise that the buyers know perfectly well is stolen. The professional thieves who place such merchandise on the market are unlikely to be affected by calls to virtue. Forget them. Be concerned with your own role in such a drama. The next time someone offers you stolen goods—automobiles, TV sets, radios, guns, whatever—listen carefully, nod as if thinking over the possibility, and then go at once to the nearest telephone and call the police. There's no need to identify yourself though the authorities would appreciate it if you did, but the wish to avoid "becoming involved" is, in some if not all cases, at least understandable. All you have to say is: "Look, I'm not going to give you my name, but listen carefully, because I have important information about the sale of a sizable amount of stolen property. I was just offered the opportunity to buy some of the goods. I was told that they were for sale at 479 South Whatever Street."

Ask the policeman to repeat the address back to make sure he gets it correct; there are almost as many dummies working on police departments these days as there are everywhere else.

That sort of gesture costs nothing beyond the price of a ten-cent phone call, but if even fifty people a day in one city made such calls a hell of a lot of good could be done and the high price of stolen merchandise would drop, thus making the entire process less attractive to both professional and amateur thieves and burglars.

Another thing you can do: if stolen goods are offered for sale at your factory, your gas station, church club, or office, try saying to your co-workers who have heard the pitch, "Say, man, I'll bet those are mighty fine TV sets that guy just offered us. I'd love to have one, but I just can't talk myself into buying stolen stuff because I figure that makes me just as much of a thief as the guy that stole it. What do you think?"

You might find agreement and you might get disagreement, but at least you'll have initiated a debate about a moral question, which itself can do some good.

*Another thing you can do is stop playing your own small role, if any, in the corruption of police. The next time you get a ticket, take the damned thing like an adult. Send in your ten, fifteen or twenty bucks and let it go at that. Don't ever again wrap your driver's license in a ten-spot. Parenthetically you shouldn't try this in Western states anyway. There's a strong likelihood that it can get you arrested, a fate you'll well deserve. But even in Eastern cities it's part of the large problem and you ought to knock it off.

*Another solution: Praise virtue where you encounter it. Diogenes would have been happy to discover a Richmond, Virginia, man named Thomas Cannon, who is something of a self-made pauper. Cannon earns $13,000 a year as a postal worker but gives most of it away. One of his 1977 contributions was a $1,000 gift to a sixteen-year-old Norfolk, Virginia, boy who, after finding $40 on a school bus, turned it in to the driver. Cannon announced that he presented the gift to young John Thompson because he was touched by his "monumental honesty and integrity." He has also made $1,000 contributions to help prisoner rehabilitation in the Virginia penal system, to help pay medical expenses for an Egyptian child flown to Richmond for surgery, and an annual donation to his alma mater, Hampton Institute.

In past centuries people who behaved like that were often considered saints. Perhaps Cannon's example might prove an inspiration to others.

*Another prescription: Shake up the judiciary. Some judges seem either out of touch with street reality, or corrupt. It has for some time been a cliché that the poor man—particularly if he is black or brown-skinned—may get a heavy prison sentence for a crime that will not cause nearly as much suffering for a white criminal with access to money and influence. One could fill boxcars with documentation; one example here will suffice: In 1977 "Operation Sting," a successful undercover project of the Washington, D.C., Police Department and the Federal Bureau of Investigation, pulled some 200 crooks into its trap as investigators pretending to be Mafiosi paid out over two million dollars for stolen items in laying their intricate trap. So competently was the project conducted that the law-enforcement personnel were able to take 110 reels of videotape to use as evidence.

But when it was all over one law enforcement officer, understandably bitter about the plea-bargaining and other legal finagling that soured the triumph, was in a mood to say to hell with American justice if "all it took was smart lawyers to walk the guilty out of court."

Campaigns encouraging respect for law and order, for example, will probably increase the understanding of law and order among magistrates. In the great city of Philadelphia, by way of illustration, as of 1976 there were 28 magistrates who handled traffic violators, heard civil cases involving 100 dollars or less, tried minor criminals, and made decisions as to whether to hold suspects in serious crimes. Despite these grave responsibilities only one of these was a lawyer, another dropped out of school in the sixth grade, four never got beyond grammar school and only nine graduated from high school. The explanation is that the magistrate's job is awarded as a political pay-off. As might be expected in a situation where ignorance prevails, corruption is rampant, too.

*Another solution: Stop the stupid personal defensiveness that makes us totally or partially blind to acts of corruption and crime committed by social groups with which we personally are identified. There is too damned much cover-up now—by millions of people who are reluctant to point a critical finger at a notorious offender simply because he's a member of their church, their nationality, their race, their political party, their philosophical camp. Realize this: all camps are contaminated now. The rascals aren't the other guys, they're all around us. When is a Democratic or Republican President of the United States going to have the guts and decency to criticize the corruption of his own party, both of which ought to be ashamed of themselves because of offenses by party members?

When is a Catholic leader—in a state like New Jersey—and I'm talking about Cardinals and Bishops—going to have enough sense of Christian honesty to stand up and concede that he presides over a flock in which corruption is not only tolerated but frequently envied and honored?

When is a parish priest going to look a Mafia leader in the eye and say, "Tony, God knows we could use the five thousand dollars you're offering us. Our parish needs that and then some. But I know how you got this money. I know you earned it from selling narcotics, from the prostitution rackets, from pornography, from having people maimed and terrorized and murdered and because of that I wouldn't take a penny of your money."

When are Jewish and Protestant religious leaders going to say the same about offenders in their camps?

When are conservatives and liberals going to stop the stupidity of assuming that corruption is something chiefly carried on by the opposition?

Corruption is now so rampant in our midst that a truly honest man is considered noteworthy if not peculiar. Corruption on the financial level, of course, is often accompanied by political corruption, the corruption of power.

It is crucial to understand that the soil in which the crimes of Watergate grew was upper middle-class country-club conservatism. Not the admirable conservatism of high principle, of honesty, of respect for the moral verities, of libertarianism, but the conservatism of reaction, social expediency and selfishness. *All the players in this tragic national drama were cast from the political right.* Gordon Liddy and H. Howard Hunt are long-time cold warriors. Liddy once ran for office as a Conservative party candidate; Hunt is the close political associate of conservative intellectuals.

The four convicted Cuban burglars, too, are veterans of the anti-Communist movement. Nor has anyone ever described ex-CIA-FBI agent McCord as liberal. Colson, Haldeman, Ehrlichman, Mitchell—all were well right-of-center.

Patrick Buchanan, that paragon of unrepentance, author of hard-hitting conservative statements and speeches delivered by those high-minded statesmen Nixon and Agnew, and an active leader of the militant Right, was revealed as a pusher of certain vulgarities and excesses in the Dirty Tricks department.

Gentlemen, is it not time to cut the sickening hypocrisy? As between the American form of Capitalism and the limited alternative of Soviet or Chinese-style Communism, practically all Americans much prefer our system. But the common Conservative pretension that our economic system is *sanctified*, that it has an inherent philosophical dignity, is stomach-turning nonsense.

What does have dignity, what does deserve our respect

is, again, *freedom*. The commodity has always been rare, throughout history, and, for that matter, is precious on our planet today. That American Communists or Fascists would, in power, place severe restrictions on our freedoms is known to every schoolchild. But what is more remarkable is that some of those who have the word *freedom* most frequently on their lips would—it has been determined by polling— revise the Bill of Rights if they had it within their power to do so. In the opinion of these self-described defenders of freedom there is far too much preaching of doctrines they distrust, far too much assembling, marching, protesting, publishing, on behalf of views of which they disapprove.

But for all the sins committed by its alleged champions, liberty is still a dear and holy commodity. Now it is obvious that a free *political* system is congenial to free *economic* practices. But to equate the one with the other—out of either stupidity or dishonesty—is reprehensible.

*Suggestion: Support the Consumer Revolution, a grand, inspiring instance of the common sense of the American people. Americans are tired of being ripped off, cheated, swindled, lied to by certain advertisers, and sold shoddy, overpriced merchandise. That's Capitalism, too, baby, and what the public is at last saying to the corporate powers and their Conservative philosophical apologists is this: Don't give us any more crap about "the glories of free enterprise." Just give us good merchandise, at fair prices, and pay us decent wages. That's what will preserve our economic system and its material blessings. Your hypocritical speeches only make us sick.

Well-intentioned Marxists have long pondered the question as to how it may be possible to achieve "Communism with a human face." It is indeed one of the most serious questions facing the Marxist camp. But in the light of the growing dilemma in our own country, the daily enlarging statistics not only about corruption, but also sexual anarchy, murder, rape, armed robbery, mugging, child abuse—the perpetrators being the *parents* of the suffering children— the roughly 25,000-per-year deaths by gunshot and all the rest of the sickening list, it is time to ask whether we should not now concern ourselves with the search for Capitalism with a human face.

It has been the common U.S. assumption for over half a century that the true superiority of Capitalism to Communism is on the moral level. Sure, some Capitalists were greedy, heartless bastards, but at least we had our civil rights, our political freedoms. Purely economic and materialist claims were also advanced and can be easily defended. But it is theoretically possible that at some future moment the scales will tip in favor of the Marxists as regards the question of the greatest good to the greatest number. The important question remaining at that point will be the moral one. And what then will we have to say, to the world or our consciences, if Marxist lands are relatively peaceful and ethical internally whereas some as yet not identified combination of forces in our own culture has led to even more destructive excesses of violence, child-abuse, sexual perversion, white-collar crime, civic corruption and general dog-eat-dog dishonesty?

       *It is frequently argued that a return to formal religion is the solution to the problem. But the prescription leaves something to be desired, for one finds practically no formal humanists, agnostics or atheists in the ranks of the corrupt. Most of the embezzlers, swindlers, con men and thieves—God help us—are card-carrying members of one religious denomination or another that formally pays respect to the Old and/or New Testaments.

Recently, Dr. John M. Steiner, a professor of sociology, made a study of shoppers who switch price tags on merchandise, thereby paying less for their purchases by defrauding the merchant. The typical tag-switcher was between the ages of 18 and 35, white, middle through upper-class and with a religious affiliation.

I naturally do not suggest that age-old rules forbidding theft are irrelevant. If enough people felt seriously obliged to be guided by the commandment "Thou shalt not covet thy neighbor's goods," the situation would certainly be improved. Obviously thieves should stop stealing. But it is also important that those who are not quite thieves themselves— whether by virtue or cowardice—*stop condoning the activities of the successful thieves.* If ours were a morally sane society, criminals and swindlers, no matter how materially successful, would be viewed with revulsion. In the eyes of far too many now they are only envied.

If the adherents of the various major churches would now statistically demonstrate serious interest in obeying the ethical and moral strictures of their own faiths—as do Quakers and Unitarians, for example—the problem would, obviously, be partly solved. But the suggestion carries the implication that the offenders are those who have abandoned their respective faiths. In reality the problem is more tragic. The point bears repetition: a depressingly large percentage of the crooked politicians, lawyers, judges, bureaucrats and grafters are affiliated with one denomination or another. In neighborhoods and cities where certain church loyalties are dominant, this sad fact is a particular scandal. It has frequently been observed, for example, that in those Eastern American cities plagued by widespread police corruption the law-breaking policemen constitute a large percentage of those who may be seen at any Sunday Mass or Communion breakfast. There is also no shortage of Protestants or Jews whose religious affiliations have no discernible effect upon their ethical behavior.

Indeed, far from making them feel guilty about their civic depredations, the fact that they are Baptists, Catholics, Jews or whatever seems to further deaden their consciences, as has for centuries been the case in the Mafia culture, so that their self-image is that of a generally civically virtuous individual, perhaps formally charitable, occasionally feeling certain glimmerings of religious sentiment. The image is far out of touch with moral reality.

An important part of Aristotle's theory of education was that it must embody moral training. In the American future there must be greater emphasis on this Aristotelian idea. Some may interpret this as a plea for a partial union of church and state, at least in the schools. On the contrary, churches must have no connection whatever with *public* education, for reasons which any student of European history does not have to be told. There is no necessary connection whatever between morality and religion. The argument that "if there is not a God there is no morality," is fallacious. If, for purposes of discussion, we assume that there is no God, it follows that morality is even *more* important than if there is a Deity. If God exists, his unlimited power can certainly redress imbalances in the scale of human justice. But if there is no God, then it is up to man to be as moral as he can. With the United States undergoing a profound moral crisis we must begin to impress upon our young people more firmly than ever the importance of moral and ethical considerations.

*Contending that fraudulent business practices of all kinds should be headed off long before illicit impulses lead to deceit, an organization called the Center for the Study of Values thinks that the country's business schools should teach ethics as part of the regular curriculum. Noting that law and medical schools now give instructions in ethical procedure but that business schools do not, the group has put together a team of professors, academic philosophers, and businessmen (including advertising agency executives). The team, called the Committee for Education in Business Ethics, will look into advertising, product safety, pricing, reliability and value, and environmental pollution, among other factors. A program of instruction will be worked out "that is directed toward sensitizing business students to the tremendous power of corporations whose acts have increasing consequences for public good or ill."

It will take time—perhaps decades—before this kind of approach produces practical results. Meanwhile a variety of other solutions have been proposed. Total censorship of all advertising? Partial censorship? Regulation in advance by special committees or the Federal Trade Commission? A new, specially-created bureaucracy concerned only with advertising? Self-regulation of the part of advertisers?

There are pluses and minuses on each side of every proposal, and a single answer that works in every instance has yet to be found. Ultimately the advertising industry may succeed in policing itself so that even youngsters can believe what they see and hear. But until the industry succeeds in this we need all the boards, panels and review committees we can find.

*One thing that's for damned sure required now is moral leadership. Not the pain-in-the-ass, hypocritical kind that came out of the Nixon White House, but the kind, for example, projected by a man named Eddie Robinson. For the past 37 years football coach at Louisiana's Grambling University, Robinson has not only turned out 160 professional football players—more than any other coach—but, more importantly, has strengthened the moral fiber in a far greater number of young blacks who have had the good fortune to have the benefit of his influence. He is, in some respects, an old-fashioned Negro who comes down hard on irresponsible sex, drug-abuse, drinking, bad manners, but his method produces results. "I tell 'em, 'Now, don't steal the towels when we're at some nice hotel,' " Robinson explains.

*We might also profitably congratulate and support men such as Stanley Sporkin, chief of the Enforcement Section of the Securities and Exchange Commission, whom Mary McGrory has called "simply the most honest and effective man in government." Sporkin, by 1977, had put the finger on some 400 corporations that had paid bribes to foreign governments and their representatives, purely for business reasons. Sporkin, as well as the executives involved, knows that an evil has been done. He thinks it should be stopped. "The competitive system," he says, "is the greatest system in the world but it works only in public confidence. If it goes unchecked, it will destroy itself. Some of our corporations were making foreign policy—look at ITT and Chile—and they weren't elected to do that. And I don't think you should take our best and brightest people and train them to be dishonest."

"Realists" in the business world sometimes say, "Look, I

know what we're doing is dishonest. But my company has to do it because everybody else does. Without such payments we'd be at a competitive disadvantage."

The solution, dear readers, is to support Sporkin and others who argue that all games should be played by the rules. If everybody is forced to act honestly, that solves the problem of competitive disadvantage, doesn't it?

*We might also begin by broadcasting the message that corruption is un-American. To our philosophical enemies it would seem self-evident that the truth is precisely the opposite, that in fact corruption is quite American in that it is an inevitable consequence of an economic system motivated, at its heart, by the idea of every-man-for-himself. Adam Smith's "unseen hand" does exist and even functions productively, but can be justified only insofar as the participants in such a drama agree to abide by an even minimum moral standard. Once the majority, or even a significant minority, is prepared to throw ethical standards overboard, then the resulting structure is no longer morally defensible. At that point one can only argue that, for all its admitted moral depravity, it still ought to be retained because (a) it produces certain material benefits more effectively than its theoretical rivals, and (b) it is, at least to a degree, more consistent with the natural human appetite for political freedom than are Marxist economic structures. But what thoughtful American could possibly be content with such a line of defense?

No, corruption—in its present degree—is clearly un-American in that it is fundamentally opposed to the political vision dreamed by our Founding Fathers. This is not said in that lamentably hazy and close-to-meaningless way in which such phrases as "the Founding Fathers" or "the American way of life" are commonly used by not notably intelligent "defenders of freedom," but rather in as precise a way as possible. Corruption is *anti*-American because in the general absence of ethical standards and conduct, our system courts the danger of actual collapse. Is it, for example, really news that corruption contributes to inflation?

*Another solution: Help the Law. My participation in the contempt that every honest citizen ought to feel for cops who have sold out to the enemy, who are, quite literally, traitors to the decent segment of society they are sworn to protect, is equalled by my admiration for honest cops. I know some of these men personally. They're the salt of the earth. They get paid very little, they work hard, are often in danger, and get precious little attention or praise. Many of these heroic and unsung soldiers work against Organized Crime and corruption in the FBI, the IRS and the government's Organized Crime Strike Forces. I have admired and respected such men since I first worked with ex-cops Bill Keating and Walter O'Meara on the anti-crime TV documentary in 1954.

Although I have never mentioned this publicly before—and do so now only because it is relevant to my argument—I have in a number of instances provided these courageous soldiers in the anti-corruption army with information about criminal behavior. One of my recommendations is that the reader do the same.

I am saying nothing original; thousands of Americans have already individually decided that they can no longer stomach the thievery and corruption they see in their communities and have gone to the law with important information. Inevitably there will be a certain number of paranoids and trouble-makers who will add static to such channels of communication by troubling law enforcement agencies unnecessarily, or deliberately providing false information. But every human institution has been misused. I repeat, if the reader has important information about Organized Crime or corruption he should channel that information to a law-enforcement source. No one can force the informant to testify publicly if he does not wish to, but odds-and-ends of information can still be useful when fitted into a larger jigsaw puzzle, some pieces of which the police will already have assembled. Information may be delivered by mail, in person or by phone. A warning: local police forces, sad to say—especially in larger cities—inevitably have a few men who have sold out to the enemy. Informants should therefore keep this factor in mind, especially when making initial contacts. You're safer with IRS or FBI contacts.

*Radio and television executives should encourage their news departments to increase their already significant investigative reports on crime and corruption. The CBS TV series "60 Minutes" deserves particular praise for its examinations of such instances as that involving GLACAA, The Greater Los Angeles Community Action Agency.

Largely as a result of the "60 Minutes" report, Martin Saminiego, Executive Director of the agency, was fired in October of 1978 and Board Chairman Otillo Barron resigned, as did fellow boardmember Porfirio Miranda. The Internal Revenue Service, in part goaded by the CBS report, began a formal audit of the agency's financial records. Earlier the Los Angeles County Board of Supervisors of the Los Angeles City Council had voted to close down the GLACAA operation, but it was the "60 Minutes" treatment that was the coup de grace. The problem, of course, was that some of the agency's officials had been devoting more time to benefiting themselves and their friends than to attending to the needs of the poor.

*The particularly concerned citizen would be well advised to develop his own library of books about corruption. The bibliography at the end of this book will serve to introduce him to a wealth of information already compiled by specialists. Study such books. Trade them with friends who share your concern.

*Suggestion: Encourage the training of more computer crime specialists such as Los Angeles Deputy District Attorney Phil Wynn. Wynn learned the ropes on his own after being handed a puzzling case involving computer-time theft. He studied the field, learned enough to bring in a conviction, and is now recognized as a specialist in such cases. As of 1980 no major city should be without one.

*Solution: The reader will have noted that in many instances of civic corruption the crimes were made possible because enormously profitable contracts had been agreed to by city or state officials without competitive bidding. There may have been a day when we could assume that, since most public servants were honest, individual communities ought to have the freedom to decide whether they wanted to institute competitive bidding procedures or not.

I'm afraid that, as regards all American communities of more than one million population, that day is long past. Competitive bidding procedures should now be guaranteed by law.

*Suggestion: Do your homework about one particular labor union, the Teamsters. It may be wondered why, in a book dealing with corruption in America, I have included relatively little information about the Teamsters. The reason is that the corruption of that particular union is documented by such an enormous amount of data that one could do little more than scratch the surface of it in so brief an overall survey. I strongly recommend, however, that the reader familiarize himself with the facts. A good way to begin is to read a book by Lester Velie titled *Desperate Bargain: Why Jimmy Hoffa Had to Die*. Clark Mollenhoff, Pulitzer Prize-winning journalist, says, "It reads like fiction, but its major fascination is that it is a chilling, real story of *a ruthless underworld group that has seized control of a powerful union that has economic power with impact upon every man, woman, and child in the United States*. It is more than the compilation of all available evidence on Jimmy Hoffa's killers, for it is a much-needed reminder that the disappearance of Hoffa was a *startling new era of insidious underworld control that has threatened to use the Teamsters Union to take over law enforcement in America through unionization of police*." (Italics added.)

One of the many interesting stories the book deals with is the connection between corrupt unionism and the Nixon White House. Lest anyone suggest such statements are nothing more than part of the on-going "liberal campaign of vilification" of Nixon, I point out that Velie's book is published by Reader's Digest Press. The *Digest* has long been one of the leading organs of responsible political conservatism, not of liberalism, in the U.S.

Then read Walter Sheridan's *The Fall and Rise of Jimmy Hoffa* for background on the notorious criminality of leading Teamster officials. After that try Bobby Kennedy's old report, *The Enemy Within, The Teamsters* by Steve Brill, and *The Hoffa Wars* by Dan E. Moldea.

*Suggestion: Urge your service club to take a formal position on corruption. Raymond Chandler, master of hard-boiled detective fiction, once wrote that "the emotional basis of the standard detective story was and had always been that murder will out and justice will be done." Chandler added, however, that in many cases justice is not done "unless some very determined individual makes it his business to see that justice is done."

I am not, God knows, presenting myself as that determined individual. Even if one assumed such determination it would be unequal to the task of doing much now to balance the terribly askew scales of justice in America. What one does want to see is an army of determined individuals, average citizens from various walks of life who, like the overwrought TV newscaster in the film *Network*, are prepared to announce that they have finally had enough. Nothing short of such a personal position, taken by millions, will be equal to the challenge facing us.

*So that's it. Not a very pretty picture. One more national problem to worry about. Thousands of people are already doing something about it. They are the crooks, shysters, con-men, grafters and mobsters who are stealing Uncle Sam blind. *You* are Uncle Sam. You personally may not be able to do very much to help.

But you'd better do something.

ℬibliography

America, Inc.: Who Owns and Operates the U.S., Morton Mintz and Jerry S. Cohen (New York: The Dial Press).

The Anderson Papers, Jack Anderson with George Clifford (New York: Random House, Inc.).

Barbarians in Our Midst: A History of Chicago Crime and Politics, Virgil W. Peterson (Boston: Little, Brown and Company).

The Beauties and the Beasts: The Mob in Show Business, Hank Messick (New York: David McKay Co., Inc.).

The Big Bankroll, Leo Katcher (New York: Harper & Row, Publishers).

Big Bill of Chicago, Lloyd Wendt and Herman Kogan (Indianapolis: The Bobbs-Merrill Co., Inc.).

The Big Fix, Norton Mockridge and Robert Prall (New York: Henry Holt & Co.).

Boss: Richard J. Daley of Chicago, Mark Royko (New York: E. P. Dutton & Co., Inc.).

Bosses in Lusty Chicago: The Story of Bathhouse John and Hinky Dink, Lloyd Wendt and Herman Kogan (Bloomington: Indiana University Press).

Bribery and Extortion in World Business, Neil H. Jacoby, Peter Nehemkis, and Richard Eells (New York: Macmillan, Inc.).

Brotherhood of Evil: The Mafia, Frederic Sondern, Jr. (New York: Farrar, Straus & Cudahy, Inc.).

Capone, John Kobler (New York: G. P. Putnam's Sons).

Captive City: Chicago in Chains, Ovid Demaris (Secaucus, N.J.: Lyle Stuart Inc.).

The Case against Congress, Drew Pearson and Jack Anderson (New York: Simon & Schuster, Inc.).

The Crime Confederation, Ralph Salerno and John S. Tompkins (Garden City, N.Y.: Doubleday & Company, Inc.).

The D.A.'s Man, Harold Danforth and James Horan (New York: Crown Publishers, Inc.).

The Deadly Silence, Renée Buse (Garden City, N.Y.: Doubleday & Company, Inc.).

Dirty Business: The Corporate-Political Money-Power Game, Ovid Demaris (New York: Harper & Row, Publishers).

The Dollar Barons, Christopher Elias (New York: Macmillan, Inc.).

"Ethics in America: Norms and Deviations," *Annals of the American Academy of Political and Social Science*, volume 363, January 1966.

The Fall and Rise of Jimmy Hoffa, Walter Sheridan (New York: Saturday Review Press).

Fleecing the Lambs, Christopher Elias (Chicago: Henry Regnery Company).

Gambler's Money, Wallace Turner (Boston: Houghton Mifflin Company).

"Gambling," *Annals of the American Academy of Political and Social Science*, Thorste and Ellian.

The Greedy War, James Hamilton Paterson (New York: David McKay Co., Inc.).

The Green Felt Jungle, Ed Reid and Ovid Demaris (New York: Trident Press).

In a Few Hands: Monopoly Power in America, Estes Kefauver (New York: Pantheon Books, Inc.).

Investigation of Improper Activities in the Labor or Management Field, 86th Congress, January 27–February 2, 1959 (Washington: Government Printing Office).

James R. Hoffa and Continued Underworld Control of New York Teamster Local #239, Hearings before the permanent Subcommittee on Investigations of the Committee on Government Operations, U.S. Senate, 87th Congress, January 10, 11, 12, 24, and 25, 1961 (Washington: Government Printing Office).

The Mafia Is Not an Equal Opportunity Employer, Nicholas Gage (New York: McGraw-Hill Book Company).

The Medical Messiahs: A Social History of Health Quackery in Twentieth-century America, James Harvey Young (Princeton, N.J.: Princeton University Press).

Merchant of Menace: The Mafia, Edward J. Allen (Springfield, Ill.: Charles C. Thomas, Publisher).

The Operators, Frank Gibney (New York: Harper & Row, Publishers).

Pay-off! Walter Arm (New York: Appleton-Century-Crofts).

The Private Lives of Public Enemies, Hank Messick, with Joseph L. Nellis (New York: Peter H. Wyden, Inc.).

Revolt in the Mafia, Raymond V. Martin (New York: Duell, Sloan & Pearce).

The Rise of Teamster Power in the West, Donald Garnel (Berkeley: University of California Press).

The Robber Barons, Matthew Josephson (New York: Harcourt, Brace & World, Inc.).

Sam the Plumber, Henry Zeiger (New York: The New American Library Inc.).

The Secret Boss of California, Arthur H. Samish and Bob Thomas (New York: Crown Publishers, Inc.).

Secret File, Hank Messick (New York: G. P. Putnam's Sons).

The Secret Rulers: Criminal Syndicates and How They Control the U.S. Underworld, Fred Cook (New York: Duell, Sloan & Pearce).

Syndicate in the Sun, Hank Messick (New York: Macmillan, Inc.).

Syndicate Wife, Hank Messick (New York: Macmillan, Inc.).

This Labor Union Racket, Edward Dean Sullivan (New York: Hillman Curl, Inc.).

Underworld, U.S.A., Joseph Dinneen (New York: Farrar, Straus & Cudahy, Inc.).

The Valachi Papers, Peter Maas (New York: G. P. Putnam's Sons).

Waterfront Priest, Allan Raymond (New York: Henry Holt & Co.).